PEDIATRICS, CHILD AND ADOLESCENT HEALTH

BUILDING YOUTH FOR THE FUTURE

A PATH TOWARDS SUICIDE PREVENTION

PEDIATRICS, CHILD AND ADOLESCENT HEALTH

JOAV MERRICK - SERIES EDITOR

NATIONAL INSTITUTE OF CHILD HEALTH AND HUMAN DEVELOPMENT, MINISTRY OF SOCIAL AFFAIRS, JERUSALEM

Building Youth for the Future: A Path towards Suicide Prevention
Hatim A Omar and Joav Merrick (Editors)
2018. ISBN: 978-1-53613-768-2 (Hardcover)
2018. ISBN: 978-1-53613-769-9 (e-book)

Child Health and Human Development Yearbook 2017
Joav Merrick (Editor)
2018. ISBN: 978-1-53613-628-9 (Hardcover)
2018. ISBN: 978-1-53613-629-6 (e-book)

Child and Adolescent Health Yearbook 2017
Joav Merrick (Editor)
2018. ISBN: 978-1-53613-594-7 (Hardcover)
2018. ISBN: 978-1-53613-595-4 (e-book)

Chronic Disease and Disability: The Pediatric Gastrointestinal Tract
Donald E Greydanus, Orhan Atay, and Joav Merrick (Editors)
2018. ISBN: 978-1-53612-948-9 (Hardcover)
2018. ISBN: 978-1-53612-949-6 (e-book)

Multiple Sclerosis in Children and Adolescents
Hatim Omar and Joshua Chalkley (Editors)
2018. ISBN: 978-1-53612-979-3 (Hardcover)
2018. ISBN: 978-1-53612-980-9 (e-book)

Childhood and Adolescence: Tribute to Emanuel Chigier, 1928-2017
Joav Merrick (Editor)
2018. ISBN: 978-1-53613-574-9 (Softcover)
2018. ISBN: 978-1-53613-575-6 (e-book)

Chronic Disease and Disability: The Pediatric Lung
Donald E Greydanus, Myrtha M Gregoire-Bottex, Kevin W Cates and Joav Merrick (Editors)
2018. ISBN: 978-1-53613-577-0 (Hardcover)
2018. ISBN: 978-1-53613-578-7 (e-book)

Bicycles: Helmet Use of Adolescents at Independent Schools
Ronald Chow, Michael Borean, Drew Hollenberg, Jaclyn Viehweger, Tharani Anpalagan and Anna Rzepka (Editors)
2017. ISBN: 978-1-53612-458-3 (Hardcover)
2017. ISBN: 978-1-53612-459-0 (e-book)

Positive Youth Development: Long Term Effects in a Chinese Program
Daniel TL Shek, Cecilia MS Ma, Janet TY Leung and Joav Merrick (Editors)
2017. ISBN: 978-1-53612-539-9 (Hardcover)
2017. ISBN: 978-1-53612-540-5 (e-book)

Adolescence: Bicycle and Helmet Use of Adolescents and Young Adults
Ronald Chow and Joav Merrick (Editors)
2017. ISBN: 978-1-53612-039-4 (Hardcover)
2017. ISBN: 978-1-53612-060-8 (e-book)

Suicide: A Global View on Suicidal Ideation among Adolescents
Mazyanga L. Mazaba, Seter Siziya and Joav Merrick (Editors)
2017. ISBN: 978-1-53611-788-2 (Hardcover)
2017. ISBN: 978-1-53611-799-8 (e-book)

Children and Youth: Post-Traumatic Stress Disorder and Motor Vehicle Crashes
Donald E. Greydanus, Roger W. Apple, Kathryn White, and Joav Merrick (Editors)
2017. ISBN: 978-1-53611-102-6 (Hardcover)
2017. ISBN: 978-1-53611-255-9 (e-book)

Child and Adolescent Health Yearbook 2016
Joav Merrick (Editor)
2017. ISBN: 978-1-53610-948-1 (Hardcover)
2017. ISBN: 978-1-53610-957-3 (e-book)

Child Health and Human Development Yearbook 2016
Joav Merrick (Editor)
2017. ISBN: 978-1-53610-946-7 (Hardcover)
2017. ISBN: 978-1-53610-958-0 (e-book)

Chronic Disease and Disability: The Pediatric Kidney
Donald E Greydanus, Vimal Master Sankar Raj, and Joav Merrick (Editors)
2016. ISBN: 978-1-63483-793-4 (Hardcover)
2015. ISBN: 978-1-63483-809-2 (e-book)

Child and Adolescent Health Yearbook 2015
Joav Merrick (Editor)
2016. ISBN: 978-1-63484-512-0 (Hardcover)
2016. ISBN: 978-1-63484-543-4 (e-book)

Child Health and Human Development Yearbook 2015
Joav Merrick (Editor)
2016. ISBN: 978-1-63484-513-7 (Hardcover)
2016. ISBN: 978-1-63484-544-1 (e-book)

Pain Management Yearbook 2015
Joav Merrick (Editor)
2016. ISBN: 978-1-63484-515-1 (Hardcover)
2016. ISBN: 978-1-63484-545-8 (e-book)

Children and Childhood: Some International Aspects
Joav Merrick (Editor)
2016. ISBN: 978-1-63484-587-8 (Hardcover)
2016. ISBN: 978-1-63484-594-6 (e-book)

Children and Adolescents: Future Challenges
Daniel TL Shek, Tak Yan Lee, and Joav Merrick (Editors)
2016. ISBN: 978-1-63484-616-5 (Hardcover)
2016. ISBN: 978-1-63484-627-1 (e-book)

Adolescence: Positive Youth Development Programs in Chinese Communities
Daniel TL Shek, Florence KY Wu, Janet TY Leung, and Joav Merrick (Editors)
2016. ISBN: 978-1-63484-044-6 (Hardcover)
2016. ISBN: 978-1-63484-677-6 (e-book)

Sexuality: Some International Aspects
Joav Merrick and Donald E Greydanus (Editors)
2016. ISBN: 978-1-63484-707-0 (Hardcover)
2016. ISBN: 978-1-63484-719-3 (e-book)

Growing Up in the Middle East: The Daily Lives and Well-Being of Israeli and Palestinian Youth
Yossi Harel-Fisch, Ziad Abdeen and Miriam Navot
2016. ISBN: 978-1-63484-746-9 (Hardcover)
2016. ISBN: 978-1-63484-765-0 (e-book)

Chronic Disease and Disability: The Pediatric Heart
Donald E Greydanus, Devika Malhotra and Joav Merrick (Editors)
2016. ISBN: 978-1-63484-828-2 (Hardcover)
2016. ISBN: 978-1-63484-842-8 (e-book)

Diabetes Mellitus: Childhood and Adolescence
Manmohan K Kamboj, Donald E Greydanus and Joav Merrick (Editors)
2016. ISBN: 978-1-53610-095-2 (Hardcover)
2016. ISBN: 978-1-53610-104-1 (e-book)

Chronic Disease and Disability: Abuse and Neglect in Childhood and Adolescence
Donald E Greydanus, Vincent J Palusci and Joav Merrick (Editors)
2016. ISBN: 978-1-53610-129-4 (Hardcover)
2016. ISBN: 978-1-53610-142-3 (e-book)

Clinical Aspects of Psychopharmacology in Childhood and Adolescence, Second Edition
Donald E Greydanus, Joseph L Calles, Jr, Dilip R Patel, Ahsan Nazeer and Joav Merrick (Editors)
2016. ISBN: 978-1-53610-241-3 (Hardcover)
2016. ISBN: 978-1-53610-253-6 (e-book)

Chronic Disease and Disability: The Pediatric Pancreas
Donald E Greydanus, Manmohan K Kamboj and Joav Merrick (Editors)
2016. ISBN: 978-1-53610-055-6 (Hardcover)
2016. ISBN: 978-1-53610-065-5 (e-book)

A Pediatric Resident Pocket Guide: Making the Most of Morning Reports
Arthur N Feinberg
2015. ISBN: 978-1-63482-141-4 (Softcover)
2015. ISBN: 978-1-63482-186-5 (e-book)

Tropical Pediatrics: A Public Health Concern of International Proportions Second Edition
Richard R Roach, Donald E Greydanus, Dilip R Patel and Joav Merrick (Editors)
2015. ISBN: 978-1-63463-381-9 (Hardcover)
2015. ISBN: 978-1-63463-404-5 (e-book)

Child and Adolescent Health Issues (A Tribute to the Pediatrician Donald E Greydanus)
Joav Merrick (Editor)
2015. ISBN: 978-1-63463-574-5 (Hardcover)
2015. ISBN: 978-1-63463-576-9 (e-book)

Child and Adolescent Health Yearbook 2014
Joav Merrick (Editor)
2015. ISBN: 978-1-63482-162-9 (Hardcover)
2015. ISBN: 978-1-63482-206-0 (e-book)

Child Health and Human Development Yearbook 2014
Joav Merrick (Editor)
2015. ISBN: 978-1-63482-163-6 (Hardcover)
2015. ISBN: 978-1-63482-207-7 (e-book)

Behavioral Pediatrics, 4th Edition
Donald E Greydanus, Dilip R Patel, Helen D Pratt, Joseph L Calles Jr, Ahsan Nazeer and Joav Merrick (Editors)
2015. ISBN: 978-1-63483-027-0 (Hardcover)
2015. ISBN: 978-1-63483-052-2 (e-book)

Disability, Chronic Disease and Human Development
Joav Merrick
2015. ISBN: 978-1-63483-029-4 (Hardcover)
2015. ISBN: 978-1-63483-057-7 (e-book)

Caribbean Adolescents: Some Public Health Concerns
Cecilia Hegamin-Younge and Joav Merrick (Editors)
2015. ISBN: 978-1-63483-341-7 (Hardcover)
2015. ISBN: 978-1-63483-343-1 (e-book)

Adolescence and Health: Some International Perspectives
Joav Merrick (Editor)
2015. ISBN: 978-1-63483-791-0 (Hardcover)
2015. ISBN: 978-1-63483-808-5 (e-book)

Youth Suicide Prevention: Everybody's Business
Hatim A Omar (Editor)
2015. ISBN: 978-1-63483-786-6 (Softcover)
2015. ISBN: 978-1-63483-820-7 (e-book)

Human Developmental Research: Experience from Research in Hong Kong
Daniel TL Shek, Cecilia Ma, Yu Lu and Joav Merrick (Editors)
2014. ISBN: 978-1-62808-166-4 (Hardcover)
2013. ISBN: 978-1-62808-167-1 (e-book)

School, Adolescence and Health Issues
Joav Merrick, Ariel Tenenbaum and Hatim A Omar (Editors)
2014. ISBN: 978-1-62948-702-1 (Hardcover)
2014. ISBN: 978-1-62948-707-6 (e-book)

Adolescence and Sexuality: International Perspectives
Joav Merrick, Ariel Tenenbaum and Hatim A Omar (Editors)
2014. ISBN: 978-1-62948-711-3 (Hardcover)
2014. ISBN: 978-1-62948-724-3 (e-book)

Child and Adolescent Health Yearbook 2013
Joav Merrick (Editor)
2014. ISBN: 978-1-63117-658-6 (Hardcover)
2014. ISBN: 978-1-63117-668-5 (e-book)

Adoption: The Search for a New Parenthood
Gary Diamond and Eva Arbel (Israel)
2014. ISBN: 978-1-63117-710-1 (Hardcover)
2014. ISBN: 978-1-63117-713-2 (e-book)

Adolescence: Places and Spaces
Myra F Taylor, Julie Ann Pooley and Joav Merrick (Editors)
2014. ISBN: 978-1-63117-847-4 (Hardcover)
2014. ISBN: 978-1-63117-850-4 (e-book)

Pain Management Yearbook 2013
Joav Merrick (Editor)
2014. ISBN: 978-1-63117-944-0 (Hardcover)
2014. ISBN: 978-1-63117-959-4 (e-book)

Child Health and Human Development Yearbook 2013
Joav Merrick (Editor)
2014. ISBN: 978-1-63117-939-6 (Hardcover)
2013. ISBN: 978-1-63117-958-7 (e-book)

Born into this World: Health Issues
Donald E Greydanus, Arthur N Feinberg, and Joav Merrick (Editors)
2014. ISBN: 978-1-63321-667-9 (Hardcover)
2014. ISBN: 978-1-63321-669-3 (e-book)

Caring for the Newborn: A Comprehensive Guide for the Clinician
Donald E Greydanus, Arthur N Feinberg and Joav Merrick (Editors)
2014. ISBN: 978-1-63321-760-7 (Hardcover)
2014. ISBN: 978-1-63321-781-2 (e-book)

Environment and Hope: Improving Health, Reducing AIDS and Promoting Food Security in the World
Leslie Rubin and Joav Merrick (Editors)
2014. ISBN: 978-1-63321-772-0 (Hardcover)
2014. ISBN: 978-1-63321-782-9 (e-book)

Pediatric and Adolescent Dermatology: Some Current Issues
Donald E Greydanus, Arthur N Feinberg and Joav Merrick (Editors)
2014. ISBN: 978-1-63321-853-6 (Hardcover)
2014. ISBN: 978-1-63321-863-5 (e-book)

Adolescence and Behavior Issues in a Chinese Context
Daniel TL Shek, Rachel CF Sun, and Joav Merrick (Editors)
2013. ISBN: 978-1-62618-614-9 (Hardcover)
2013. ISBN: 978-1-62618-692-7 (e-book)

Advances in Preterm Infant Research
Jing Sun, Nicholas Buys and Joav Merrick
2013. ISBN: 978-1-62618-696-5 (Hardcover)
2013. ISBN: 978-1-62618-775-7 (e-book)

Child Health and Human Development: Social, Economic and Environmental Factors
Leslie Rubin and Joav Merrick (Editors)
2013. ISBN: 978-1-62948-166-1 (Hardcover)
2013. ISBN: 978-1-62948-169-2 (e-book)

Children, Violence and Bullying: International Perspectives
Joav Merrick, Isack Kandel and Hatim A Omar (Editors)
2013. ISBN: 978-1-62948-342-9 (Hardcover)
2013. ISBN: 978-1-62948-345-0 (e-book)

Chinese Adolescent Development: Economic Disadvantages, Parents and Intrapersonal Development
Daniel TL Shek, Rachel CF Sun and Joav Merrick (Editors)
2013. ISBN: 978-1-62618-622-4 (Hardcover)
2013. ISBN: 978-1-62618-694-1 (e-book)

Chronic Disease and Disability in Childhood
Joav Merrick
2013. ISBN: 978-1-62808-865-6 (Hardcover)
2013. ISBN: 978-1-62808-868-7 (e-book)

Environmental Health Disparities in Children: Asthma, Obesity and Food
Leslie Rubin and Joav Merrick (Editors)
2013. ISBN: 978-1-62948-122-7 (Hardcover)
2013. ISBN: 978-1-62948-135-7 (e-book)

Environmental Health: Home, School and Community
Leslie Rubin and Joav Merrick (Editors)
2013. ISBN: 978-1-62948-155-5 (Hardcover)
2013. ISBN: 978-1-62948-158-6 (e-book)

Guidelines for the Healthy Integration of the Ill Child in the Educational System: Experience from Israel
Yosefa Isenberg
2013. ISBN: 978-1-62808-350-7 (Hardcover)
2013. ISBN: 978-1-62808-353-8 (e-book)

Internet Addiction: A Public Health Concern in Adolescence
Artemis Tsitsika, Mari Janikian, Donald E Greydanus, Hatim A Omar and Joav Merrick (Editors)
2013. ISBN: 978-1-62618-925-6 (Hardcover)
2013. ISBN: 978-1-62618-959-1 (e-book)

Playing with Fire: Children, Adolescents and Firesetting
Hatim A. Omar, Carrie Howell Bowling and Joav Merrick (Editors)
2013. ISBN: 978-1-62948-471-6 (Softcover)
2013. ISBN: 978-1-62948-474-7 (e-book)

Promotion of Holistic Development of Young People in Hong Kong
Daniel TL Shek, Tak Yan Lee and Joav Merrick (Editors)
2013. ISBN: 978-1-62808-019-3 (Hardcover)
2013. ISBN: 978-1-62808-040-7 (e-book)

University and College Students: Health and Development Issues for the Leaders of Tomorrow
Daniel TL Shek, Rachel CF and Joav Merrick (Editors)
2013. ISBN: 978-1-62618-586-9 (Hardcover)
2013. ISBN: 978-1-62618-612-5 (e-book)

Break the Cycle of Environmental Health Disparities: Maternal and Child Health Aspects
Leslie Rubin and Joav Merrick (Editors)
2013. ISBN: 978-1-62948-107-4 (Hardcover)
2013. ISBN: 978-1-62948-133-3 (e-book)

Child and Adolescent Health Yearbook 2012
Joav Merrick (Editor)
2012. ISBN: 978-1-61942-788-4 (Hardcover)
2012. ISBN: 978-1-61942-789-1 (e-book)

Child Health and Human Development Yearbook 2011
Joav Merrick (Editor)
2012. ISBN: 978-1-61942-969-7 (Hardcover)
2012. ISBN: 978-1-61942-970-3 (e-book)

Child and Adolescent Health Yearbook 2011
Joav Merrick (Editor)
2012. ISBN: 978-1-61942-782-2 (Hardcover)
2012. ISBN: 978-1-61942-783-9 (e-book)

Tropical Pediatrics: A Public Health Concern of International Proportions
Richard R Roach, Donald E Greydanus, Dilip R Patel, Douglas N Homnick and Joav Merrick (Editors)
2012. ISBN: 978-1-61942-831-7 (Hardcover)
2012. ISBN: 978-1-61942-840-9 (e-book)

PEDIATRICS, CHILD AND ADOLESCENT HEALTH

BUILDING YOUTH FOR THE FUTURE

A PATH TOWARDS SUICIDE PREVENTION

HATIM A OMAR
AND
JOAV MERRICK
EDITORS

nova
science publishers
New York

Library of Congress Cataloging-in-Publication Data

Names: Omar, Hatim A., editor. | Merrick, Joav, 1950- editor.
Title: Building youth for the future : a path towards suicide prevention / editors, Hatim A Omar, M.D., and Joav Merrick, M.D. (Director, National Institute of Child Health and Human Development, Jerusalem, Israel, and others).
Description: Hauppauge, N.Y. : Nova Science Publishers, Inc., [2018] | Series: Pediatrics, child and adolescent health | Includes index.
Identifiers: LCCN 2018024791 (print) | LCCN 2018031362 (ebook) | ISBN 9781536137699 (ebook) | ISBN 9781536137682 (hardcover)
Subjects: LCSH: Young adults--Suicidal behavior. | Suicide--Prevention.
Classification: LCC HV6546 (ebook) | LCC HV6546 .B85 2018 (print) | DDC 362.28/70835--dc23
LC record available at https://lccn.loc.gov/2018024791

Published by Nova Science Publishers, Inc. † New York

CONTENTS

INTRODUCTION

In: Building Youth for the Future ISBN: 978-1-53613-768-2
Editors: H. A Omar and J. Merrick

Chapter 1

TEENS AND SUICIDE

Hatim A Omar[1,*], MD and
Joav Merrick[1-4], MD, MMedSci, DMSc
[1]Division of Adolescent Medicine,
Kentucky Children's Hospital, University of Kentucky,
Lexington, Kentucky, US
[2]National Institute of Child Health and Human Development,
Jerusalem, Israel
[3]Department of Pediatrics, Mt Scopus Campus,
Hadassah Hebrew University Medical Center, Jerusalem, Israel
[4]Center for Healthy Development, School of Public Health,
Georgia State University, Atlanta, Georgia, US

ABSTRACT

While a lot is left to be done in order to minimize the suicide attempts and suicides of Kentucky's adolescents, the work of Stop Youth Suicide Campaign (SYS) and the comprehensive grassroots' approach is showing

* Correspondence: Hatim A Omar, MD, Professor of Pediatrics and Obstetrics/Gynecology, Chief, Division of Adolescent Medicine and Young Parents Program, KY Clinic, L412, Lexington, KY 40536-0284, United States. Email: haomar2@uky.edu.

signs of success in the state of Kentucky. The 2013 nation Youth Risk Behavior Survey (YRBS) showed that for the 1st time, indicators of youth suicide in the state are at or below the national average, while they were always above that before. In the three rural counties where the school systems have partnered with SYS and the Division of Adolescent Medicine in Lexington there is an actual absence of completed suicides compared to the average of three per year prior to this partnership. In order to maintain and improve that, we must ensure that students do not have easy access to weapons, guns, and drugs by ensuring that these are properly stored in homes where children are present. Kentucky's educators must continue to develop ways to provide safe and supportive school environments. Physicians, teachers, parents, and students all must be able to recognize an adolescent at suicidal risk, be able to ask difficult questions about suicide, and have a variety of resources to seek help or offer support. Open dialogue and sharing stories about suicide can help spread awareness throughout the Kentucky community.

INTRODUCTION

In 2013, Suicide was the second leading cause of death among United States young adolescents (15-19 years of age), accounting for 18.4% of all deaths in this age group (1). According to a nationally representative study on the lifetime prevalence of adolescent suicidal behaviors, 12.1% of United States (US) adolescents experience suicidal ideation, 4.0% develop a plan and 4.1% attempt suicide (2). The same study estimated that approximately 60% of young people with a suicide plan will attempt suicide, and most of the adolescents who subsequently make an attempt do so within the first year after the onset of ideation.

These findings support the importance of the early identification of youths at risk of developing suicidal thoughts, monitoring their behavior, and providing the necessary help to address the risk factors that could act as catalysts for self-inflicted harm.

Research studies show that there were many factors, beyond genetic predisposition and mental illness that could influence suicide risk during adolescence. The adolescent phase is associated with physical, emotional, and social changes. Lack of family support, unrealistic expectations, academic pressure, social isolation, or victimization, can lead to disappointment, depression, or simply overreaction that may result in a self-inflicted injury or death.

Researchers found that patients who survived suicide attempts often acted impulsively, with very little time between thinking about suicide and actually attempting suicide (3). Having access to a firearm increases the chances that the suicide attempt will result in death (4-7). Adolescents, who were victims of dating violence were at higher risk for planning and/or attempting suicide (8, 9). There was a strong association between sexual assault and suicide risk in US adolescents, for both males and females (10). Kindrick and colleagues (11) found that "being forced to have sex," the early onset of sexual activity, and having more than one partner, were risk factors for depression, suicide ideation, suicide planning and attempts among Arkansas high-school students (11). Similar results were published by Epstein and Spirito (12), who found that being forced to have sex, having sex before age 13 years, early alcohol onset, and injection drug use, were associated with planning and attempting suicide (12).

Bullying victimization (school bullying or/and cyberbullying or brooming) is associated with higher risk of sadness and attempting suicide. Messias and colleagues reported (13) that according to the 2011 national Youth Risk Behavior Survey (YRBS) data, among the high-school students who reported not being bullied 4.6% reported having made a suicide attempt, compared with 21.1% of those reporting victimization of school and cyber bullying (13). Depression and hopelessness developed as a result of being bullied are related to suicidal ideation and attempts (14). Based on a meta-analysis, Holt et al. (15) concluded that involvement in bullying in any capacity (victim or perpetrator) was associated with suicidal ideation and behavior (15). "Feeling unsafe at school" was a significant risk factor for depression and suicide among high-school students (16). Adolescents who engaged in substance use were more likely to experience suicide ideation and behavior (17-19). Preteen alcohol use initiation was found to be an important risk factor for suicidal ideation and suicide attempts (20). Effective public health prevention of youth suicide is focused on reducing the suicide risk factors.

Stop Youth Suicide campaign

Youth suicide has been a major contributing factor to mortality and morbidity over the past five decades. It has consistently been one of the leading causes of death among teenagers 10-24 years of age and has been the third leading cause of death in the United States among this age group. According to the Centers for Disease Control and Prevention (CDC), 2003 Risk Youth Behavior Survey, an average of 8.5 percent of youth have actually attempted suicide (21). A 21 year old longitudinal study by Ferguson reported (22) suicide ideation in 28.8% of youth and suicide attempts in 7.5% by age 21 years. Autopsies of youth successfully completing suicide have identified numerous factors more significantly associated with suicide completers than with controls. These factors include non-intact family of origin, less frequent and satisfying communication with parents, history of mood disorder in mother, history of legal problems in father, family history of suicidal behavior, recent discipline (especially school suspension and juvenile court appearance), recent break up with boyfriend or girlfriend, recent separation of parents, lack of employment or school attendance, or grade failure (23) and the presence of DSM-III diagnosis (24) especially mood disorder, anxiety disorder and disruptive disorders.

According to prior studies, predictors of suicide attempts include parental depression, poor family functioning (25), large number of parental changes, poor attachment to parents, exposure to sexual abuse (26), depression, hopelessness (27), anxiety disorder and substance abuse (28). Primary reasons reported for suicide attempts when given a list to choose from include: to die, relief from state of mind, escape from a situation and to make others understand how desperate one feels (29). We have previously found that one of the most quoted reasons for attempted suicide in Central Kentucky, as reported by teenagers who were admitted to emergency rooms for attempted suicide, was conflict with parent followed by conflict with significant other (30).

The program was named "Stop Youth Suicide Campaign" (SYS) and started officially in October 2000. The campaign was started by a coalition including thirty agencies in the Central Kentucky area such as the Adolescent Medicine program at the University of Kentucky (leader of the coalition), the Coroner's Office, the Health Department, several local media outlets, participants from the school system, parent groups and many others. The goal of the program was:

- To improve community awareness of the problem of youth suicide.
- To assess the need in the community and provide basic knowledge about youth suicide.
- To start a public education campaign targeting parents, teachers and everyone who has anything to do with teens.
- To provide for improved education of medical care providers that deal with adolescents and to improve their knowledge and comfort level in screening and assessing for depression and suicide.
- To provide around the clock, available help to any teenagers in the area who were suicidal or needed help in that regard.

To accomplish these goals, the campaign started with a media press conference and an announcement by the Mayor's Office in Lexington, Kentucky to inform the people in the area about the program. This was followed by several days of media information on the government television channel in the area. The campaign then started a website (www.stopyouthsuicide.com) that is available to anyone to access information on youth suicide and in order to contact the campaign in case help is needed.

The campaign then produced local video showing teenagers, who had attempted suicide and survived, parents of youth who committed suicide and friends or peers of young people who had completed suicide, as well as experts discussing ways and means on how to understand youth suicide and work on youth suicide prevention. The next step was to educate providers, which was done through numerous lectures and workshops. From October 2000 to December 2004, a total of 60 lectures and workshops and three full day conferences was devoted to youth suicide prevention training to medical care providers of all levels. The campaign has also participated in working with the state government and local agencies to build and establish a State-wide youth suicide prevention program. In addition, the Stop Youth Suicide Campaign had participated in church and school activities in multiple visits to all area middle and high schools as well as religious activities to educate parents on the problem of youth suicide.

Over the first four years, between October 2000 and 2004 the Stop Youth Suicide Campaign had received a total of 861 e-mails and 976 phone calls from teenagers who were contemplating suicide and asking for help and 26 e-mails and 112 phone calls from parents of teens at risk. These patients were appropriately treated in the area and referred to appropriate people if they were out of the area. A total of thirteen teenagers who were acutely suicidal with a plan and readiness to complete it at the time of contacting the program were helped to change their minds and to continue to be alive as of this date. Several of the teens helped by the program have joined the campaign to help other teens. Public awareness in the area regarding youth suicide has improved based on surveys done before the launching of the program and years after. Also, the Stop Youth Suicide Campaign played a significant role in working with the state on establishing a state suicide program that is now ongoing.

Another event that the Stop Youth Suicide campaign hosts is the annual Spread the Love-a-thon. The founder of this event is Leslie Aslam, MD and the event is held immediately prior to Valentine's Day. High school students from Fayette County as well as surrounding counties attend the event. During the Spread the Love-a-thon, students learn several facts about suicide. They then reach out to others via phone calls, texts, emails, social media, or in person to make "life lines." When they make a life line, they must tell the other person a few facts about suicide and give them three genuine complements. The atmosphere is very festive with Valentine's decorations and donated pizza. The annual event has several hundred teens attending and resulting in several thousands of life lines contacts. Many teens have commented on how positive it was to hear the responses they got from those they reached out to. The teens also report feeling good about reaching out to so many others in such a positive way.

SOME DATA

It is claimed that 72% of all deaths among adolescents and young adults in the United States is due to four causes: car accidents, other unintentional injuries, homicides and suicide (1, 31). The Centers for Disease Control and Prevention (CDC) developed the Youth Risk Behavioral Surveillance System (YRBS) (32) to monitor priority health risk behaviors among high school students, including risk behaviors known to be related to suicide ideation, planning and suicide attempts. A brief introduction to the survey methodology is presented in this chapter, for a more detailed discussion the reader is referred to Brener et al. (33). The YRBS is a survey of a sample of students in grades 9-12 in the 50 US States and District of Columbia. The sampling frame for this sample consisted of all public and private schools catering for students in at least one of grades 9-12. A three-stage cluster sampling design was adopted to produce a nationally representative sample of students in grade 9-12 in public and private schools (32).

In the first-stage 1,276 primary sampling units (PSUs) were selected consisting of counties, subareas of large counties, or groups of smaller, adjacent counties (32). The 1,276 PSUs were stratified into 16 strata according to their metropolitan statistical area (MSA) status (i.e., urban city) and the percentages of black and Hispanic students in the PSUs (32). From the 1,276 PSUs, 57 were sampled with probability proportional to overall school enrolment size for the PSU.

Sampling of schools and students was carried out in stage two and three (32). In the second stage of sampling, 194 schools with any of grades 9–12 were sampled with probability proportional to school enrolment size. The third stage of sampling consisted of random sampling in each of grades 9–12, one or two classrooms from either a required subject (e.g., English or social studies) or a required period (e.g., homeroom or second period). All students in sampled classes were eligible to participate. Schools, classes, and students that refused to participate were not replaced (32). A self-administered questionnaire during a class period was used for data collection. This process included data collection under the US's data protection and privacy laws including obtaining parental consent (32).

Information about the reliability of the standard questionnaire has been published elsewhere (34). The standard and national YRBS questionnaires are available at http://www.cdc.gov/healthyyouth/yrbs/ questionnaire_rationale.htm. Data were analysed as follows (32): "Statistical analyses were conducted on weighted data using SAS (35) and SUDAAN (36) software to account for the complex sampling designs. Prevalence estimates and confidence intervals were computed for all variables and all data sets. In addition, for the national YRBS data, t tests were used to determine pairwise differences between subpopulations (37). Differences between prevalence estimates were considered statistically significant if the t test p value was <0.05 for main effects (sex, race/ethnicity, and grade) and for interactions (sex by race/ethnicity, sex by grade, race/ethnicity by sex, and grade by sex). In the results section, only statistically significant differences in prevalence estimates are reported in the following order: sex, sex by race/ethnicity, sex by grade, race/ethnicity, race/ethnicity by sex, grade, and grade by sex. To identify long-term temporal changes in health-risk behaviors nationwide, prevalence estimates from the earliest year of data collection to 2011 for each variable assessed with identically worded questions in three or more survey years were examined. Logistic regression analyses were used to account for all available estimates; control for sex, grade, and racial/ethnic changes over time; and simultaneously assess orthogonal linear and quadratic time effects (37)."

As described above, YRBS data are publically available through Youth Online (31). Youth Online is a data tool that allows national and state-level analysis, including by race/ethnicity, gender, grade, and health topics. Youth Online allows comparison between two groups or two time periods, provides a p-value from a t-test to determine if the percentage of students engaged in a particular risky behavior is significantly different between the two groups/time points, and offers an interpretation of the test results at level of significance?=0.05. For this chapter, the percentage of Kentucky High School Students (KyHSS) engaged in a specific risky behavior in 2013 is compared to the percentages reported for 2011 in order to identify areas of improvement as well as areas where more work is needed in the coming years. KyHSS were also compared with US HSS in 2013. Significant gender-specific differences on given questions were highlighted. The readers can find complete data on the youth risk behavior survey by querying Youth Online (http://nccd.cdc.gov/YouthOnline/).

Using YRBS data, the objectives of this study were to assess recent changes, 2011-2013, in prevalence of suicide-related risk behaviors among Kentucky High School Students (KyHSS), to assess how the KyHSS compared to their US peers, and to identify areas where state and local interventions are needed to reduce the suicide risk among KyHSS.

FINDINGS

The Stop Youth Suicide Campaign is a holistic suicide awareness campaign. In other words, the programme seeks to provide appropriate information and assist all stakeholders, e.g., individuals, communities and governments/ policy makers to make informed decisions. In Kentucky, the Campaign has been successful in changing some laws, introduce suicide education and training at schools and provide interventional services as well as prevention strategies throughout Kentucky. A measure of success is a sustained drop in suicide rates over time. As mentioned before, the suicide rates in Kentucky began to decline annually following the Stop Youth Suicide Campaign. However, of interest is whether the Campaign has had any impact on changing attitudes and perceptions and hence behavior, if so, how has this change been affected. The CDC data set provides a number of behavioral outcome measures on adolescents which are collected independently of the Campaign. These variables can be used to assess and evaluate the effect of the Campaign across Kentucky.

Suicide ideation, planning and attempt

According to the Kentucky 2013 YRBS data, 15% of the Kentucky High School Students (KyHSS) reported seriously considering attempting suicide during the 12 months before the survey (see Table 1).

Table 1. Prevalence of risk behaviors among Kentucky high school students, 2011-2013, and United States high school students, 2013

YRBS (selected questions)	Ky 2013	U.S. 2013	p-value[a]	Ky 2011	p-value[b]
Carried a weapon	20.7	17.9	0.07	22.8	0.34
Carried a gun	7.5	5.5	0.05	8.6	0.39
Carried a weapon on school property	6.4	5.2	0.18	7.4	0.50
Were threatened or injured with a weapon on school property	5.4	6.9	0.03	7.4	0.08
Were in a physical fight	21.2	24.7	0.02	28.7	0.00
Were injured in a physical fight	2.8	3.1	0.59	4.2	0.05
Were in a physical fight on school property	6.0	8.1	0.04	11.4	0.00
Did not go to school because they felt unsafe at school or on their way to or from school	7.0	7.1	0.96	8.4	0.29
Were electronically bullied	13.2	14.8	0.19	17.4	0.01
Were bullied on school property	21.4	19.6	0.25	18.8	0.20
Were ever physically forced to have sexual intercourse	9.6	7.3	0.01	11.0	0.27
Experienced physical dating violence	9.8	10.3	0.73	—	—
Experienced sexual dating violence	9.8	10.4	0.61	—	—
Felt sad or hopeless	25.7	29.9	0.02	27.0	0.52
Seriously considered attempting suicide	15.0	17.0	0.23	14.8	0.94
Made a plan about how they would attempt suicide	12.6	13.6	0.45	13.7	0.43
Attempted suicide	7.7	8.0	0.72	10.9	0.04
Attempted suicide that resulted in an injury, poisoning, or overdose that had to be treated by a doctor or nurse	2.9	2.7	0.72	4.6	0.08
Drank alcohol before age 13 years	19.0	18.6	0.78	20.5	0.47
Currently drank alcohol	30.4	34.9	0.01	34.6	0.05
Had five or more drinks of alcohol in a row	19.4	20.8	0.36	23.2	0.04
Reported that their largest number of drinks in a row was 10 or more	6.3	6.1	0.81	—	—
Ever used marijuana	34.0	40.7	0.01	37.4	0.23
Tried marijuana before age 13 years	8.5	8.6	0.88	10.0	0.26
Currently used marijuana	17.7	23.4	0.00	19.2	0.48
Ever used cocaine	4.5	5.5	0.16	7.5	0.00
Ever used hallucinogenic drugs	—	7.1	—	—	—
Ever used inhalants	7.1	8.9	0.03	11.4	0.00

YRBS (selected questions)	Ky 2013	U.S. 2013	p-value[a]	Ky 2011	p-value[b]
Ever used ecstasy	4.2	6.6	0.00	6.6	0.01
Ever used heroin	—	2.2	—	5.2	—
Ever used methamphetamines	3.7	3.2	0.48	5.6	0.03
Ever took steroids without a doctor's prescription	2.9	3.2	0.55	5.3	0.00
Ever took prescription drugs without a doctor's prescription	12.4	17.8	0.00	19.0	0.00
Ever injected any illegal drug	—	1.7	—	4.2	—
Were offered, sold, or given an illegal drug on school property	20.6	22.1	0.32	24.4	0.04
Ever had sexual intercourse	44.7	46.8	0.47	51.8	0.05
Had sexual intercourse before age 13 years	5.4	5.6	0.82	7.2	0.10
Had sexual intercourse with four or more persons	12.6	15.0	0.10	16.6	0.07
Were currently sexually active	31.7	34.0	0.39	37.7	0.09
Did not use a condom	46.9	40.9	0.04	49.4	0.43
Did not use birth control pills	80.1	81.0	0.71	78.8	0.62
Did not use an IUD (e.g., Mirena or ParaGard) or implant (e.g., Implanon or Nexplanon)	97.4	98.4	0.21	—	—
Did not use a shot (e.g., Depo-Provera), patch (e.g., OrthoEvra), or birth control ring (e.g., NuvaRing)	95.1	95.3	0.92	—	—
Did not use birth control pills; an IUD or implant; or a shot, patch, or birth control ring	72.7	74.7	0.45	73.8	0.74
YRBS (selected questions)	Ky 2013	U.S. 2013	p-value[a]	Ky 2011	p-value[b]
Did not use both a condom during and birth control pills; an IUD or implant; or a shot, patch, or birth control ring before last sexual intercourse	93.4	91.2	0.11	90.5	0.12
Did not use any method to prevent pregnancy	15.1	13.7	0.46	16.2	0.64
Drank alcohol or used drugs before last sexual intercourse	18.7	22.4	0.10	16.8	0.49
Were never taught in school about AIDS or HIV infection	19.3	14.7	0.03	16.1	0.19
Were never tested for HIV	—	87.1	—	—	—

[a] p-value for the t-test comparing prevalence between Kentucky and U.S. high school student risk behaviors, 2013.

[b] p-value for the t-test comparing prevalence between Kentucky high school student risk behaviors in 2013 and 2011.

Table 2. Prevalence of risk behaviors among Kentucky high school students, 2013, by gender

Kentucky 2013 YRBS (selected questions)	All	Female	Male	p-value[a]
Unintentional Injuries and Violence				
Carried a weapon	20.7	7.6	33.5	0.00
Carried a gun	7.5	2.5	12.3	0.00
Carried a weapon on school property	6.4	2.7	9.7	0.00
Were threatened or injured with a weapon on school property	5.4	3.8	6.6	0.02
Were in a physical fight	21.2	13.4	28.8	0.00
Were injured in a physical fight	2.8	1.6	3.8	0.00
Were in a physical fight on school property	6	4.1	7.7	0.00
Did not go to school because they felt unsafe at school or on their way to or from school	7	7.2	6.6	0.64
Were electronically bullied	13.2	16.4	9.9	0.00
Were bullied on school property	21.4	24.1	18.6	0.01
Were ever physically forced to have sexual intercourse	9.6	11.9	7.2	0.00
Experienced physical dating violence	9.8	11.8	7.6	0.03
Experienced sexual dating violence	9.8	13.1	6.4	0.00
Felt sad or hopeless	25.7	31.7	20	0.00
Seriously considered attempting suicide	15	19.2	10.9	0.00
Made a plan about how they would attempt suicide	12.6	14.3	10.9	0.03
Attempted suicide	7.7	9.2	5.9	0.02
Attempted suicide that resulted in an injury, poisoning, or overdose that had to be treated by a doctor or nurse	2.9	3.2	2.6	0.51
Alcohol and Other Drug Use				
Drank alcohol before age 13 years	19	16.8	21	0.13
Currently drank alcohol	30.4	28	32.6	0.12
Usually obtained the alcohol they drank by someone giving it to them	34.1	42.9	27	0.00
Had five or more drinks of alcohol in a row	19.4	15.4	23.3	0.00
Reported that their largest number of drinks in a row was 10 or more	6.3	4	8.6	0.00
Ever used marijuana	34	30.6	36.9	0.06
Tried marijuana before age 13 years	8.5	6	10.6	0.01
Currently used marijuana	17.7	15.3	20	0.04
Ever used cocaine	4.5	2	6.5	0.00
Ever used hallucinogenic drugs	—	—	—	

Kentucky 2013 YRBS (selected questions)	All	Female	Male	p-value[a]
Ever used heroin	—	—	—	
Ever used methamphetamines	3.7	2.5	4.3	0.09
Ever took steroids without a doctor's prescription	2.9	1.5	3.8	0.02
Ever took prescription drugs without a doctor's prescription	12.4	12	12.6	0.71
Ever injected any illegal drug	—	—	—	
Were offered, sold, or given an illegal drug on school property	20.6	15.9	24.8	0.00
Sexual Behaviors				
Ever had sexual intercourse	44.7	43.3	45.9	0.42
Had sexual intercourse before age 13 years	5.4	3.2	7.5	0.00
Had sexual intercourse with four or more persons	12.6	10.5	14.4	0.07
Were currently sexually active	31.7	32.3	31	0.65
Did not use a condom	46.9	54.9	37.9	0.00
Did not use birth control pills	80.1	75.8	84.7	0.02
Did not use an IUD (e.g., Mirena or ParaGard) or implant (e.g., Implanon or Nexplanon)	97.4	97.3	97.5	0.83
Did not use a shot (e.g., Depo-Provera), patch (e.g., OrthoEvra), or birth control ring (e.g., NuvaRing)	95.1	93.2	97.1	0.01
Did not use birth control pills; an IUD or implant; or a shot, patch, or birth control ring	72.7	66.3	79.4	0.00
Did not use both a condom during and birth control pills; an IUD or implant; or a shot, patch, or birth control ring before last sexual intercourse	93.4	91.5	95.4	0.04
Did not use any method to prevent pregnancy	15.1	18.6	11.2	0.01
Drank alcohol or used drugs before last sexual intercourse	18.7	13.6	23.8	0.00
Were never taught in school about AIDS or HIV infection	19.3	19.7	18.5	0.58
Were never tested for HIV	—	—	—	

[a] p-value for the t-test comparing prevalence between Kentucky male vs female high school student risk behaviors, 2013.

The prevalence of suicide ideation didn't change significantly from 2011 (14.8%) and showed no significant difference with the 2013 US prevalence (17%). There was no significant change in the prevalence of suicide planning among KyHSS in 2013 (12.6%) compared with 2011

Kentucky data (13.7%) and with the 2013 US prevalence (13.6%). There was a significant decrease in the percentage of KyHSS who reported attempting suicide (one or more times during the 12 months before the survey) in 2013 compared to 2011 (7.7% vs. 10.9%), and a significant decrease in the 2013 reported attempted suicide that resulted in an injury, poisoning, or overdose that had to be treated by a doctor or a nurse (2.9% vs. 4.6%). In 2013, KyHSS were as likely as their US peers to attempt suicide (7.7% vs. 8.0%) and to attempt suicide that required medical treatment (2.9% vs. 2.7%). Kentucky high school female students were more likely than male students to have seriously considered attempting suicide (during the 12 months before the survey) (19.2% vs. 10.9%) (see Table 2). More females than males made a plan about how they would attempt suicide (during the 12 months before the survey) (14.3% vs. 10.9%). While females were more likely than males to report having attempted suicide one or more times during the 12 months before the survey (9.2% vs 5.9%), there was no significant gender difference in attempted suicide that resulted in an injury, poisoning, or overdose that had to be treated by a doctor or nurse (during the 12 months before the survey) (3.2% for females, 2.6% for males).

Felt sad or hopeless

KyHSS were less likely to feel sad or hopeless (almost every day for two or more weeks in a row so that they stopped doing some usual activities during the 12 months before the survey) compared with their US peers in 2013 (25.7% vs. 29.9%), but there was no significant change from the reported 27% in 2011 in Kentucky (see Table 1). Kentucky female students were significantly more likely to feel sad or hopeless than males in 2013 (31.7% vs. 20.0%) (see Table 2).

Bullying

More than one fifth (21.4%) of the KyHSS reported being bullied on school property (during the 12 months before the survey) in 2013, percentage that is not significantly different from the one reported in 2011 (18.8%) and from the reported school bullying among the US-HSS in 2013 (19.6%) (see Table 1). The prevalence of having been electronically bullied (including being bullied through e-mail, chat rooms, instant messaging, websites, or texting during the 12 months before the survey) in 2013 among the KyHSS (13.2%) was comparable to the one for the US-HSS (14.8%). The KyHSS however reported significantly lower prevalence of being electronically bullied in 2013 than in 2011 (17.4%). Kentucky female students were much more likely than the male students to be bullied on school property (24.1% vs. 18.6%) or electronically bullied (16.4% vs. 9.9%) (see Table 2).

Dating violence (physical or sexual)

Among the KyHSS who dated or went out with someone during the 12 months before the 2013 survey, 9.8% reported that they experienced physical dating violence (one or more times during the 12 months before the survey, including being hit, slammed into something, or injured with an object or weapon on purpose by someone they were dating or going out with) (see Table 1). There was no significant difference between the KyHSS and the US-HSS in the prevalence of physical dating violence (9.8% vs. 10.3%) as well as the prevalence of the sexual dating violence (9.8% vs. 10.4%), 2013. Both questions were not included in the 2011 Kentucky YRBS. Kentucky female HSS were at significantly higher risk than male HSS for experiencing physical dating violence (11.8% vs. 7.6%) and sexual dating violence 913.1% vs. 6.4%) (see Table 2).

Forced to have sexual intercourse

KyHSS reported significantly higher prevalence of ‘ever being physically forced to have sexual intercourse when they did not want to’, compared with their US peers, 2013 (9.6% vs. 7.3%). The Kentucky prevalence did not improve significantly in 2013 from the reported 11.0% in 2011. Kentucky female students were significantly more likely to reply 'yes' to the question 'ever forced to have sexual intercourse' than the male students, 2013 (11.9% vs. 7.2%).

Did not go to school because they felt unsafe at school or on their way to or from school

Seven percent of the KyHSS reported they did not go to school, because they felt unsafe at school or on their way to or from school (on at least 1 day during the 30 days before the survey). This is a small, but insignificant decrease from the 8.4% reported in 2011. The corresponding prevalence for the U.S. High School Students in 2013 was 7.1%. There was no significant difference in the percentage of female and male KyHSS who didn't go to school at least once during the 30 days before the 2013 surveys because they felt unsafe (7.2% vs. 6.6%).

Physical fight

KyHSS were significantly less likely to be in a physical fight (one or more times during the 12 months before the survey) in 2013 (21.2%) than in 2011 (28.7%), and significantly less likely than their US peers in 2013 (24.7%) (Table 1). The prevalence of being in a physical fight on school property (one or more times during the 12 months before the survey) among KyHSS was significantly lower in 2013 than in 2011 (6.0% vs. 11.4%); the 2013 Kentucky prevalence was significantly lower than the 2013 US prevalence (6.0% vs. 8.1%). Although, there was no significant difference in the percentage of HSS injured in a physical fight in Kentucky and in the US, 2013 (2.8% vs. 3.1%), the reported 2013 Kentucky prevalence suggested a decrease from the reported 2011 Kentucky prevalence (2.8% vs. 4.2%, p-value = 0.05). As expected, Kentucky high school boys were significantly more likely than the girls to be in a physical fight (28.8% vs. 13.4%), to be injured in a physical fight (3.8% vs. 1.6%), or to be in a physical fight on school property (7.7% vs. 4.1%).

Risk behaviors related to weapons

From 2011 to 2013 there were no significant changes in the percentage of KyHSS who (on at least one day during the 30 days before the survey): 1) carried a weapon (such as a gun, knife, or club) (22.8% vs. 20.7%); 2) carried a gun (8.6% vs. 7.5%); or 3) carried a weapon on school property (such as a gun, knife, or club) (7.4% vs. 6.4%) (see Table 1). There were no significant differences between the 2013 Kentucky and US prevalence on carrying a weapon (20.7% vs. 17.9%), carrying a gun (7.5% vs. 5.5%), or carrying a weapon on school property (6.4% vs. 5.2%). However, KyHSS were less likely than the US-HSS to being threatened or injured with a weapon on school property (5.4% vs. 6.9%).

Significantly higher percentage of Kentucky high school boys than girls carried a weapon on at least one day during the 30 days before the survey (33.5% vs 7.6%), carried a gun (12.3% vs. 2.5%), carried a weapon on school property (9.7% vs. 2.7%), or were threatened or injured with a weapon on school property during the 12 months before the survey (6.6% vs. 3.8%).

Alcohol use

KyHSS were as likely as the US-HSS to had drank alcohol before age 13 years (for the first time other than a few sips) (19.0% vs. 18.6%), and no substantial change in the early onset of alcohol use among KyHSS was observed since 2011 (20.5%) (see Table 1). Significantly lower percentage of KyHSS reported having five or more drinks of alcohol in a row (within a couple of hours on at least 1 day during the 30 days before the survey) in 2013 than in 2011 (19.4% vs. 23.2%); no differences in the prevalence among the Kentucky and the US- HSS, 2013 (19.4% vs. 20.8%).

The Kentucky high school girls were as likely as the boys (16.8% vs. 21.0%) to start drinking alcohol before age of 13 years, according to 2013 Kentucky YRBS (see Table 2). However, the boys were more likely than the girls to have five or more drinks of alcohol in a row (within a couple of hours on at least 1 day during the 30 days before the survey) (23.3% vs. 15.4%).

Drug use

Although KyHSS were less likely than US-HSS to report in 2013 that they have ever used marijuana in their life (34.0% vs. 40.7%) and that they used marijuana one or more times during the 30 days before the survey (17.7% vs. 23.4%), no change in marijuana usage (ever or during the last 30 days) was seen among Kentucky students between 2011 and 2013 (see Table 1).

The 2013 Kentucky YRBS did not include the questions on the use of heroin and the injection of illegal drugs. The most recent Kentucky data is from the 2011 YRBS, showing that 5.2% of the KyHSS ever used heroin, a significantly higher percentage than the reported 2.9% for the US-HSS in 2011 (p-value = 0.01, data not shown in the tables). Also, 4.2% of the KyHSS reported in 2011 that they ever injected any illegal drugs, compared with 2.3% for the U.S.HSS in 2011 (p-value = 0.00; data not shown in the tables).

The KyHSS reported significantly lower prevalence in 2013 than in 2011 on several risk behaviors related to drug use: 1) ever used any form of cocaine (powder, crack, or freebase) one or more times in their lifetime (4.5% vs. 7.5%); 2) ever used inhalants (7.1% vs. 11.4%); 3) ever used ecstasy (4.2% vs. 6.6%); 4) ever used methamphetamines (3.7% vs. 5.6%); 5) ever took steroids without a doctor's prescription (2.9% vs. 5.3%); 6) ever took prescription drugs without a doctor's prescription (12.4% vs. 19.0%); 7) were offered, sold, or given an illegal drug on school property (during the 12 months before the survey) (20.6% vs. 24.4%).

Kentucky high school boys were more likely than the girls to try marijuana before age 13 years, currently used marijuana, ever used cocaine, ever used ecstasy, took steroids without a doctor's prescription, or were offered, sold, or given an illegal drug on school property (see Table 2).

Discussion

In 2011, Kentucky high school students were no more likely than their US peers to be seriously considering suicide or planning to attempt suicide, yet Kentucky students were significantly more likely to carry out their suicide plan (38). It is not clear why Kentucky students were more likely to follow through with their suicide plan. One explanation could be that adolescents often make decisions on impulse and easy access to firearms and lack of engagement with their support network lead to making a serious/fatal suicide attempt.

A study of 82 psychiatric patients post-suicide attempts found that although about 83% of patients were alone when the decision (87%) to commit suicide came about, 76% had personal contact with a family member, partner, or friend via phone during which 25-40% hinted of their wish to die (3). Kentucky residents need to better identify/recognize students at risk for suicide and who are planning suicide, so that future attempts can be prevented. When it comes to risk factors, Kentucky adolescents have a specific set of risk behaviors with a higher prevalence than their US peers. For example, in 2011, when suicide attempts peaked, Kentucky students were more likely than US students to carry a weapon or gun, to not go to school because they felt unsafe at school or on their way to or from school, to have 'ever been physically forced to have sexual intercourse,' to have 'ever used a needle to inject any illegal drug into their body,' or have 'ever used heroin one or more times.' For these risk factors, no change was seen in Kentucky students from 2011 to 2013. Unfortunately, the questions for injecting illegal drugs or using heroin were not even included in the Kentucky Youth Risk Behavioral Surveillance System (YRBS) in 2013, but it is known that these are growing issues for Kentucky youth.

Interestingly enough, in 2013, the percentage of Kentucky students who attempted suicide decreased but those who were seriously considering or planning suicide did not. This could suggest a couple of things. Either the risk factors for suicide which did decrease during this time were the factors which made those who were thinking about suicide more likely to attempt, or that students had greater access to resources which kept those who were thinking about suicide from attempting.

The risk factors for suicide which decreased from 2011 to 2013 for Kentucky high school students were being in a physical fight both on and off school property, having been subjected to cyber bulling, drug use (except for injecting illegal drugs, heroin use, alcohol, and marijuana).

Although Kentucky females were more likely than Kentucky males to report suicidal ideation, make plans, or attempt, they were less likely than males to report for the remaining suicidal risk factors that were covered by YRBS. As Kentucky adolescents have a specific set of risk behaviors with a higher prevalence than their US peers, so does each gender when compared with the other. In the same manner that Kentucky residents need to be aware of their adolescents' suicidal risk factors, they should also be particularly conscientious of each gender's increased suicidal risk, while not overlooking the opposite gender for those same risks.

In 2010, Kentucky's governor signed Senate Bill 65 and House Bill 51 as suicide prevention education for Kentucky's high school students and staff. Senate bill 65 amended KRS 158.070 to require principals, guidance counsellors, and teachers to complete a minimum of two hours of instruction in suicide prevention each school year. House bill 51 amended KRS 156.095 to require the Cabinet for Health and Family Services to post suicide prevention awareness and training information on its Web page by August 1, 2010; requiring every public middle and high school administrator to disseminate suicide prevention awareness information to all middle and high school students by September 1, 2010, and September 1 of each year thereafter.

The Stop Youth Suicide Campaign (SYS) is a community-based youth suicide prevention program, led by the University of Kentucky Division of Adolescent Medicine (39). It raises awareness and educates government agencies, teachers, parents, and students about the high risk behaviors that can lead to youth suicide. It provides education for medical care agencies to recognize and screen for adolescent depression and suicide, connects youth, parents, citizens, caregivers, and professionals with appropriate support services (40). SYS was also instrumental in creating and initially leading the state wide effort through the KY suicide prevention group. The Kentucky Suicide Prevention Group, unites people who have been affected, personally or professionally, by suicide (41). A few of the suicide prevention programs that are posted on their website include Signs of Suicide (SOS) and Question, Persuade, and Refer (QPR) Suicide Prevention Gatekeeper Training. QPR seek to train ordinary citizens in sessions lasting 90 minutes in questioning, persuading and referring. SOS is a two day program during which students are screened for depression and suicide risk and referred for professional help where necessary. Students are taught to recognize signs of depression and suicide in others to acknowledge them, and let that person know they care about them, and to also inform a responsible adult. Aside from suicide awareness, this program strives to develop productive attitudes toward suicide and encourages seeking help.

Another way to keep Kentucky's youth from turning suicidal ideation/plans into an attempt is to restrict their means of committing suicide. One study found that those with firearms in their home were no more likely to report suicidal ideation or plan, but among those with a plan, having a firearm in the home increased the chances completing suicide using firearm seven-fold (42). Schuster et al. (5) estimated from the National Health Interview Survey that 35% of homes in the United States with children younger than 18 years reported owning at least one firearm, and that 43% of these homes had at least one unlocked firearm (5). This is troublesome, because if adolescents have easy access to a firearm and choose to attempt suicide with it, there is an 86% chance that their attempt will result in death. A 2014 study reporting 30 to 50% reduction in suicide rates was observed in other countries by restricting access to lethal suicide methods such as guns (43). As for gun access among Kentucky's youth, according to the 2013 YRBS, no improvements have been made.

Other restriction methods for suicide include reducing the availability of prescription drugs. Kentucky has made great strides in limiting the availability of prescription drugs through House Bill 1 that expanded the use of the state prescription drug monitoring program to limit the illicit use of controlled substances dispensed by pharmacies (44). Prescription and over-the-counter drug disposal locations are available across the state to help remove unneeded medications from homes (45). According to the YRBS, Kentucky's youth are less likely to have ever taken a prescription drug without a doctor's prescription in 2013 compared to 2011. The Kentucky Office of Drug Control Policy has posted Public Service Announcements (PSAs) about the "Heroin epidemic" in Kentucky and will continue to work towards increased public education, increased access to treatment, enhanced penalties for major traffickers, and greater access to naloxone (46).

Another category of the YRBS which has not seen improvement is sexual violence. A program called Green Dot is an initiative to spread knowledge on how to stop sexual violence, sexual harassment, stalking and dating violence. Interventions are mostly geared to high school and college students. A recent study found that there was more than a 50% reduction in the self-reported frequency of sexual violence at schools that received the Green Dot training, compared with a slight increase in schools that did not (47). The 2013 YRBS added two new questions "experienced physical dating violence" and "experienced sexual dating violence" in order to monitor the prevalence of sexual violence in Kentucky. teaches everyone personalized skills needed to stop rape, partner violence and stalking from happening teaches everyone personalized skills needed to stop rape, partner violence and stalking from happening.

Although the percentage of Kentucky students who were cyber bullied was significantly lower in 2013, the percentage of Kentucky students who were bullied on school property and who did not go to school because they felt unsafe did not change during the period 2011 to 2013. This is despite Kentucky's anti-bullying legislation House Bill 91 from 2008 which warns students that hazing, bullying, menacing, taunting, intimidating, verbal or physical abuse of others or other threatening behavior is not tolerated and those who violate the policy are subject to the appropriate disciplinary action (48). Additionally, students that believe they are victims of bullying/hazing will be provided with a process to enable them to report such incidents to District personnel for appropriate action.

Conclusion

While a lot is left to be done in order to minimize the suicide attempts and suicides of Kentucky's adolescents, the work of SYS and the comprehensive grassroots' approach is showing signs of success in the state. The 2013 YRBS shows that for the 1st time, indicators of youth suicide in the state are at or below the national average while they were always above that before. In the three rural counties where the school systems have partnered with SYS and the Division of adolescent medicine there is an actual absence of completed suicides compared to the average of 3 per year prior to this partnership. In order to maintain and improve that, we must ensure that students do not have easy access to weapons, guns, and drugs by ensuring that these are properly stored in homes where children are present. Kentucky's educators must continue to develop ways to provide safe and supportive school environments. Physicians, teachers, parents, and students all must be able to recognize an adolescent at suicidal risk, be able to ask difficult questions about suicide, and have a variety of resources to seek help or offer support. Open dialogue and sharing stories about suicide can help spread awareness throughout the Kentucky community.

The work to establish the "Stop Youth Suicide Campaign (SYS)" has resulted in contact with many young adults. We realized that the most important thing for the kids was finding a caring person they can trust and talk to. This project has been a learning process for all involved. We learned that we can help and so can everyone else. This community and grassroot approach showed tangible results. It needs caring and dedication and most importantly desire to make a difference. It is hard work, but well worth it. Lessons learned:

- We will never completely eliminate youth suicide
- We can reduce both completed and attempted youth suicide
- Mental health treatment plays a significant role in suicide prevention, but it is not a primary prevention in many cases.
- The health care system needs to eliminate the discrepancy between medical and mental. We are dealing with an individual as a whole and separating mental from medical does more harm than good.
- Teens who feel alone, hopeless and desperate need to have someone they can turn to, but they feel they do not. To change that we need to educate parents, school teachers and personnel, religious leaders and athletic coaches as well as health care providers to use every encounter with teens to tell them whom they can talk to.
- Organizations such as the American Academy of Pediatrics, Society for Adolescent Health and Medicine (SAHM) and many others need to make youth suicide a focal point of their conferences every year. Just as an example, SAHM which is supposed to be the leader in teen health has not dedicated a plenary on teen suicide for years and very few workshops, which is unacceptable.

Youth suicide prevention is a public health project for all of us to work on.

References

[1] Leading Causes of Death Reports. WISQARSTM. National Center for Injury Prevention and Control, Centers for Disease Control and Prevention. URL: http://webappa.cdc.gov/ sasweb/ncipc/leadcaus10_us.html.

[2] Nock MK, Green JG, Hwang I, McLaughlin KA, Sampson NA, Zaslavsky AM, et al. Prevalence, correlates, and treatment of lifetime suicidal behavior among adolescents: results from the National Comorbidity Survey Replication Adolescent Supplement. JAMA Psychiatry 2013;70(3):300-10.

[3] Deisenhammer EA, Ing CM, Strauss R, Kemmler G, Hinterhuber H, Weiss EM. The duration of the suicidal process: how much time is left for intervention between consideration and accomplishment of a suicide attempt? J Clin Psychiatry 2009;70(1) 19-24.

[4] Rivara FP. Youth Suicide and Access to Guns. JAMA pediatrics 2015 Mar 9. Doi: 10.1001/jamapediatrics.2015.104.

[5] Grossman DC, Mueller BA, Riedy C, Dowd MD, Villaveces A, Prodzinski J, et al. Gun storage practices and risk of youth suicide and unintentional firearm injuries. JAMA 2005;293(6):707-14.

[6] Brent DA, Perper JA, Allman CJ, Moritz GM, Wartella ME, Zelenak JP. The presence and accessibility of firearms in the homes of adolescent suicides. A case-control study. JAMA 1991;266(21):2989-95.

[7] Brent DA, Perper JA, Moritz G, Baugher M, Schweers J, Roth C. Firearms and adolescent suicide. A community case-control study. Am J Dis Child 1993;147(10):1066-71.

[8] Belshaw SH, Siddique JA, Tanner J, Osho GS. The relationship between dating violence and suicidal behaviors in a national sample of adolescents. Violence Victim 2012;27(4):580-91.

[9] Olshen E, McVeigh KH, Wunsch-Hitzig RA, Rickert VI. Dating violence, sexual assault, and suicide attempts among urban teenagers. Arch Pediatr Adolesc Med 2007;161(6):539-45.

[10] Anderson LM, Hayden BM, Tomasula JL. Sexual Assault, Overweight, and Suicide Attempts in U.S. Adolescents. Suicide Life Threat Behav 2014 Dec 19. Doi: 10.1111/sltb.12148.

[11] Kindrick C, Gathright M, Cisler JM, Messias E. Sadness, suicide, and sexual behavior in Arkansas: results from the youth risk behavior survey 2011. J Ark Med Soc 2013;110(7):134-6.

[12] Epstein JA, Spirito A. Gender-specific risk factors for suicidality among high school students. Arch Suicide Res 2010;14(3):193-205.

[13] Messias E, Kindrick K, Castro J. School bullying, cyberbullying, or both: correlates of teen suicidality in the 2011 CDC Youth Risk Behavior Survey. Comprehen Psychiatry 2014;55(5):1063-8.

[14] Shireen F, Janapana H, Rehmatullah S, Temuri H, Azim F. Trauma experience of youngsters and Teens: A key issue in suicidal behavior among victims of bullying? Pak J Med Sci 2014;30(1):206-10.

[15] Holt MK, Vivolo-Kantor AM, Polanin JR, Holland KM, DeGue S, Matjasko JL, et al. Bullying and suicidal ideation and behaviors: a meta- analysis. Pediatrics 2015;135(2):e496-509.

[16] Kindrick K, Castro J, Messias E. Sadness, suicide, and bullying in Arkansas: results from the Youth Risk Behavior Survey — 2011. J Ark Med Soc 2013;110(5):90-1.

[17] Burge V, Felts M, Chenier T, Parrillo AV. Drug use, sexual activity, and suicidal behavior in U.S. high school students. J Sch Health 1995;65(6): 222-7.

[18] Vijayakumar L, Kumar MS, Vijayakumar V. Substance use and suicide. Curr Opin Psychiatry 2011;24(3):197-202.

[19] Kaley S, Mancino MJ, Messias E. Sadness, suicide, and drug misuse in Arkansas: results from the Youth Risk Behavior Survey 2011. J Ark Med Soc 2014;110(9):185-6.

[20] Swahn MH, Bossarte RM. Gender, early alcohol use, and suicide ideation and attempts: findings from the 2005 youth risk behavior survey. J Adolesc Health 2007;41(2):175-81.

[21] Centers for Disease Control and Prevention. Surveillance summaries, May 21, 2004. MMWR 2004;53:25-7.

[22] Fergusson DM, Woodward LJ, Horwood LJ. Risk factors and life processes associated with the onset of suicidal behavior during adolescence and early adulthood. Psychol Med 2000;30:23-39.

[23] Gould MS, Fisher P, Parides M, Flory M, Shaffer D. Psychological risk factors of child and adolescent completed suicide. Arch General Psychiatr 1996;53:1155-62.

[24] Shaffer D, Gould MS, Fisher P, Trautman P, Moreau D, Kleinman M, Flory M. Psychiatric diagnosis in child and adolescent suicide. Arch General Psychiatr 1996;53:339-48.

[25] Garber J, Little S, Hilsman Ruth, Weaver KR. Family predictors of suicidal symptoms in young adolescents. J Adolesc 1998;21:445-57.

[26] Overholser JC, Freiheit SR, DiFilippo JM (1987), Emotional distress and substance abuse as risk factors for suicide. Can J Psychiatr 1997;42: 402-8.

[27] Gould MS, King R, Greenwald S, Fisher P, Schwab-Stone M, Kramer R, et al. Psychopathology associated with suicidal ideation and attempts among children and adolescents. J Am Acad Child Adolesc Psychiatr 1998;37:915-23.

[28] Boergers J, Spirito A, Donaldson D. Reasons for adolescent suicide attempts: associations with psychological functioning. J Am Acad Child Adolesc Psychiatr 1998;37:1287-93.

[29] Negron R, Placentini J, Graae F, Davies M, Shaffer D. Microanalysis of adolescent suicide attempters and ideators during the acute suicidal episode. J Am Acad Child Adolesc Psychiatr 1997;36:1512-9.

[30] Omar HA, Hagedorn J. Retrospective analysis of youth evaluated for suicide attempt or suicidal ideation in an emergency room setting. Int J Adolesc Med Health 2001;14(1):55-60.

[31] CDC, NCHS. Mortality data file for 2008 with all state identifiers. Atlanta, GA: CDC, CD-ROM, 2011.

[32] Youth Risk Behavior Surveillance System (YRBSS). Centers or Disease Control and Prevention. URL: www.cdc.gov/yrbss.

[33] Brener ND, Kann L, Kinchen S, Grunbaum JA, Whalen L, Eaton D, et al. Methodology of the Youth Risk Behavior Surveillance System. MMWR 2004;53:RR-12.

[34] Brener ND, Kann L, McManus T, Kinchen SA, Sundberg EC, Ross JG. Reliability of the 1999 Youth Risk Behavior Survey questionnaire. J Adolesc Health 2002;31:336–42.

[35] SAS Institute, Inc. SAS,® version 9.2 [software and documentation]. Cary, NC: SAS Institute, 2008.

[36] Research Triangle Institute. SUDAAN® version 10 [software and documentation]. Research Triangle Park, NC: Research Triangle Institute, 2008.

[37] Hinkle DE, Wiersma W, Jurs SG. Applied statistics for the behavioral sciences. 5th ed. Boston, MA: Houghton Mifflin, 2003.

[38] Centers for Disease Control and Prevention. Youth Risk Behavior Surveillance. Compare State/District and National Results. URL: http://www.cdc.gov/ healthyyouth/yrbs /factsheets/index.htm#compare.

[39] Stop Youth Suicide Campaign. URL: http://www.stopyouthsuicide.com/

[40] Omar HA. A model program for youth suicide prevention. Int J Adolesc Med Health 2005;17(3):275-8.

[41] Kentucky Suicide Prevention Group. URL: http://kentuckysuicideprevention.org/.

[42] Betz ME, Barber C, Miller M. Suicidal behavior and firearm access: results from the second injury control and risk survey. Suicide Life Threat Behav 2011;41(4):384-91.

[43] Barber CW, Miller MJ. Reducing a suicidal person's access to lethal means of suicide: a research agenda. Am Journal Prevent Med 2014; 47(3 Suppl 2):S264-72.

[44] Kentucky House Bill 1. URL: http://www.lrc.ky.gov/record/12ss/hb1.htm

[45] Kentucky Office of Drug Control Policy. Prescription drug disposal locations. URL: http://odcp.ky.gov/Pages/Prescription-Drug-Disposal- Locations.aspx.

[46] Kentucky Office of Drug Control Policy. The heroin epidemic. URL: http://odcp.ky.gov/Pages/The-Heroin-Epidemic.aspx.

[47] "Green Dot" effective at reducing sexual violence. URL: http://uknow.uky.edu/ content/green-dot-effective-reducing-sexual- violence.

[48] Kentucky House Bill 91. URL: http://www.lrc.ky.gov/record/08rs/HB91.htm.

SECTION ONE: THE ADOLESCENT BRAIN

In: Building Youth for the Future ISBN: 978-1-53613-768-2
Editors: H. A Omar and J. Merrick

Chapter 2

ADOLESCENT BRAIN DEVELOPMENT AND SELF-ESTEEM

Maria H Rahmandar, MD
and Frank M Biro*[*], MD
Ann and Robert H. Lurie Children's Hospital of Chicago, Chicago, Illinois and Division of Adolescent and Transition Medicine, Cincinnati Children's Hospital Medical Center, Cincinnati, Ohio, US

ABSTRACT

Puberty can be a vulnerable time for adolescents as their body, brain, and self-esteem undergo changes. Low self-esteem is an important risk factor for suicide, which is a major cause of mortality in teens. On the other hand, high self-esteem can protect against suicidality. Building self-esteem could be an approach that saves lives.

* Correspondence: Frank Biro, MD, Professor, Adolescent and Transition Medicine, UC Department of Pediatrics, Cincinnati Children's Hospital Medical Center, 3333 Burnet Avenue, Cincinnati, Ohio 45229-3026, United States. Email: frank.biro@cchmc.org.

INTRODUCTION

Suicide is, and has been, one of the most serious issues impacting adolescents. Suicide ranks number three as a cause of death in United States teens, and many more teens experience an attempt, yet survive (1). Rates of suicide attempts, and serious consideration of suicide, are greater in adolescent females than males. The Youth Risk Behavior Survey (YRBS) 2013 (2) noted that 17.0% of high school students seriously considered suicide, with nearly twice as many females (22.4%) reporting they seriously considered suicide contrasted to 11.6% of males. There was also a significant difference in suicide attempts by gender; 10.6% of high school females reported one or more attempts contrasted to 5.4% of high school males (2). Although the rate of suicide attempts is higher in females, completion in males is four times the rate in females (1), as males tend to use deadlier means (i.e., firearms in males vs. drug overdoses in females). This review will explore some of the reasons in this important difference between the two genders, examining biologic changes and relative timing of puberty, maturation of the brain and cognitive growth, and how these changes potentially impact self-esteem.

HOW ADOLESCENTS CHANGE

Adolescents mature in several areas, including cognitive, social, and biologic realms. Maturation in each of these areas impacts the others. For example, biologic maturation (puberty) has both direct and indirect effects on cognitive (thought) development and neurodevelopment (brain), as noted below. Cognitive changes include development of formal operational thought. Formal operational thought, also known as abstract thought, includes the ability to understand complex relationships, such as algebra concepts and nuances in communication, as well as how current behaviors affect future outcomes. One becomes more reflective and develops a sense of egocentrism (for example, if adolescents are thinking about something, those around them may, and perhaps, should be thinking about the same thing). The clinician and parent should be aware that responses from the adolescent patient at this time may reflect partial answers, not necessarily from a sense of misdirection, but rather that the adolescent may assume that the clinician has already drawn the same conclusion from the response that the adolescent client has drawn. For example, an adolescent may present with headaches and abdominal pain and assume that the clinician is already aware that the adolescent is concerned that she is pregnant. It is important for the clinician to engage in reflective listening, summarize the issues with the adolescent, and then ask directly if (s)he is concerned about anything else. Of note, not all adolescents develop abstract thought, and they are less likely to do so if they have intellectual delays (that is, mental retardation).

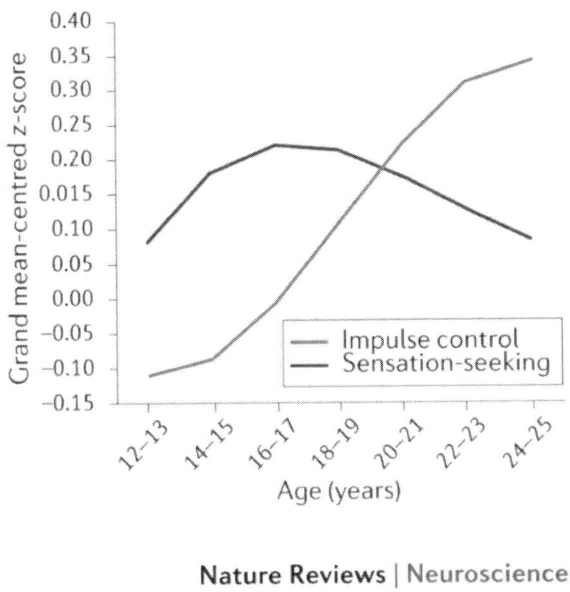

Figure 1. Sensation-seeking and impulse control. The different developmental trajectories of self-reported sensation-seeking and impulse control based on an analysis of data from National Longitudinal Study of Youth (NLSY79) Children and Young Adults (CNLSY), a longitudinal, nationally representative survey of more than 7,000 American children and young adults ranging in age from 12 to 24 years (see National Longitudinal Surveys) (3).

During the mid- to late- teen years, there is typically transition from "hot" (high emotional content) to "cool" (less emotional, more rational content) cognition; this likely results from both from the development of abstract thought processes described above as well as neuromaturation. As an example of the differences between hot and cool cognition, the reader should take a moment to recall a very emotional, stressful event in the past month and how that situation was resolved. Were you at the top of your game and trying to determine the best outcome for everybody involved? You likely were experiencing hot cognition at that time, with a significant amount of affective (emotional) input into conscious processing. This unusual state for an adult is not unlike the typical state of the adolescent brain.

Both hot cognition, as well as engaging in risk-taking or emotionally charged behaviors, may reflect neuromaturation of the adolescent brain. There is later maturation of prefrontal cortex and mismatch of incentive processing over cognitive control during teen years (see Figure 1) (3). Several have proposed that risky behavior during adolescence is a result of this imbalance, with a predominance of the emotional, sensation-seeking areas of the brain, such as the limbic and paralimbic structures, over the cognitive-control (executive functioning) areas of the brain, such as the prefrontal cortex (4). The "self-regulatory" (impulse-control) system may be overwhelmed by the "incentive-processing" (reward-seeking) system (4). Indeed, there are distinct changes in brain volume, structure, and connections that occur during puberty, and some of these changes are impacted differently in individuals undergoing relatively earlier or later pubertal maturation (5). Additionally, these maturation changes occur at an earlier age in females than males; that is, maturation of the prefrontal cortex occurs in the late teens in females contrasted to the early twenties in males.

Another result of neurodevelopment and biologic maturation is the gender-specific increase in depression. Prior to adolescence, males have a slightly higher rate of depression that do females, but by mid-adolescence and, more precisely, mid-puberty, the rate of depression among girls is twice as great as the rate in boys (6). Further, when depression is examined with respect to the hormones estradiol and testosterone, hormone levels are more important than pubertal status (7).

PUBERTY AND THE RAPIDLY CHANGING BODY

Puberty is represented by a series of changes throughout the body and includes the pubertal growth spurt, changes within the hypothalamic/ pituitary/gonadal axis, development of secondary sexual characteristics, changes in body composition, and the achievement of fertility. Puberty begins with an increase in the pulsatile secretion of gonadotropin-releasing hormone (GnRH), typically at night. This pulsatile secretion stimulates the release of follicle-stimulating hormone (FSH) and luteinizing hormone (LH) and the subsequent production of the sex steroids estradiol and testosterone from the gonads (in girls, ovaries and in boys, testicles). Estradiol stimulates the growth of breast tissue, and both estrogen and testosterone stimulate the growth plates in bones and lead to the pubertal growth spurt.

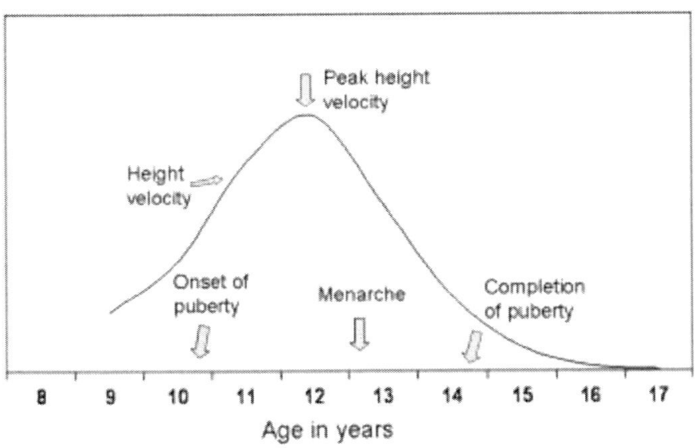

Figure 2. Sequence of puberty in girls.

The sequence of events is demonstrated in Figure 2 (8). With pubertal maturation, there are associated changes in body composition. Both girls and boys have an increase in lean body mass, but girls experience a rapid increase in the total, as well as relative, body fat during pubertal maturation (9). These changes in body composition occur during a vulnerable period of the development of self-esteem, as noted in the following section.

CHANGES IN GLOBAL SELF-WORTH IN ADOLESCENT GIRLS

Adolescence is a time when youth become more independent and think of themselves as a separate "self" (10). Self-esteem may become more salient with this increased awareness of self. Adolescent boys typically have greater self-esteem than girls (11-12). As girls go through the teen years, measures of self-esteem, or self-worth, increase slightly or remain stable in African-American girls, whereas measures of self-esteem decrease in white girls, which appears to be driven by a decrease in body satisfaction (9) (see Figure 3). There is a significant interaction of body mass index (BMI), race, and age on self-esteem. Self-esteem is greater among African-American girls with a typical BMI (between the 20th and 80th percentile, corresponding to the average BMI plus or minus one standard deviation), whereas self-esteem is greatest in white girls in the lowest BMI group (below the 20th percentile) (9). Self-esteem in white girls increases in mid- to late adolescence, and research has suggested that this increase in self-worth is associated with a decrease in the importance that white adolescent girls place on body satisfaction.

A decrease in self-worth during puberty can impact resiliency (the ability to cope with negative experiences) and, subsequently, increase the likelihood of substance abuse, risky sexual behaviors, depression, and suicidal thoughts (13, 14). Of these factors, depression is considered as the most significant risk for suicidal behavior (15). Negative body attitudes and feelings are predictive of suicidal ideation beyond the effects of depression, perhaps because those with negative image are less invested in protecting their bodies from harm (16). Of note, the standardized mortality ratio (SMR, risk of death compared to the general population of similar age and gender) for psychiatric diagnoses is greatest for eating disorders rather than depression; the SMR for anorexia nervosa was 32.4 times, whereas the SMR for depression was 21.2 times the expected rate of suicide in the general population (17).

On the other hand, increasing the level of self-esteem improves resiliency and protects against suicidality (18). Self-esteem influences adolescent suicide risk behaviors for youth with low as well as high family support. However, teens with low family support may have to rely on themselves more often, so self-esteem may be of heightened importance in these adolescents (18). Depression and low self-esteem in the family context (e.g., perceiving minimal family support or feeling unloved) are each independently associated with suicidal ideation and attempts; screening for depression and low self-esteem in the family context may help identify adolescents at risk for suicide attempts (15).

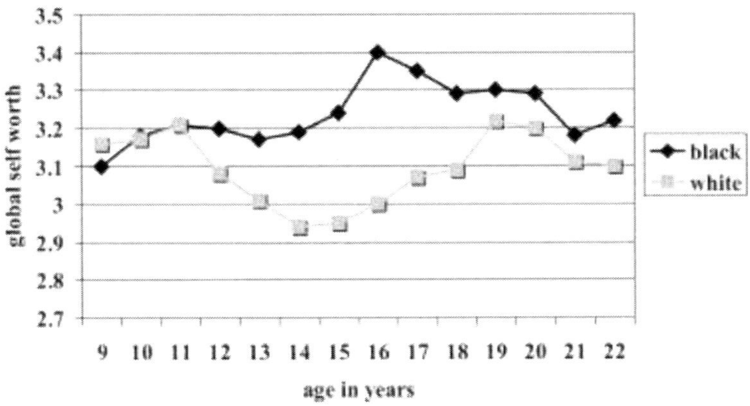

Figure 3. Global self-worth, by race and age. Longitudinal analysis of 1213 black and 1166 white girls, aged 9 and 10 years at intake. Black diamonds = black participants; gray squares = white participants.

BUILDING SELF-ESTEEM IN ADOLESCENTS

Self-worth is stable for some individuals, but for others, as discussed earlier, self-esteem can change over time as factors, such as body composition, change (9). If self-esteem is not always a static personality trait, how can it be enhanced and thus hopefully decrease the risk of suicide?

Low levels of peer/parental/family support and low self-esteem predict suicidality and, conversely, high levels of each could serve as protective factors (10, 18). However, more awards and praise are not necessarily the answer. Contemporary teens are part of what is sometimes referred as the "Trophy Generation," with a surplus of superficial accolades; despite this, the rates of suicide and depression in adolescents have not changed (19).

Some school-based programs have been developed that effectively build self-esteem in a meaningful way. Such programs could be used to intervene in a variety of mental health, social, and behavioral issues that are linked to levels of self-esteem. Through this approach, multiple issues could be tackled by a single program (20). Additionally, school could be the ideal setting for this work, potentially reaching a large number of children in an efficient manner (20). One program that proved its effectiveness was a mentoring program that focused on relationships, self-esteem, goal setting, and academics. The youths' self-esteem increased; they felt more connected to school, peers, and family; and they also were less likely to be depressed (21). It has been previously shown that connectedness, especially in school, protects against depression and suicidality as well as other negative outcomes (22). Another example was a school-based self-esteem education program that addressed body image, along with eating attitudes and behaviors, and resulted in positive effects that persisted one year after completion (23). Although these programs show promise, more research needs to be done on long-term data regarding these interventions in order to determine lasting impact.

In addition to the programs that can be implemented within local schools, there are approaches geared toward parents and other interested caretakers. See the tips below from the American Academy of Pediatrics website HealthChildren.org, along with the Mayo Clinic and Substance Abuse and Mental Health Services Administration (SAHMSA) websites (24, 25). The following are recommendations for the parents of teenagers from HealthyChildren.org (24):

- Provide sincere praise for accomplishments as well as effort.
- When teens make mistakes, offer constructive criticism.
- In matters in which your teen can have a choice, ask for your teen's opinion.
- Encourage teens to explore their interests and build on their talents

The following are recommendations to adolescents from The Mayo Clinic based on concepts of cognitive behavioral therapy (25):

- Reflect on situations that lower your self-esteem.
- Pay attention to your negative thoughts.
- Test the truthfulness of your negative thoughts.
- Replace the negative thoughts with truthful, positive thoughts.

Another recommendation from The Mayo Clinic is based on acceptance and commitment therapy (25):

- Reflect on situations that lower your self-esteem.
- Pay attention to your negative thoughts.
- Repeat the negative thoughts over and over until the words sound strange in order to distance yourself from the negative thoughts.
- Instead of fighting them, accept the thoughts so as to decrease their power. You do not need to control your thoughts, and your negative thoughts do not need to control you.

Conclusion

Puberty can be a vulnerable time for adolescents as their body, brain, and self-esteem undergo changes. Low self-esteem is an important risk factor for suicide, which is a major cause of mortality in teens. On the other hand, high self-esteem can protect again suicidality. Building self-esteem could be an approach that saves lives.

Suggested Readings

- SAHMSA has a short booklet that can be found at no cost online to help improve self-esteem and practice affirmations (26): https://store.samhsa.gov/shin/content/SMA-3715/SMA-3715.pdf.
- The following book, "Living with depression: A survival manual for families" by Kim Poling, LSW, can be downloaded free of charge (27). https://www.starcenter.pitt.edu/Files/PDF/Manuals/Living_With_Depression.pdf.

References

[1] Centers for Disease Control and Prevention. Suicide prevention: Youth suicide. URL: http://www.cdc.gov/violenceprevention/pub/youth_suicide.html.

[2] Kann L, Kinchen S, Shanklin SL, Flint KH, Kawkins J, Harris WA, et al. Youth risk behavior surveillance—United States, 2013. MMWR Surveill Summ 2014;63 (suppl 4):1-168.

[3] Steinberg L. The influence of neuroscience on US Supreme Court decisions about adolescents' criminal culpability. Nat Rev Neurosci 2013;14(7):513-8.

[4] Steinberg L. A dual systems model of adolescent risk-taking. Dev Psychobiol 2010;52(3):216-24.

[5] Goddings AL, Mills KL, Clasen LS, Giedd JN, Viner RM, Blakemore SJ. The influence of puberty on subcortical brain development. Neuroimage 2014;88:242-51.

[6] Angold A, Costello EJ, Worthman CM. Puberty and depression: The roles of age, pubertal status and pubertal timing. Psychol Med 1998;28(1):51-61.

[7] Angold A, Costello EJ, Erkanli A, Worthman CM. Pubertal changes in hormone levels and depression in girls. Psychol Med 1999;29(5):1043-53.

[8] Biro FM. Puberty—Whither goest? J Pediatr Adolesc Gynecol 2006;19:163-5.

[9] Biro FM, Striegel-Moore RH, Franko DL, Padgett J, Bean JA. Self-esteem in adolescent females. J Adolesc Health 2006;39(4):501-7.

[10] Brausch AM, Decker KM. Self-esteem and social support as moderators of depression, body image, and disordered eating for suicidal ideation in adolescents. J Abnorm Child Psychol 2014;42(5):779-89.

[11] Birndorf S, Ryan S, Auinger P, Aten M. High self-esteem among adolescents: longitudinal trends, sex differences, and protective factors. J Adolesc Health 2005;37(3):194-201.

[12] Gordon Rouse KA, Ingersoll GM, Orr DP. Longitudinal health endangering behavior risk among resilient and nonresilient early adolescents. J Adolesc Health 1998;23(5):297-302.

[13] Ethier KA, Kershaw TS, Lewis JB, Milan S, Niccolai LM, Ickovics J. R. Self-esteem, emotional distress and sexual behavior among adolescent females: Inter-relationships and temporal effects. J Adolesc Health 2006;38(3):268-74.

[14] Salazar LF, Crosby RA, DiClemente RJ, Wingood GM, Lescano CM, Brown LK, et al. Self-esteem and theoretical mediators of safer sex among African American female adolescents: Implications for sexual risk reduction interventions. Health Educ Behav 2005;32(3):413-27.

[15] Wild LG, Flisher AJ, Lombard C. Suicidal ideation and attempts in adolescents: Associations with depression and six domains of self-esteem. J Adolesc 2004;27(6):611-24.

[16] Brausch AM, Muehlenkamp JJ. Body image and suicidal ideation in adolescents. Body Image 2007;4(2):207-12.

[17] Harris EC, Barraclough B. Excess mortality of mental disorder. Br J Psychiatry 1998;173(1):11-53.

[18] Sharaf AY, Thompson EA, Walsh E. Protective effects of self-esteem and family support on suicide risk behaviors among at-risk adolescents. J Child Adolesc Psychiatr Nurs 2009;22(3):160-8.

[19] Healthy People 2020. Healthy People 2020 leading health indicators: Mental health. Published 2014 May. URL: http://www.healthypeople.gov/sites/default/files/HP2020_LHI_Mental_Hlth.pdf.

[20] Mann M, Hosman CMH, Schaalma HP, de Vries NK. Self-esteem in a broad-spectrum approach for mental health promotion. Health Educ Res 2004;19(4):357-72.

[21] King KA, Vidourek RA, Davis B, McClellan W. Increasing self-esteem and school connectedness through a multidimensional mentoring program. J School Health 2002;72(7):294.

[22] Resnick MD, Bearman PS, Blum RW, Bauman KE, Harris KM, Jones J, et al. Protecting adolescents from harm: Findings from the National Longitudinal Study on Adolescent Health. JAMA 1997;278(10):823-32.

[23] O'Dea JA, Abraham S. Improving the body image, eating attitudes, and behaviors of young male and female adolescents: A new educational approach that focuses on self-esteem. Int J Eat Disord 2000;28(1):43-57.

[24] American Academy of Pediatrics. Ways to build your teenager's self-esteem. URL: http://www.healthychildren.org/English/ages-stages/teen/Pages/Ways-To-Build-Your-Teenagers-Self-Esteem.aspx.

[25] Mayo Clinic Foundation. Self-esteem: Take steps to feel better about yourself. URL: http://www.mayoclinic.org/healthy-lifestyle/adult-health/in-depth/self-esteem/art-20045374.

[26] Curie CG, Arons BS. Building self-esteem: A self-help guide. URL: https://store.samhsa.gov/shin/content/SMA-3715/SMA-3715.pdf.

[27] Poling K. Living with depression: A survival manual for families, 3rd ed. Pittsburgh, PA: University of Pittsburgh Health System, 1997.

In: Building Youth for the Future
Editors: H. A Omar and J. Merrick
ISBN: 978-1-53613-768-2

Chapter 3

THE ADOLESCENT BRAIN AND SUBSTANCE ABUSE

Patrick J Withrow**, *MD, FACC, FSCAI
Outreach, Baptist Health Paducah, Paducah, Kentucky, US

ABSTRACT

A few years ago an event took place at a local high school in McCracken County, Kentucky where four students were caught smoking marijuana in the parking lot. This event resulted in a collaboration amongst a 23 year old opioid addict in recovery, a captain in the city police department and a physician actually involved in substance and addictive activity education for caregivers and educators. The presentation or program in the schools is offered to any school in Western Kentucky that request it. The collaboration has presented "The Adolescent Brain and Substance Abuse" to approximately 9,000 middle school kids in nine counties. The presentation includes some sound advice to the kids that in order to avoid withdrawal, craving tolerance and the compulsion to use drugs is to "Never start!" Caring people such as parents, caregivers, family, teachers,

* Correspondence: Patrick J Withrow, MD, FACC, FSCAI, Director of Outreach Baptist Health Paducah, 2501 Kentucky Avenue, Paducah, KY 42003, United States. Email: pwithrow@bhsi.com.

counselors and friends are urged to let kids depend on them to talk in order to make a difference in behavioral outcomes.

Introduction

About three years ago at a local high school in McCracken County, Kentucky, four students were caught smoking marijuana in the parking lot. As part of the school's action to stop this activity, three citizens from varied backgrounds were asked to counsel these students; a 23 year old opioid addict in recovery, a captain in the city police department and a physician actually involved in substance and addictive activity education for caregivers and educators. All of our efforts seemed to be successful based on follow-ups with the teachers and the students that had gotten into trouble with marijuana.

After discussion with the teachers, we decided to present a program to other middle school kids. We offered this program to any school in Western Kentucky that requested it. Thus far, we have presented "The Adolescent Brain and Substance Abuse" to approximately 9,000 middle school kids in nine counties. Arguably, it may be more efficacious to talk with younger kids than middle schoolers, but we gave our program to the children that the school offered to us, namely 6-8th graders (around age 11-14 years).

Our Goal

Our goal was to reinforce each one of our messages in three different ways. Matt would tell his very compelling life story of how he started drug abuse at age 11 years. His presentation included his progression from alcohol to marijuana to opioids to methamphetamines. Foster care, reform school, treatment centers and jail were all described as well as the paralysis and death of his older brother, because of addiction. Captain Copeland of the

Paducah Police Department would detail many of the addicts, innocent victims and situations he had observed, while working as a police officer.

If the audience was not too large, I brought in a brain specimen to the presentation. This stimulated the interest in many of the kids. I allowed the kids to put on a single surgical glove so they could touch the brain (see Figure 1).

The immature adolescent prefrontal cortex function may explain why poor judgement and decision making are present in youth. The adolescent prefrontal cortex does not mature until the middle 20s. Specifically, brain maturation occurs with "pruning and decrease of gray matter" that is not being used and when glial cell myelination or insulation of nerve cells and "connections" are occurring. Poor judgement and decision making is in part why adolescents are prone to risk-taking and are vulnerable to substance abuse. Exposure to substances at this critical time of brain development may affect the propensity of future multiple drug addictions.

I jokingly use the example of functioning with an immature prefrontal cortex is like playing cards with a half deck or driving a car with poor brakes and a super accelerator pedal (see Figure 3).

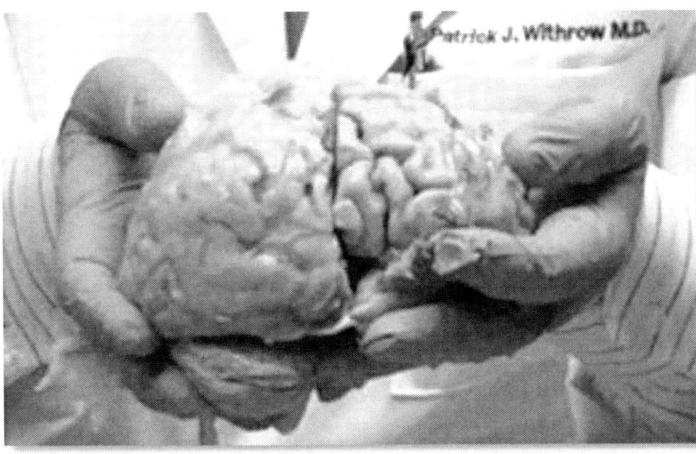

Figure 1. We bring a brain specimen for those kids who want to get close and are very interested in biology. If the audience is not too large, we allow the children to put on one latex glove and gently touch the brain.

The Adolescent Brain

The adolescent brain does NOT mature until 22-27 years old

Figure 2. The adolescent brain does not mature until the mid-twenties. Maturation results when neurons that are not used are "pruned" and when the glial cells laying down of an insulating myelin sheath is complete. Neurons make many new connections after birth to improve neural transmissions

The Front of the Adolescent Brain

Figure 3. Driving a car with poor brakes and a super accelerator pedal.

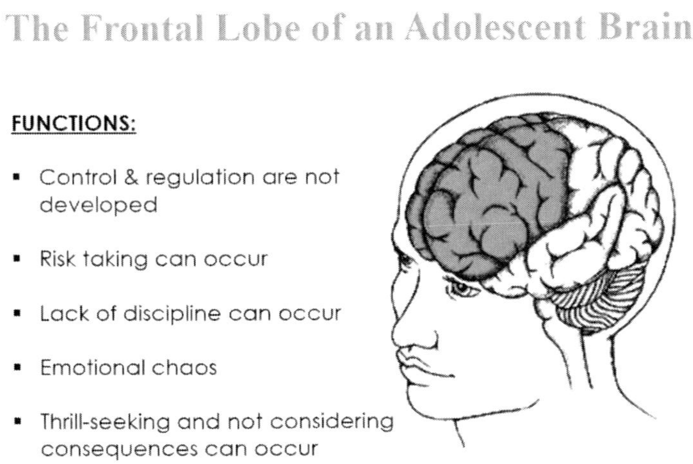

Figure 4. The immature frontal lobe in the adolescent brain explains many behaviors that occur during youth.

As compared to the adolescent prefrontal cortex, the “instinct” or “reptilian brain” develops around 10-12 years. In our culture, possibly around 7 years, quick reflex or instinctive decisions are made through the more developed premature limbic or reptilian brain. Poor judgement decisions may be made from the immature prefrontal cortex. The excitable, reward oriented, risk taking and peer driven “instinct brain” in conjunction with the “immature prefrontal cortex” (poor judgement) may be a recipe for thrill seeking and addiction (see Figure 4).

WHY DO KIDS USE DRUGS?

As part of our program, we ask the middle school children: Why would kids use drugs anyway? The answers are variable, but the themes are remarkably similar; impulsive feelings, hopelessness and depression, anxiety, sensitivity or panic disorder, and sensation or thrill seeking. I suppose these reasons could be reduced to “I just don’t like the way I feel” (see Figure 5).

Figure 5. Here are just a few responses I get when I ask middle school children why they use drugs. Does this mean you take drugs because you don't like the way you feel?

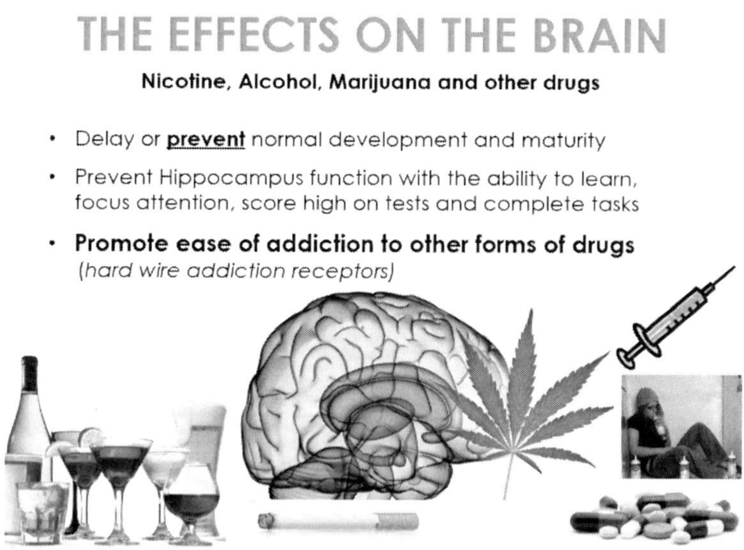

Figure 6. How many of you know a 30-year-old that acts like a 13-year-old? Wonder why? Don't squander your God-given brain ability to learn and achieve by using drugs. Multiple addictions are possible with drug exposure at a critical time of brain immaturity.

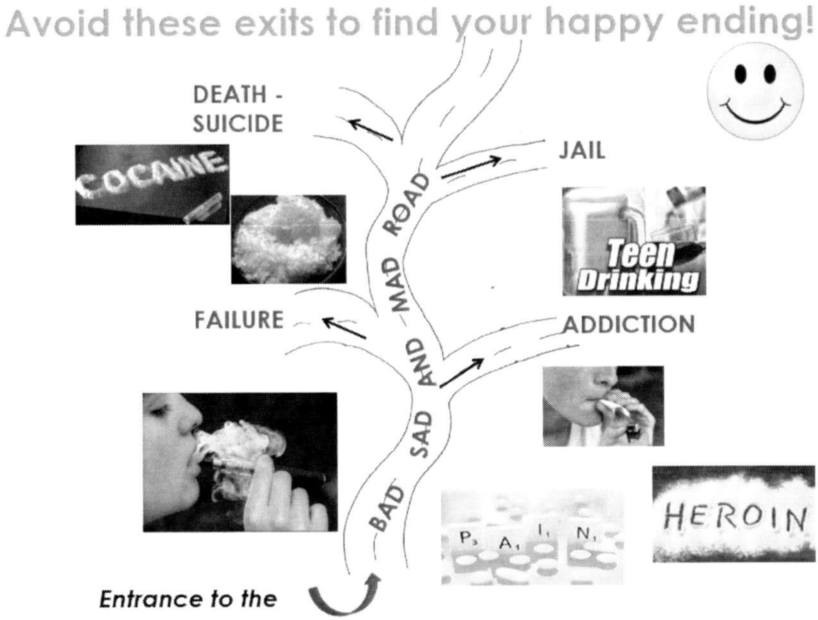

Figure 7. The bad, sad and mad road is one to be avoided. This road can be an unforced error of life.

True to the topic of this program, I think it is very important to explain to the children the detrimental effects of the substances on the adolescent brain. We address nicotine, alcohol, marijuana, opioids, bath salts, methamphetamines and "downers".

"Do you kids know a 30 year old that acts like a 13 year old?" The kids invariably hold up their hands in affirmation. A follow-up question: "Why do you think that is?" I explain to the kids that drugs delay or even prevent normal development and maturation of the brain. It is common for a 30 year old person who used drugs at a young age to act like a 13 year old, because that is the age their brain maturation was arrested (see Figure 6).

Drugs and other substances impair scoring well on tests, being able to complete tasks, and the ability to learn. These substances and effects can be compared to the brain damage caused by lead contamination in drinking water. Since the primitive instinct brain is excitable and reward-aware, the use of drugs at a young age can result in many drug addictions. With adolescent drug use, there is no way of predicting the detrimental and permanent brain defects.

Just like other medical conditions, such as heart attack and stroke, there are risk factors for the disease of addiction. If there is a family history of alcoholism or drug addiction, then a hereditary risk for the disease may be present. The age of first use is a risk factor for addiction. The younger a person is at first use, the more likely addiction will occur. Availability of the drugs, whether it is from peers or from the home medicine cabinet, is a clear risk for addiction (see Figure 7).

A recent study found that 43% of automobile fatalities were drug related (illegal or abused prescription) and 37% related to alcohol levels above the legal limit (see Figure 8). This data is felt by some to be associated with the legalization of medical and recreational marijuana. Currently, there are 29 states and the District of Columbia where marijuana is legal to use is some form.

Figure 8. 43% tested positive for drugs and 37% over the legal alcohol limit in fatal crashes.

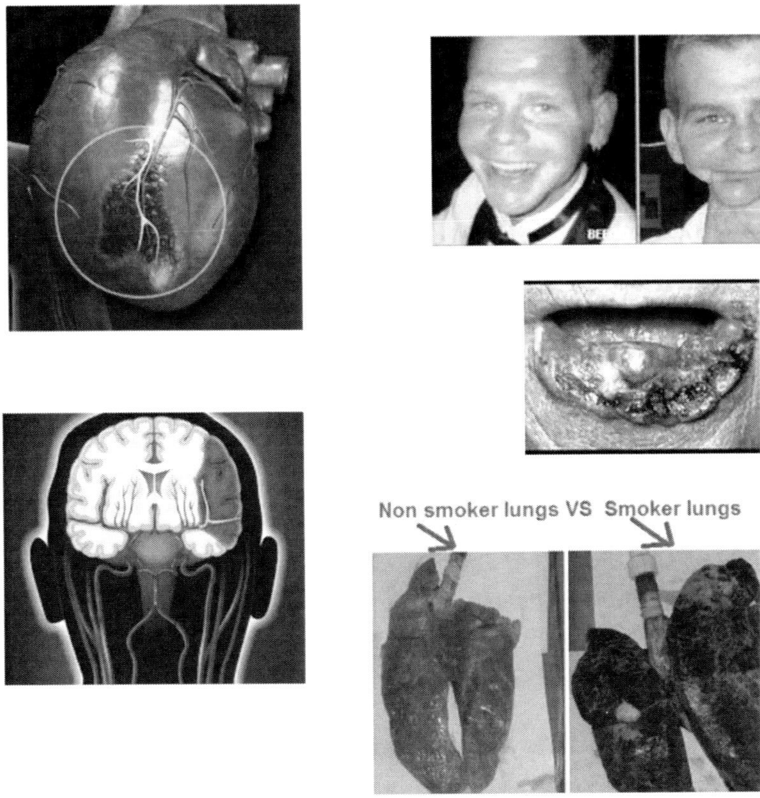

Figure 9. With tobacco, let's not forget about heart attack, stroke, oral cancer, lung cancer and chronic lung disease.

According to the Kentucky Center for School Safety published in April 2015, marijuana, hashish and alcohol were responsible for more school violations than any other drugs. Almost a quarter of the students involved with these violations were 9th graders.

BIG TOBACCO

Tobacco companies are estimated to spend $26 million per day to market cigarettes, e-cigarettes, smokeless tobacco and lobby for marijuana legalization. Big tobacco is now using some of the same advertising techniques which were effective in marketing tobacco to children; cartoon characters, Joe Camel, skate boarding kids, Beyoncé, etc. The target is e-cigarettes and kids. It seems to be working in that more Kentucky children are smoking e-cigarettes more frequently. This of course will result in an entire generation of Kentucky youth addicted to nicotine from e-cigarettes that do not smoke combustibles yet (see Figures 9-12).

KENTUCKY RANKINGS

- #1 state for smoking
- #1 state for lung cancer
- #8 state for heart attack/stroke death rate
- United States rates 1 death per hour due to oral cancer (smokeless tobacco).

Figure 10. Where is the State of Kentucky?

Tobacco Companies spend $26 Million per day marketing Cigarettes, e-Cigarettes and Smokeless Tobacco

http://www.nytimes.com/1991/12/11/us/smoking-among-children-is-linked-to-cartoon-camel-in-advertisements.html?pagewanted=all

Figure 11. Big tobacco needs more addicts (nicotine) to support their business. They advertise to kids because it works.

Figure 12. "Big Tobacco" currently is using its marketing and proven techniques to promote E-Cigs and marijuana. Again, the focus seems to be on the youth.

In order for the children who hear this presentation to better understand the addiction concept, we attempt to define some terms related to the process and disease of addiction. No one starts out intending to develop an addiction. Nearly 23 million Americans or 1 in 10 are addicted to alcohol or other drugs and nearly 2/3 of people with addiction abuse alcohol. The top three drugs causing addiction is marijuana, opioid narcotics and cocaine (see Figure 7).

Addictive drugs hijack the pleasure or reward center of the reptilian brain by causing extremely high pleasurable neurotransmitters (dopamine) release in these areas as a result of drug use or certain behaviors. The mesolimbic system remembers the experience and causes intense craving to use more drug to get the same or similar effect on the pleasure center.

Tolerance or the need for more drug use to get the same rewarding effect develops with time. Tolerance will go away if the drug is not used regularly. This loss of tolerance can lead to death from drug overdose in certain drugs (example: opioids). Withdrawal from a drug of addiction can lead to a characteristic set of symptoms especially with opioids; withdrawal, nausea, vomiting, diarrhea, chills, sweating and the sense that someone has a severe case of the flu. The combination of craving and withdrawals often results in drug relapse if an individual is off the addicting drug for a time.

CONCLUSION

Some sound advice to the kids to avoid withdrawal, craving tolerance and the compulsion to use drugs is to "Never start!" Frequently, the experience of trauma in many forms followed by post-traumatic stress can lead to substance abuse. Caring people such as parents, caregivers, family, teachers, counselors and friends to talk with can make a huge difference in behavioral outcomes.

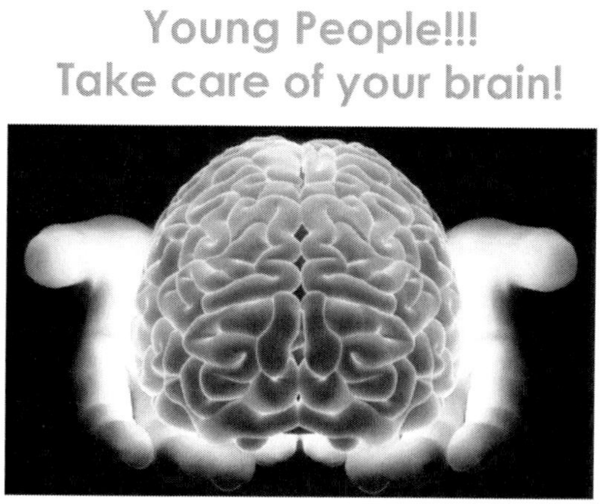

Figure 13. Advice to young people.

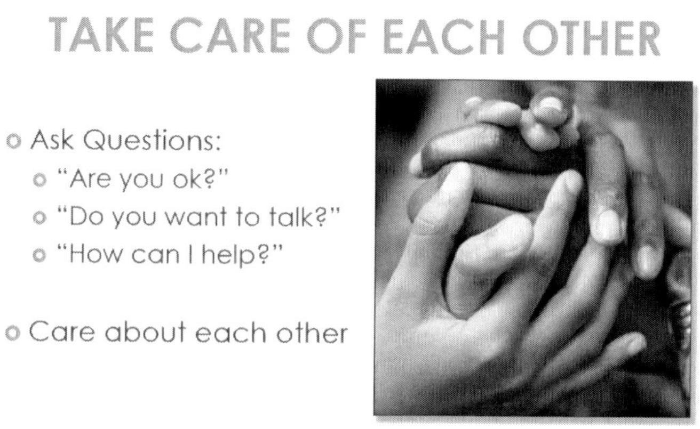

Figure 14. Take care of each other.

THE TAKE AWAY

- The adolescent brain is still maturing at your age.
- Think and take time before acting
- You DO NOT have to smoke, drink or use drugs to "fit in"!
- DO NOT pressure yourself or be pressured!
- Take care of your brain
- Alcohol and drugs can make you feel good temporarily but also can destroy your future
- Take care of each other
- Don't be afraid to get help

Figure 15. The take home message from our presentation.

SECTION TWO: AWARENESS AND PRESENTATION

In: Building Youth for the Future ISBN: 978-1-53613-768-2
Editors: H. A Omar and J. Merrick

Chapter 4

EVAN'S STORY BY HIS FATHER: SUICIDE AWARENESS AND PREVENTION

Charles W Peoples*[*], *Sheriff
Sheriff's Office, Pendleton County, Falmouth, Kentucky, US

ABSTRACT

As a law enforcement officer for many years, I have been involved in many tragic events, but had not expected suicide in my own family. In this chapter, I describe the suicide and death of our son, Evan, and my journey in trying to understand why people and especially teenagers commit suicide. This journey led me to undertake a program to explain to the community, children, youths and parents the issue of teen suicide, explain my own story and hopefully prevent other stories like this in the future.

---

[*] Correspondence: Charles William (Craig) Peoples, Sheriff, Sheriff's Office, 202 Chapel Street, Falmouth Kentucky 41040, United States. Email: craigpeop.pendsheriff@gmail.com.

INTRODUCTION

Being in law enforcement for nearly 20 years, I had been subjected to responding to someone's calls for help because they had attempted to take their own life or by a third party caller finding someone, a loved one or friend, who had completed the act of suicide. Little did I know that suicide had multiple warning signs and that the majority of those signs and the majority of the websites that address the issue of suicide awareness and prevention place it in the category of mental health with paranoia, schizophrenia, or bipolar disorder, but that may not always be the case (1-3).

EVAN'S STORY

August 2013: the start of the 2013-2014 Pendleton County High School year and, more importantly, it was the beginning of my oldest son Evan's senior year. Boy was he excited! The first couple of months were pretty typical for Evan. He would go to school then to work at Edwardo's Pizza and Subs, and if he was not at either of those two places he was at his mother Tanja's house, at our house, or at his girlfriend to who he had been dating for about a year. Everything seemed to be rolling along as normal at our homes, work, and school, but on October 8 while on a college visit to Northern Kentucky University with Bradford, Evan's little brother, Tanja and I, she informed me that Evan's girlfriend had broken up with him the night before, which explained the lack of enthusiasm he seemed to have. After walking the campus we went to see the criminal justice professor in order for Evan to get an understanding of what the criminal justice course of study was about and what it would require to obtain a bachelor's degree in criminal justice. At the conclusion of the meeting, Professor Shelley had invited Evan to come back and sit in on a college lecture to get a feel as to what college life was like. Evan agreed and by the end of that week he had arranged to go to one or more of her classes on October 18th.

Evan's goal for his future was to obtain a college degree in criminal justice, become employed by a law enforcement agency, and after about five years apply to work for the United States Marshals Service. Of course, I was excited about him following in my footsteps to become a law enforcement officer and to serve his community.

On the Sunday prior to October 18th it had been decided that we would have family photos taken at the farm with my parents, my brothers, sister, and their families and my mom's brother, sister, their families, her mother, and my family. As you can imagine, getting twenty people together on-time and gathered up to do this was quite a chore. But none the less we all gathered at the family farm and had a wonderful time. Afterwards, it was time to have fun. So, all of the little kids and some of the adults dressed down to some old clothes and white t-shirts to have a powdered paint party.

Well, Evan was not willing to get dirty and do something silly, but oh to the contrary when "EF Hutton" spoke my mom, his grandmother, by telling him to get one of his grandpa's white t-shirts on and go out there and have fun, she did not have to tell him twice! He went out and had fun with the rest of them. After everyone had cleaned that paint from their eyes, ears, and hair, Evan, Bradford, Miranda and I left to go eat at "Red Lobster," one of Evan's favorite places to eat, and boy could he eat crab legs! We had a great day together and he seemed to be dealing with the breakup just fine, so I thought.

During the week his mom and stepdad, myself, Miranda and numerous other people talked to Evan about the breakup and to help him to understand why and that possibly someday they would get back together. My understanding of the breakup was that she had started in her specific studies at Northern Kentucky University to become a pharmacist and she needed to focus on those in order to keep on track with her career.

The week seemed to be going fairly normal. Miranda and I went to work, Bradford to school and Evan would do a combination of school and work. On Wednesday evening Evan went to work and I attended a project grad meeting, where we discussed senior events for the year and fundraising for project grad. Project grad is an event for seniors that takes place on the night of graduation after the formal ceremonies. All seniors are expected to attend and they stay until 6:00 am the next morning. During this time there is a lot of food to eat, games to play, and prizes to win to assist them in their college life. It also serves as maybe one last time for them to see each other as classmates.

After arriving home shortly thereafter Evan arrived home from work and we talked about what I had learned. We talked about ordering his cap and gown, senior memorabilia, he particularly wanted a "2014" key chain and name cards and graduation invitations, that turned into a discussion. Evan did not see the need in ordering invitations, because he was only allowed to have eight tickets for family members to attend graduation and that was not enough! I explained to him that you send out the invitations in hopes that people will send you a congratulatory card with money to go towards your college fund. After all of those discussions he told us that on Thursday night he was going to stay at his mom's in Alexandria, because on Friday morning he was going to Northern Kentucky University to sit in on the criminal justice classes. That Thursday morning Miranda left for work and as I left with Bradford to take him to school, Evan was in the shower and I hollered at him to have a good day at school and work and to have fun at Northern Kentucky University tomorrow and we would talk after lunch. Little did I know that was to be the last conversation I would have with him!

Black Friday

Friday morning October 18, 2013 was a day that started like any other, but would become the worst day of my life. Around 9:30 am I had received information about the location of someone with warrants so I decided to go and attempt serving them. I went to the residence and located the two people in a garage apartment and arrested the male on warrants. Upon affecting the arrest I discovered items used to manufacture methamphetamine in said apartment at which time both parties were charged with manufacturing of methamphetamine and I began collecting evidence and writing citations. It was around 1:30 pm; myself, Todd Dennie, and Jailer Ken Kells were at the sheriff's office eating lunch and afterwards I was going to call Evan to see how Evan's morning had went.

At approximately 2:10 to 2:15 pm I received a phone call from the ex-girlfriend stating that she and Evan had been texting back and forth and the last message she received was a picture of him holding a gun in his lap and stating "I hope you're happy!" I asked her to send me the picture knowing it would tell me whether he was at my house or at his mom's. As she did so I began calling him, texting him "where are you," "answer the phone" with no response. I told Todd and Ken what was going on and I left. While driving I called Tanja, Evan's mom, and explained to her what was going on and that I was en route to her house. A twenty-minute drive, that only took me seven minutes with lights and sirens. While all the way praying I would not find the outcome, which my heart and mind knew was probably going to be the case. I also spoke with Bill, Evan's stepdad, who contacted his neighbor and friend Norm who is a police officer and asked him to go make entry into the house and check on Evan. The next call stated that I had better hurry! Upon my arrival which was prior to EMS and fire department I was met by George Schreiner, Tim Vinson, and JB Brown, my academy classmate, all officers with the Alexandria Police Department. George is a rather large man and I was bound and determined that if he tried to stop me from getting to my son I was going to plow him over, he did not. I made entry into the house and to Evan's room and saw my son in a sitting position on his bed bleeding from a self-inflicted gunshot wound to the head, with Norm sitting beside him. They advised me there was no pulse and they were waiting on EMS who walked in just a few minutes behind me.

I immediately went to Evan's side and held his hand and told him that "I LOVED HIM!," and sobbed. I then turned to Norm and hugged him and thanked him for being there. Soon after other officer's from Campbell County, Alexandria and Kentucky State Police, that I had specific ties to, arrived and so did Tanja. I stopped her in the yard and would not let her go into the house, at this point I told her that our son had died, we both hugged each other and cried the hardest tears you could imagine. After regaining some sense of composure and waiting on Bill I asked someone to contact my preacher Evan Meyer to come to the scene, while I contacted Todd Dennie my friend and Chief Deputy to go to Miranda's work at the doctor's office and pick her up and take her to my mom and dad's to wait for me there. Soon thereafter Bill arrived and we consoled each other and he and Tanja did as more of their friends and family began to arrive. As we waited for the coroner's office to arrive I called Miranda to tell her and to let everyone know what was going on and that I would be there as soon as I could that I was not leaving the house until Evan did, Todd wanted to come and get me and I told him NO!, that I needed him there to take care of my family until I could get there. Once the livery service arrived I performed the last most important gesture that I could do. I assisted in carrying my son down the steps and loaded him into the van myself.

In talking with Tanja she stated that she had spoken to him on the phone at approximately 1:45 pm for about 10-15 minutes and that he seemed very happy. In that, that morning on her way to work and Evan's travels to Northern Kentucky University they stuck their tongues out at one another in passing and my brother Nathan even played along. Her last conversation with Evan had been about going to Northern Kentucky University and how much he enjoyed sitting in on the college lecture. This was also later confirmed by the professor that Evan was engaging and focused. They also talked about him having lunch at Taco Bell and that he was going to work at Edwardo's that afternoon and would be back at her house that evening. She believed that he sounded in good spirits and that everything was fine. So the question was and still remains what was the "impulse" that gave Evan the "desire" to want to take his own life?

WHY DO PEOPLE COMMIT SUICIDE?

In November 2013, I started doing the research into "Why" people commit suicide, especially in youth. This is when I started to get angry! Everything I was researching and reading talked about a laundry list of warning signs and mental illness.

As I read through the warning signs, I thought of Evan and checked off any that I though fit his situation. That list consisted of:

- Ideation-making threats or talking about wanting to hurt themselves
- Looking for ways to kill themselves, or talking or writing about death and suicide
- Substance abuse-increased use of alcohol or drugs
- No reason to live-no sense of purpose in life
- Anxiety- agitation unable to sleep
- Trapped – there's no way out of the situation
- Withdrawal – from family/friends
- Anger – reckless or engaging in risky behavior.

As I compared Evan's activities over those last two weeks none of these warning signs were present as I have discussed earlier. As I continued reading through 2010 data of the American Association of Suicidology (3), it stated that suicide is the second leading cause of death among ages 15-24 years and that it is estimated that there are 25 attempts for every completed suicide. Their finding also showed that mental health diagnosis are generally associated with a higher rate of suicide.

Autopsy studies showed that more than 90% of completed suicides had one or more mental disorders, those being depression, schizophrenia, paranoia, or drug and alcohol dependency.

As I looked on other sites closer to home I found the Kentucky Suicide Prevention Group and discovered the following (2):

- That Kentucky loses over 600 people per year to suicide
- Three times more to homicides, that it is the second leading cause of death for Kentuckians ages 15-34 years
- Firearms are used 62% of the time
- Experts believe that most suicidal people do not want to die, they just want to end their pain

- Another fact is that major depression is the most common psychiatric diagnosis most commonly associated with suicide.

We do not deny that Evan was depressed at least to this level or even "clinically depressed by definition. Experts believe that suicide is preventable. Most suicidal individuals desperately want to live; they are just unable to see alternatives to their problems.

The pediatrician Hatim A Omar, MD, states in his book "Youth suicide prevention" (1), that "the first problem with identifying those at risk and then referring them to treatment is that many teens fall in the category of "same day suicide," meaning kids who could not be identified as at risk, because they do not have any mental health problems. They just run into a problem that feels unsolvable and have no one to run to," so they think.

I believe this is where Evan fell into the cracks, no warning signs to speak of, no diagnosed mental illness, and had not been seen by a doctor or prescribed medication. We only had ten days from the date of the breakup till the day of his death. Another interesting fact from the book was that in 1910 Sigmund Freud (1856-1939) gave an opinion that suicide in youth was due to love conflicts and school pressure for achievement. I think this still resonates today in the 21st century with the inclusion of bullying in our schools.

Conclusion

After reading and asking questions I decided that I needed, wanted to do something to bring the stigma and misunderstanding of suicide in youth to the forefront in our community and elsewhere.

By February 2014 with the help and input from others I started a program entitled "Evan's story: Suicide awareness and prevention." On February 5 we had two seminars with approximately 100 people from the community in attendance. They watched a video narrated by myself about Evan's life from the day he was born till the day he died. This was followed up by a power point presentation about the "warning signs" of suicide myths and facts, survivors, and ways to assist someone in getting help if they are feeling suicidal.

Since that time I have given the presentation to churches, civic organizations, middle and high school students, college students, radio, TV and book interviews, in all a total of 44 since February 2014. I have also included a bullying segment for middle school students, My travels have been all across the Commonwealth of Kentucky and southern Ohio. The program is offered free of charge, but a donation is requested to support our 501c3, which allows us to provide $2,000 in scholarships in Evan's name to graduating seniors at Pendleton County High School, the first of them being to members of his graduating Class of 2014.

Being a survivor, someone's whose family member died by suicide, is difficult, painful, heart breaking, and confusing. I feel that I have learned a lot through this unwanted, unsolicited experience that has helped me grow stronger as a person, father, and husband. It has provided me with additional tools in my toolbox to help others while performing the duties as a law enforcement officer, and to be closer with GOD! Throughout the presentation I am filling a glass with water and each time I make a point the glass keeps getting fuller and at the end it over flows.

The statement I make is, "On October 18, 2013 my son Evan died by suicide because his glass overflowed, if you know someone whose glass is full, poke a hole in it by offering HOPE and HELP which can make all of the difference. I understand that we cannot keep suicides from happening, but on the other hand this is how we can keep them from happening less frequently."

REFERENCES

[1] Omar HA. Youth suicide prevention. Everybody's business. New York: Nova Science, Publishers, 2015.

[2] Kentucky Suicide Prevention. URL: http://kentuckysuicidepreventin.org.

[3] McIntosh JL, Drapeau CW. American Association of Suicidology Suicide in the USA based on 2010 data. Washington, DC: 2012:1-3.

In: Building Youth for the Future ISBN: 978-1-53613-768-2
Editors: H. A Omar and J. Merrick

Chapter 5

CHILD AND FAMILY POVERTY: ITS IMPACT ON CHILDREN AND WHAT WE CAN DO ABOUT IT

David L Wood*[*]*, MD, MPH
Department of Pediatrics, Quillen College of Medicine,
East Tennessee State University, Johnson City, Tennessee, US

ABSTRACT

Poverty has a toxic effect on the developing child by being associated higher likelihood of the child being faced with maternal depression, parental divorce or separation, single parent household, exposure to toxic environment, violent neighborhood and inferior schools. Poverty has a substantial impact on the health and development of children. Poverty rates among young children in the United States (US) is the highest among any age group. Poverty in the US has declined slightly since the peak in the years post the 2008 depression; however, they remain unacceptably high, especially when compared to poverty rates for

[*] Correspondence: David L Wood, MD, MPH, Professor and Chair, Department of Pediatrics, Quillen College of Medicine, East Tennessee State University, PO Box 70578, Johnson City, TN 37614, United States. Email: Wooddl@etsu.edu.

children in other developed countries. There are effective income transfer programs that can reduce child poverty. As recommended by the American Academy of Pediatrics all that is needed is the political will to implement or expand such programs.

INTRODUCTION

Poverty has a toxic effect on the developing child by being associated higher likelihood of the child being faced with maternal depression, parental divorce or separation, single parent household, exposure to toxic environment, violent neighborhood and inferior schools. Recent research shows that poverty and the stress it causes on the human organism, has a negative impact on the brain architecture and growth causing significant and lifelong consequences. In addition, through the same stress mechanisms, poverty affects the expression of genes, putting children in poverty at risk.

EPIDEMIOLOGY OF POVERTY, CHILDREN AND THE UNITED STATES

Poverty is defined as household income below the poverty level (1). To measure the degree of financial stress in families, the federal government defined the federal poverty level in the early 1960s, and that measure has not changed in 50 years. It was first conceptualized as a household's budget that was three times the cost of the basic food basket. If the total income in a family or household is less than this calculation, they are considered poor. If their income is between the poverty line and 200% of the federal poverty line, they are considered "low income." This measure continues to be used despite major changes in the relative cost of food and how families spend their money. For example, over the past 50 years rent has gone up relative to food and the cell phones is a new necessary household expenditure. A new measure was approved several years ago called the "supplemental poverty measure" (SPM), which accounts for some of these changes in how families spend money and in how family income is counted. For example, the original poverty measure did not count family income from income transfer programs, like food stamps, but the SPM does. In addition, the SPM takes into account the variation in cost of living across the United States.

Although the number of people in poverty has fluctuated, there has been a general upward trend since the 1970s. The actual poverty rate has been relatively flat, fluctuating between 12 and 15%. Recent data shows that in the United States, 12.7% of people or 40.6 million were poor (1). When looking at poverty rates by age, there is a trend of decreasing poverty among people over sixty-five, primarily due to the social security act from the mid 1960s. The poverty rate among the elderly over sixty-five in 2016 was 9.3%. The poverty rate for children was almost double that at 18%. Furthermore, when you look at poverty rates for children under eighteen, the rates are higher for younger children than for older children. When examining poverty by different family characteristics, there is a substantial difference in income rates by education of the family head of household. The average family income differs by almost $100,000 between not having a high school degree with an average income of $30,000/year/family to those with a graduate degree having a median income of $130,000.

The median income for all families in the United States in 2015 was $64,800 (2, 3). Family poverty rates vary dramatically by the family structure (2). Single parent families have a poverty rate of approximately 37% compared to families with two parents having a poverty rate of 10.5%. Poverty rates differ greatly by race and ethnicity (3). The 2017 KIDS COUNT Data Center, using data from 2011-2015, found that the national poverty average was 14% for all people, but was 32% for African-Americans, 31% for American Indians/Native Americans, 23% for Hispanics and only 5% for non-Hispanic whites. The poverty rates of children by race are very similar; 34% of African-American children are poor and only 12% of non-Hispanic whites are poor. There is also a significant variation in geographic distribution of child poverty with the poorer states being in the southeast and the southwest. Most states below the Mason Dixon Line have higher rates of poverty than those above, and the highest rates of poverty are in the southeast with child poverty rates of up to 30%.

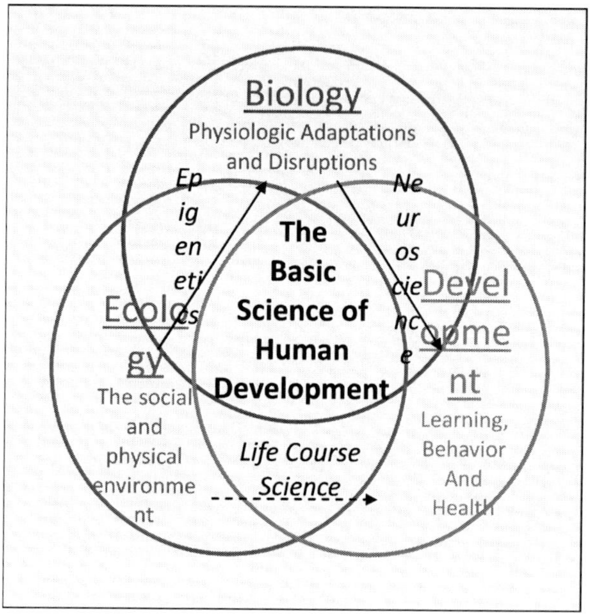

Figure 1. Eco-bio-developmental model of human health and disease.

IMPACT OF POVERTY ON CHILDREN'S HEALTH AND DEVELOPMENT

The American Academy of Pediatrics (AAP) considers poverty one of the greatest threats to the health and welfare of children. In 2015 the AAP published a technical report and a policy paper on the adverse effects of child poverty in the United States that used an Eco-bio-developmental model of human health and disease (4). This model (see figure 1) posits that the environment in which a child develops is influenced by the parents' resources which include financial, emotional, relational, and community. These multiple factors in the family and child environment have dynamic influences on the developing child that link poverty to long term physical and mental health problems of children, youth, and adults. The Eco-bio-developmental model posits that over the child's life course the ecology, social, and physical environments influence the child's biological development. The child's biology is influenced through mechanisms such as gene regulation, or epigenetics, the turning on and off genes through methylation and histone formation. As the children's ecology influences their biology over the lifetime, this leads to very different life trajectories of child development and adult achievement.

Figure 2 lists some of the poverty mechanisms that impact child development, and these mechanisms can be classified in three areas. The first mechanism, material hardships, includes the lack of basic resources like as food, housing, safe neighborhood, and stable living situation. In addition, poverty is associated with poorer early childhood education availability, less access to books, and less access to an environment that is intellectually stimulating. Family processes are the second mechanism whereby poverty affects a child's health and development. Poverty causes families to be stressed. Family stress leads to compromised parental relationships, and the reduced capacity of parents to engage warm and reciprocal relationships with their children. In poor families, there is less "serve and return" verbal and visual interaction between the child and the parents. Maternal depression is highly associated with poverty, which also causes a deterioration in the interaction between the parents and the child. The third mechanism by which poverty affects child development is the context of chaos. Families that are poor struggle to pay rent or stay in a home. This leads to multiple changes in the living situation, which is very stressful for the child. Poor communities are also associated with violence or lack of resources or inadequate schools, which leads to further stress and chaos. All three of the above mechanisms work simultaneously in the poor family to increase the allostatic load that a child experiences, which affects both the child's gene expression and their emotional and cognitive development as well as their physical health.

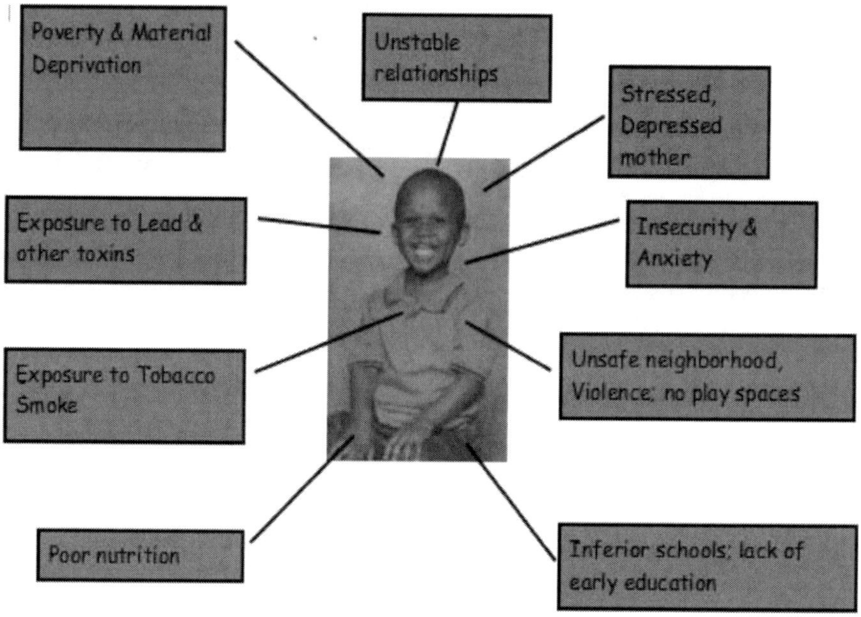

Figure 2. Cumulative risk poverty.

Poor families may have difficulty obtaining resources to support their children's development through a nurturing, stimulating home environment. Data from the National Longitudinal Survey of Youth (5) indicate that children in poor households have less access to learning materials such as books, stimulating toys, or skill building lessons. Language development studies that compare low and high socioeconomic status (SES) children show that by age three high SES children have three times as many words in the vocabulary, almost 1,200 words on average, compared to the poor child who has an average of about 400 words (6). These differences in developmental trajectories put the poor child behind from a very early age and make it very difficult for them to make up this ground when they enter formal education. In fact, we know that there is a large social gradient of school readiness that makes a huge difference in a child's ability to benefit from formal education. Children living in poverty have an uneven start that is estimated to be one to one and one-half standard deviations difference in educational achievement starting in kindergarten (7). Starting behind places poor children at risk for future failure and dramatically impacts their ability to learn to read and ultimately be successful in school. It has been estimated higher income families compared to poor families invest $8,000 more child per year in various activities that stimulate the cognitive, emotional and social development.

Table 1. Population-based health measures in poor children versus non-poor children (8)

Health Indicator (children between 0-17 years old unless otherwise noted)	Poor Children	Non-Poor Children	Ratio of Poor to Non-Poor
Reported in excellent Health	48.9%	66.9%	0.7
Reported in Fair or Poor Health	3.2%	0.8%	4.0
Obesity (2-19 yrs)	24.4%	12.7%	1.9
Currently has asthma	11.0%	8.2%	1.3
Serious emotional or behavioral difficulty (4-17 yrs)	7.8%	4.5%	1.7
Grade repetition (6-17 yrs)	18.0%	7.8%	2.3
High School Dropout	10.7%	5.7%	1.9

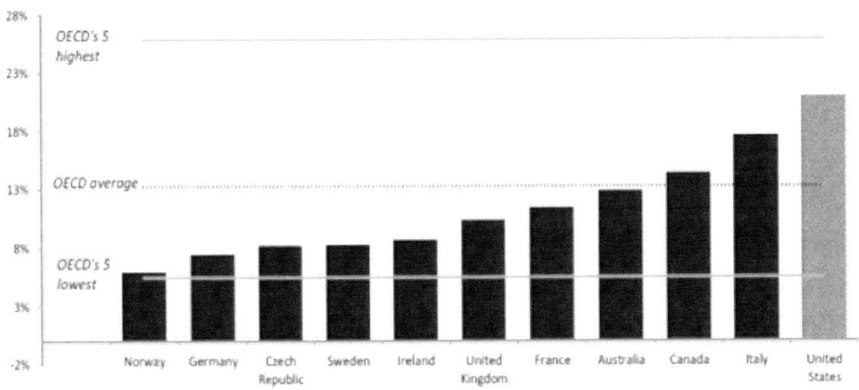

Figure 3. The United States can do more to reduce child poverty (13).

Table 1 compares health problems of poor children to non-poor children (8). On multiple measures children who are poor have worse health than children who are not poor. Only about half are reported by their parents to be in excellent health as opposed to almost 67% of non-poor.

Obesity rates are almost double, asthma rates are 30% higher, serious emotional and behavioral difficulties are 70% higher, grade repetition is over double with 18% of poorer children repeating a grade compared to only 7.8%, and high school dropout rates are almost double. On almost any measure, children that are poor have worse health and health outcomes than children who are non-poor.

INTERVENTIONS TO REDUCE CHILDHOOD POVERTY IN THE UNITED STATES

So what can we do to reduce childhood poverty? Figure 3 compares childhood poverty rates by the different countries in the Organization for Economic Cooperation and Development. Norway and Germany have the lowest child poverty rates, whereas the United States has one of the highest (9). Other studies have shown that child poverty rates prior to taking into account income transfer programs, are somewhat comparable between these countries; however, the countries with the lower child poverty rates have post-economy larger income transfer programs (13).

Figure 4 shows that poverty rates for all ages and for children under eighteen, before taxes and not counting government assistance, is 29.8% for children (10). Counting all government assistance after taxes that percentage drops to 18%. In other words, the income transfer programs in the United States reduce poverty from approximately 30% to 18%. However, in other developed countries, the income transfer programs are much more effective, larger, and reduce the effective rate of family poverty from about the same rate of 30% to less than 10% (13).

There are a number of income transfer programs in the United States including earned income tax and child tax credit (EITC), Supplemental Nutrition Assistant Program (SNAP, housing assistance programs, supplemental security income, and temporary assistance for needy families. The earned income tax credit is by far the most effective policy for reducing child and family poverty in the United States (10). The EITC lifted 5.1 million children out of poverty, and brought the families of 8 million children closer to escaping poverty. As a refundable tax credit, the EITC allows low to moderate-income workers to keep more of their earnings. The credit benefits working families of children that have annual incomes up to roughly $54,000 depending on family size, and yielding an average tax credit of about $3,200. Some states have actually added to it and increased the size of the earned income tax credit. SNAP, the food stamp program, is another major income transfer program that is almost as effective at reducing poverty as the EITC. SNAP has lifted over 5 million children out of poverty.

In their report published before the 2016 presidential elections, "The blueprint for children", the American Academy of Pediatrics made a number of policy recommendations to address income security among families and reduce the detrimental impact of poverty on children (11). First, the AAP recommends expanding and increasing the earned income tax credit, SNAP and expanding family medical leave. Second, the AAP recommends that the US make significant investments to assure access to affordable and high-quality childcare for all families through the Childcare and Development block grants. Improving access to high quality childcare and early education will help close the educational readiness gap between poor and non-poor children entering Kindergarten. Third, the AAP recommends increasing access to affordable housing for families. The United States has the resources to provide affordable housing to all families through the expansion of programs such as the rental assistance or voucher programs. Fourth, the AAP recommends increasing home visiting and improve the rate of diagnosis and intervention for mothers who are depressed. As stated earlier, maternal depression is highly associated with poverty and depressed mothers are less capable of providing a stimulating environment for their children. By reducing maternal depression through brief interventions, the health outcomes of children would be greatly improved.

Additional interventions could be put in place to continue addressing the needs of poor families and improving their health and development. The "Medical home", endorsed by the American Academy of Pediatrics and other medical societies, provides comprehensive services in the primary care setting (12).

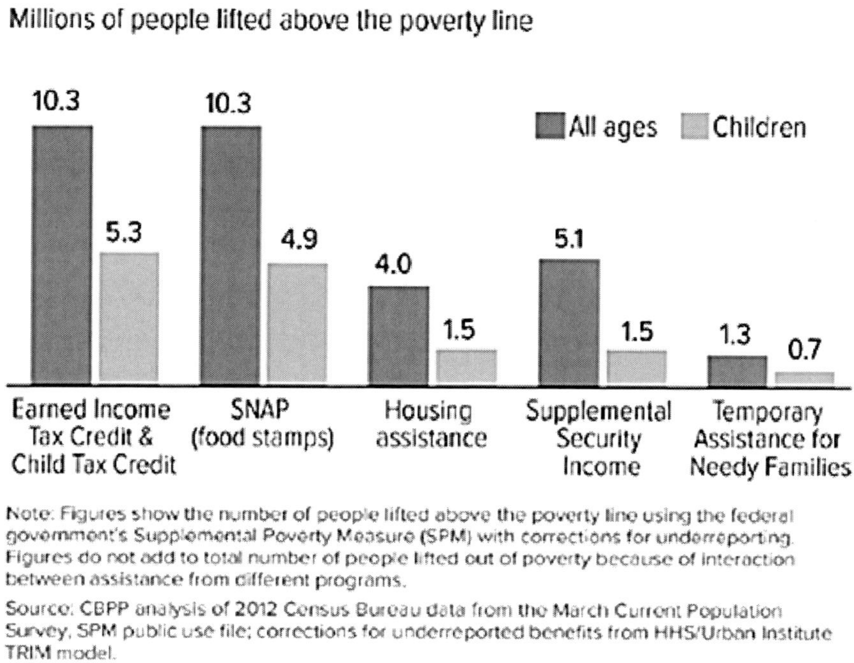

Figure 4. People out of poverty.

Within the "Medical home" setting, programs such as "Reach out" and "Read", social determinant screening, and screening for maternal depression can occur. These brief screenings and interventions can help improve a child's cognitive and social emotional development. Lastly, in the "Medical home", mental health services could be integrated to provide early intervention for families struggling to parent and provide a supportive environment for their children.

Conclusion

Poverty has a toxic effect on the developing child by being associated higher likelihood of the child being faced with maternal depression, parental divorce or separation, single parent household, exposure to toxic environment, violent neighborhood and inferior schools. Poverty has a substantial impact on the health and development of children. Poverty rates among young children in the US is the highest among any age group. Poverty in the US has declined slightly since the peak in the years post the 2008 depression; however, they remain unacceptably high, especially when compared to poverty rates for children in other developed countries. There are effective income transfer programs that can reduce child poverty. As recommended by the American Academy of Pediatrics, all that is needed is the political will to implement or expand such programs.

REFERENCES

[1] US Census Bureau. Annual Social and Economic Supplement of the Current Population Survey 2017. URL: https://www.census.gov/programs-surveys/sahie/technical-documentation/model-input-data/cpsasec.html.

[2] Wimer C, Nam J, Waldfogel J, Fox L. Trends in child poverty using an improved measure of poverty. Acad Pediatr 2016;16(3):S60–6. URL: http://dx.doi.org/10.1016/j.acap.2016.01.007.

[3] The Annie E Casey Foundation. 2017 KIDS COUNT Data Book 2017. URL: http://www.aecf.org/resources/2017-kids-count-data-book/

[4] Pascoe JM, Wood DL, Duffee JH, Kuo A, Committee on Psychosocial Aspects of Child and Family Health, Council of Community Pediatrics. Mediators and adverse effects of child poverty in the United States. Pediatrics 2018;137(4):e20160340. URL: http://www.ncbi.nlm.nih.gov/pubmed/26962239.

[5] US Bureau of Labor Statistics. National Longitudinal Survey of Youth 1997. URL: https://www.nlsinfo.org/content/cohorts/nlsy97.

[6] Hart B, Risley TR. Meaningful differences in the everyday experience of young American children. Baltimore, MD: Paul H Brookes, 1995.

[7] Lee VE, Burkam DT. Inequality at the starting gate. Social background differences in achievement as children begin school. URL: http://library.mpib-berlin.mpg.de/toc/z2007_1747.pdf.

[8] Chaudry A, Wimer C. Poverty is not just an indicator: The relationship between income, poverty, and child well-being. Acad Pediatr 2016;16(3):S23–9.

[9] OECD. In it together: Why less inequality benefits all, 2015. URL: http://www.oecd-ilibrary.org/employment/in-it-together-why-less-inequality-benefits-all_9789264235120-en.

[10] Sherman A, Debot B, Huang CC. Boosting low-income children's opportunities to succeed through direct income support. Acad Pediatr 2016;16(3):S90–7.

[11] American Academy of Pediatrics. AAP Agenda for Children, 2018. URL: https://www.aap.org/en-us/about-the-aap/aap-facts/AAP-Agenda-for-Children-Strategic-Plan/Pages/AAP-Agenda-for-Children-Strategic-Plan.aspx.

[12] Council on Community Pediatrics. Poverty and child health in the United States. Pediatrics 2016;137(4):e20160339–e20160339. URL: http://www.ncbi.nlm.nih.gov/pubmed/26962238.

[13] Smeeding T, Thévenot C. Addressing child poverty: How does the United States compare with other nations? Acad Pediatr 2016;16(3):S67–75.

In: Building Youth for the Future ISBN: 978-1-53613-768-2
Editors: H. A Omar and J. Merrick

Chapter 6

CLINICAL OVERVIEW OF ATTENTION DEFICIT AND HYPERACTIVITY DISORDER

David L Wood*[*]*, MD, MPH
Department of Pediatrics, Quillen College of Medicine,
East Tennessee State University, Johnson City, Tennessee, US

ABSTRACT

Attention deficit hyperactivity disorder (ADHD), one of the most commonly diagnosed behavior disorders in childhood, makes it difficult for children to pay attention and control behavior. At any point in time, ADHD affects an estimated 4% to 6% and up to 9% of young people between the ages of 6 and 17 years. Three symptoms that predominant ADHD are: 1) inability to regulate activity level or hyperactivity; 2) inability to attend to task or inattention; and 3) impulsivity or inability to inhibit behavior. Although ADHD symptoms are most prominent in younger children, ADHD does have an impact across the lifespan. The Centers for Disease Control estimates that 4.4 million youth ages 4 to 17 have been diagnosed with ADHD in the United States. Most research

[*] Correspondence: David L Wood, MD, MPH, Professor and Chair, Department of Pediatrics, Quillen College of Medicine, East Tennessee State University, PO Box 70578, Johnson City, TN 37614, United States. Email: Wooddl@etsu.edu.

suggests the cause of ADHD lies in neurobiology and genetics, as ADHD tends to run in families with inheritability of about 80-85%. ADHD treatment focuses on reducing symptoms and improving functioning through three approaches: medications, behavioral therapies, and creating a structured environment to support organization and reduce distraction. Parents and teachers benefit from strategies to help manage their child's behaviors at home and help promote effectiveness in school.

INTRODUCTION

Attention deficit hyperactivity disorder (ADHD), one of the most commonly diagnosed behavior disorders in childhood, makes it difficult for children to pay attention and control behavior. At any point in time, ADHD affects an estimated 4% to 6% and up to 9% of young people between the ages of 6 and 17 years (1). Boys are two to three times more likely to develop ADHD (2). Although ADHD is usually associated with children, the disorder can persist into adulthood. Children and adults with ADHD are easily distracted by sounds, sights, and other features in the environment. Additionally, they cannot concentrate for long periods of time, are restless and/or impulsive, have a tendency to daydream, and often struggle to completing tasks.

DIAGNOSING ADHD

Three symptoms that predominant ADHD are: 1) inability to regulate activity level or hyperactivity; 2) inability to attend to task or inattention; and 3) impulsivity or inability to inhibit behavior. These three different areas of symptoms include things like difficulty paying attention or poor concentration, increased activity/hyperactivity, poor impulse control, and poor social interactions. In addition, children with ADHD may take undue risks, which is associated with acting on an impulse before thinking. Children with ADHD frequently experience sleep problems including difficulty initiating sleep or staying asleep. Often these children underperform at school; however, they are generally of normal intelligence.

The DSM-V Diagnostic Manual lists a set of nine symptoms for inattention/impulsivity and nine core symptoms for hyperactivity for ADHD diagnostic criteria (3). The child must exhibit six or more core symptoms from one or both areas. Additionally, these symptoms should be of a degree that is inconsistent with the child's developmental level and negatively impacts social and academic activities. They also should not be a manifestation of other diagnoses such as anxiety, depression, hostility, or lower intelligence. Table 1 lists the nine core activities related to inattention. These are common types of tasks for school age children and may not be as applicable to older adolescents or adults. Similarly, hyperactivity and impulsivity are grouped. The child should exhibit six symptoms that have lasted at least six months. Again, the behaviors should be inconsistent with the child's developmental level and negatively impact social and academic activities. Table 2 lists the core symptoms of hyperactivity and impulsivity. Again, these are very common characteristics of school aged children, but when they are looked at in the aggregate, they constitute a hyperactive profile. Adolescents with ADHD may have similar levels of inattention, but tend to have less hyperactivity and impulsivity. However, adolescents' impulsivity may manifest as high-risk behaviors such as sexual activity, drinking or using illicit drugs.

Table 1. Inattention

A.	Often fails to give close attention to details or makes careless mistakes in schoolwork, at work, or during other activities
B.	Often has difficulty sustaining attention in tasks or play activities
C.	Often does not seem to listen when spoken to directly
D.	Often does not follow through on instructions and fails to finish schoolwork, chores, or duties in the workplace
E.	Often has difficulty organizing tasks and activities
F.	Often avoids, dislikes, or is reluctant to engage in tasks that require sustained mental effort
G.	Often loses things necessary for tasks or activities

In addition to having these symptoms present they must also have been present prior to age twelve; inattentive or hyperactive/impulsive symptoms are present in two or more settings, for example, at home, schoolwork, with friends, or with relatives; clear evidence that the symptoms interfere or reduce the quality of social, academic, or occupational functioning; and these symptoms are not explained by another mental health disorder such as a mood disorder, anxiety disorder, personality disorder, substance intoxication, or addiction.

Table 2. Hyperactivity and impulsivity

A.	Often fails to give close attention to details or makes careless mistakes in schoolwork, at work, or during other activities
B.	Often has difficulty sustaining attention in tasks or play activities
C.	Often does not seem to listen when spoken to directly
D.	Often does not follow through on instructions and fails to finish schoolwork, chores, or duties in the workplace
E.	Often has difficulty organizing tasks and activities
F.	Often avoids, dislikes, or is reluctant to engage in tasks that require sustained mental effort
G.	Often loses things necessary for tasks or activities
H.	Is often easily distracted by extraneous stimuli

According to the DSV V, there are three subtypes of ADHD. The first subtype, Combined Type is characterized by the child meeting criteria for both inattention and hyperactivity/impulsivity. The second type, Predominantly Inattentive Type, is characterized by the child meeting criteria for inattention, but does not meet criteria for hyperactivity/ impulsivity. Children that are the Predominately Inattentive Type are often referred to as a daydreamer and are characteristically sluggish, slow moving, and/or unmotivated. The third type is the Predominantly Hyperactive Compulsive Type. This type includes children that meet criteria for hyperactivity/impulsivity but do not meet criteria for inattention. ADHD symptoms are typically most prominent during the elementary grades, and the Combined Type is by far the most common among younger children. Girls tend to typically be the Predominately

Inattentive Type. ADHD is known to occur in a wide variety of cultures with some variation among western countries arising from different diagnostic practices.

Although ADHD symptoms are most prominent in younger children, ADHD does have an impact across the lifespan. During preschool ADHD may present as disruptive behavior, aggression toward other children, hyperactivity, conduct problems, and being inattentive. In middle childhood, ADHD may be more easily seen by the tasks the child fails to complete such as unfinished games, uncovered toothpaste, incomplete homework, difficulty with completing activities at a level that is normal for that child's age. Middle childhood is a time when schoolwork suffers either due to poor attention in class, poor follow through, or lack of completion of assignments. This is also the time where children with ADHD may develop significantly lower self-esteem, depression, or conduct disorders. During adolescence, there is a high rate of accompanying disorders, or comorbidities, with ADHD that include anxiety, depression, oppositional behavior, and substance abuse. In adulthood, ADHD can present as difficulty at work, difficulty in developing and maintain work relationships or personal relationships, and significant difficulty following directions, organizing, and/or completing complex tasks. Like in adolescents, adults with ADHD may also experience a significant number of other comorbidities such as anxiety, depression, and poor social functioning. Family and peer relationships tend to be a challenging area for children with ADHD. Parents of children with ADHD report almost three times as many peer problems as those without ADHD. Parents also report that their children experience difficulty with developing and maintaining relationships with friends and family because the child's increased aggression or impulsive behavior is often viewed as off-putting to others.

EPIDEMIOLOGY OF ADHD

The Centers for Disease Control estimates that 4.4 million youth ages 4 to 17 years have been diagnosed with ADHD in the United States. Of those

4.4 million, only about 2.5 million are receiving medication treatment for the disorder (1). There is a predominance of almost three to one boys versus girls with this diagnosis (2). Part of this is due to the fact that girls are often under-diagnosed since they tend to have more inattentive ADHD profile compared to boys, who have more of a combined profile. ADHD varies somewhat by race with white children having a higher rate of diagnosis than Hispanic or Black children (2). In figure 1, regional variation can be seen in of the United States with rates of diagnoses ranging from under 7% in some states such as Nevada, to over 13% in states in the southeast and mid-Atlantic region including Ohio, Kentucky, and Tennessee.

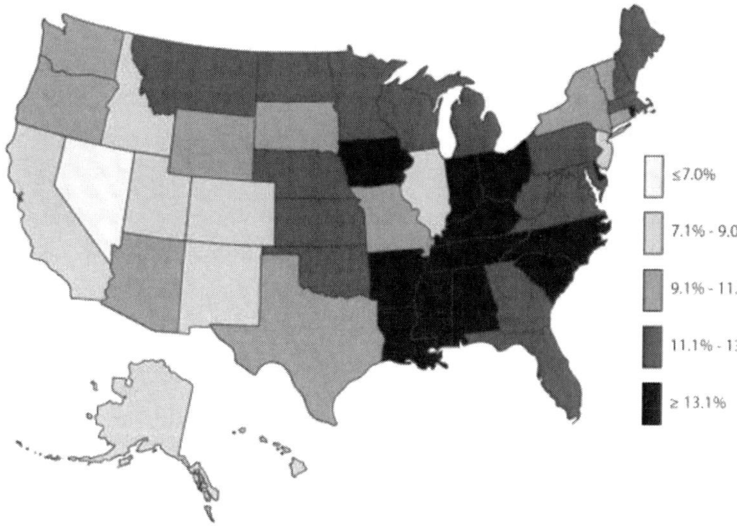

Figure 1. Percent of youth 4-17 years ever diagnosed with attention-deficit/ hyperactivity disorder: National Survey of Children's Health, 2011-2012 (7).

Comorbidities, like oppositional defiant disorder (ODD), anxiety, depression, Tourette syndrome, or learning disabilities, are common among children diagnosed with ADHD which can present challenges in treating and managing symptoms. Almost one-third to one-half of children with ADHD may also have (ODD). Children with ODD are defiant, non-compliant, belligerent, and stubborn. Determining the cause of the child's concentration issues can pose additional challenges with comorbidities like anxiety or depression since all three impact the child's ability to concentrate. A small portion of ADHD may have Tourette Syndrome. This neurological disorder includes nervous tics and repetitive mannerisms that responds well to medication. Lastly, about 20-30% of children with ADHD also have a specific learning disability such as a disability in reading or in mathematics impacting their academic abilities.

CAUSE OF ADHD

Most research suggests the cause of ADHD lies in neurobiology since some parts of the brain of children with ADHD are smaller compared to age and gender matched children without ADHD. Genetics may also play a role as ADHD tends to run in families with inheritability of about 80-85%. Some research suggests that children with ADHD may have deficiencies in dopamine and norepinephrine, the neurotransmitters thought to be related to attention. Dopamine has been associated with approach and pleasure-seeking behaviors, whereas norepinephrine plays a role in emotional and behavioral regulation. Most research suggests deficiencies in the availability of dopamine and norepinephrine among children with ADHD compared to children without the disorder. Other researchers speculate there may be structural differences in the brains of children with ADHD. The executive functioning, located primarily in the prefrontal cortex, appears to be diminished for children with ADHD. Additionally, functioning of the limbic system, including the amygdala, appears to be increased. The amygdala is associated with impulsivity and hyperactivity whereas the prefrontal cortex is concerned with executive functioning, organization, attention, special working memory, and short-term memory. Inadequate control of the prefrontal cortex over the limbic system (e.g., amygdala), is thought to the primary neuro-anatomical dysfunction of those that have ADHD.

Executive functioning processes appear to be most important in children with ADHD. On the cognitive level these include working memory, planning, use of organizational strategies, etc.; in language, they relate to verbal fluency and communication; and for motor it is response, inhibition, and motor coordination. One of the most important aspects of executive functioning is emotional regulation and tolerance of frustration, both of which are deficient in children with ADHD.

DIAGNOSIS OF ADHD

ADHD assessment has been a subject of significant research, and there is good evidence for both the approach to evaluation and diagnosis of ADHD. Children suspected of having ADHD should present to a professional that can do a comprehensive evidence-based assessment, like the Vanderbilt Scales (8), using validated questionnaires that help describe their behavior (4). An assessment by both a parent and a teacher is required to assess functioning and symptomatology in two areas or two settings. A clinical interview with parents is also important to understand the particular concerns that a parent may have regarding their child's strengths and weaknesses (4). As mentioned earlier, children with ADHD underperform at school and this can be due to ADHD, a learning disabilities or both; therefore, a full psychoeducational assessment is necessary determine the child's intelligence level and potential learning disabilities that could cause both frustration and poor self-esteem. Imaging techniques or EEGs do not play any role in the assessment of children with ADHD.

TREATMENT OF ADHD

ADHD treatment focuses on reducing symptoms and improving functioning through three approaches: medications, behavioral therapies, and creating a structured environment to support organization and reduce distraction. Stimulants are the primary treatment for ADHD, the most well researched, and most effective class of medication. They improve focus, thinking, ability to learn and work as well as reduce the symptoms of hyperactivity, impulsivity, and inattention. Stimulates are relatively safe and do not make children feel high. Also there is no evidence that stimulants, when used for the treatment of ADHD, cause drug abuse or dependence. In fact, there is evidence that the use of stimulants in a child with ADHD is protective of them later experimenting with or using substances.

Stimulants reduce ADHD symptoms by blocking the re-uptake of norepinephrine and dopamine; therefore, having those neurotransmitters persist in the synaptic cleft and increase or enhance the effect of these neurotransmitters in certain areas of the brain including the prefrontal cortex and basal ganglia or limbic system. Substantial research has been conducted on both the effect size and effect profile of stimulants. They have been shown to effectively reduce the core symptoms of ADHD, decrease disruption in the classroom, and increase academic productivity and on task behavior. Different formulations work differently for different children, and the optimal dosing is also one that has to be discovered empirically with each child. Common side effects include insomnia and decreased appetite

Table 3 lists ADHD medicines approved by the US Food and Drug Administration. As noted in the table, the medicines are generally approved for ages six years and older (5). Three medication types are commonly used: amphetamines, methylphenidate, or atomoxetine. Most studies show that methylphenidate or amphetamine/dexamphetamine are more effective than atomoxetine in terms of effects size. These medicines have been around for decades; however, recent advances have been to develop new mechanisms of drug delivery. These advances have included time release capsules, development of a pro drug that requires metabolism by the liver, and subcutaneous absorption in a patch formulation. These more recent medication formulations allow for a longer effect time compared to the generic methylphenidate or amphetamines which last only for a few hours. Additional medications used for ADHD and core symptoms include alpha2-agonists, clonidine and guanfacine. These medications can also help with sleep and the associated symptoms of aggression that sometimes accompanies impulsivity. The side effects of these drugs are sleepiness, fatigue, hypotension, constipation, and dry mouth.

Creating structured environments is another treatment option for ADHD. Children with ADHD benefit from clear structure and routines on a day-to-day basis. They should have clear rules about behavior and clear expectations for their responsibilities in school and at home. Reward systems provide immediate feedback to the child and incentivize their motivation, which has a significant impact on attention. Managing distractions by providing a quiet, distraction free area a school or in the home to complete work is another key behavioral strategy for treating ADHD. This can be accomplished by using desk dividers, having the student seated away from high traffic areas, or playing white noise or soft music (6).

Table 3. List of stimulants approved by the FDA (5)

ADHD Medications Approved by U.S. Food and Drug Administration (FDA)*

Trade Name	Generic Name	Approved Age
Adderall	amphetamine	3 and older
Adderall XR	amphetamine (extended release)	6 and older
Concerta	methylphenidate (long acting)	6 and older
Daytrana	methylphenidate patch	6 and older
Desoxyn	methamphetamine hydrochloride	6 and older
Dexedrine	dextroamphetamine	3 and older
Dextrostat	dextroamphetamine	3 and older
Focalin	dexmethylphenidate	6 and older
Focalin XR	dexmethylphenidate (extended release)	6 and older
Metadate ER	methylphenidate (extended release)	6 and older
Metadate CD	methylphenidate (extended release)	6 and older
Methylin	methylphenidate (oral solution and chewable tablets)	6 and older
Ritalin	methylphenidate	6 and older
Ritalin SR	methylphenidate (extended release)	6 and older
Ritalin LA	methylphenidate (long acting)	6 and older
Strattera	atomoxetine	6 and older
Vyvanse	lisdexamfetamine dimesylate	6 and older

Children with ADHD often benefit from working on organization or structure with daily school/home report cards, communicating about required work that is required, and using a reward system for daily accountability (5).

In addition to creating structured environments, behavioral therapies help manage behaviors directly related to the child's performance in school or with work. Behavioral plans can also be implemented for relationships with peers or family members. Parents and teachers can role-play social skills, engage them in planned activities such as shopping or going to church, and coach them to be more effective in peer and family relationships. One approach is to teach "Stop and think" before talking to encourage the child to be more mindful of where they are, who they are talking to, and what is appropriate to say (6). Teaching children to "Stop and think" is helpful since many children with ADHD have difficulty listening which negatively impacts their social interactions (9). An important aspect of behavioral management is to give the child a lot of positive support, focus on their strengths, and give them a place to unwind and reduce stress.

Parents and teachers may need strategies to help manage their child's behaviors at home and help promote effectiveness in school. Many family and parent counseling strategies are available for parents of youth with ADHD including psychotherapy, behavioral therapy, social skills training, and parenting skills training. Managing a child with ADHD can be both challenging and rewarding at the same time if the parent is given the skills to handle the child's hyperactivity, impulsivity, and inattention.

Conclusion

ADHD is a common problem of attention and behavior in children. The diagnosis and management of ADHD should be based on published guidelines which are backed up by an extensive history of research. Most research suggests the cause of ADHD lies in neurobiology and genetics, as ADHD tends to run in families with inheritability of about 80-85%. ADHD treatment focuses on reducing symptoms and improving functioning through three approaches: medications, behavioral therapies, and creating a structured environment to support organization and reduce distraction.

Parents and teachers benefit from strategies to help manage their child's behaviors at home and help promote effectiveness in school.

REFERENCES

[1] Centers for Disease Control and Prevention. Attention deficit hyperactivity disorders (ADHD), 2018. [URL: https://www.cdc.gov/ncbddd/adhd/index.html.
[2] Pastor PN, Reuben CA. Diagnosed attention deficit hyperactivity disorder and learning disability: United States, 2004-2006. Vital Health Stat 2008;237:1–14.
[3] American Psychiatric Association. Diagnostic and statistical manual of mental disorders, 5th ed. Arlington, VA: American Psychiatric Publishing, 2013.
[4] Pelham, Jr. WE, Fabiano GA, Massetti GM. Evidence-based assessment of attention deficit hyperactivity disorder in children and adolescents. J Clin Child Adolesc Psychol 2005;34(3):449–76. doi/abs/10.1207/s15374424jccp3403_5.
[5] The National Institute of Mental Health Information Resource Center. Attention deficit hyperactivity disorder. URL: https://www.nimh.nih.gov/health/topics/ attention-deficit-hyperactivity-disorder-adhd/index.shtml.
[6] ADHD in school. URL: https://addinschool.com/tag/adhd-in-school.
[7] Centers for Disease Control and Prevention. State-based prevalence data of parent reported ADHD diagnosis by a health care provider. URL: https://www.cdc.gov/ncbddd/adhd/prevalence.html.
[8] Wolraich ML, Lambert W, Doffing MA, Bickman L, Simmons T, Worley K. Psychometric properties of the Vanderbilt ADHD Diagnostic Parent Rating Scale in a referred population. J Pediatr Psychol 2003;28:559–68.
[9] Project ACHIEVE. Stop and think social skills products and resources. URL: http://www.projectachieve.info/stop-think/stop-and-think.html.

In: Building Youth for the Future ISBN: 978-1-53613-768-2
Editors: H. A Omar and J. Merrick

Chapter 7

YOUTH GUN VIOLENCE: A GROWING PUBLIC HEALTH CONCERN

Amy Burnett*, MSN, APRN
Division of Adolescent Medicine and Young Parent programs, J422 Kentucky Clinic, Department of Pediatrics, Kentucky Children's Hospital, University of Kentucky College of Medicine, Lexington, Kentucky, US

ABSTRACT

Youth gun violence is a significant public health concern around the world. There have not been any certain methods or programs implemented that have been shown to significantly decrease this issue. There are some thoughts as to what would be effective interventions, but lack of research prevents evidence-based interventions from being implemented. Without addressing gun violence in the adolescent population, there will continue to be a disproportionate level of morbidity and mortality in our youth.

---

* Correspondence: Amy L Burnett, MSN, APRN, Adolescent Medicine, University of Kentucky College of Medicine, 740 S Limestone, Lexington, KY 40536, United States. Email: amy.burnett1@uky.edu.

Introduction

Gun violence is a pervasive problem in today's society. It is difficult to watch the news without hearing of serious acts of harm toward individuals, with guns most commonly being the weapon of choice. The United States has a disproportionately high problem compared to most other developed countries, but there are growing issues around the globe. This form of violence is very frustrating for all sides involved due to the complexity of the problem. There seem to be many opinions on how to address this significant concern, but no effective solutions have been identified.

The thought as to why gun violence is more prevalent in the United States is largely due to social attitudes surrounding firearms and the ease of access. Guns are entrenched in the American culture (1). There is an extremely strong gun lobby in the United States and firearm laws are more lenient than most other countries in the world. It is currently estimated that there are over 300 million guns in circulation in the United States, which is over three times as many as the 79 million throughout the European Union (2).

Overall, gun violence rates are down significantly since the peak in the 1990s (3). Even with the decline in overall violence rates, youth gun violence prevalence remains somewhat alarming at this time. Worldwide, an average of 200,000 adolescents die from gun violence each year (4). Unintentional injury remains the leading cause of death in adolescents in the United States, followed by suicide and homicide (5). Homicide is the leading cause of death in African American males ages 10 to 24 years (6). There are roughly three times the number of non-fatal injuries due to gun violence each year, which lead to significant physical, psychological, social, and financial burden to the individuals and families involved (4). Youth homicides and assault-related injuries cost the United States alone about $18 billion annually (6).

Not all gun violence is the same. There are two very distinct classifications of youth gun violence, which are mass shootings and street violence (7). The characteristics of the perpetrator and their overall intent are generally very different between these groups. School shooters are statistically Caucasian males, little or no history of behavior problems, and have average to above average intelligence (7). Many times the reason for mass/school shootings remains unknown. Street violence offenders, on the other hand, are statistically minorities from urban areas high in poverty and crime (7). These shootings typically involve drugs, gang affiliation, neighborhood "turf" battles, and personal conflict (7). Mass shooters will often commit suicide at the end of their rampage, but street shooters rarely do (8).

In most countries, there are laws prohibiting the legal purchase of firearms by a minor. This does not seem to stop adolescents from obtaining, carrying, and using guns. Many wonder about the ease of access and the availability of guns to this population. Mass shooters often purchase a gun legally, if over the legal age, or will obtain guns from within their homes (7). It is estimated that 44% of homes in the United States have at least one gun (5). Street shooters typically obtain guns from purchasing illegally on the street, taking guns from their homes, or stealing the firearms (7). These individuals often feel the need to protect themselves and will carry guns on a regular basis (1).

It is important to be able to identify those youth that are at risk for gun violence. Statistically, males are the large majority of perpetrators of gun violence (9). It is a common misconception that those with mental illness are at higher risk for gun violence, but actually only 4% of violent acts are committed by those with diagnosed severe mental illness (10). Victims of bullying have been found to be at an increased risk of weapon carrying (11). Exposure to violence in the home seems to be a large predictor of becoming a perpetrator of violence due to the physical and emotional trauma that children face (1). One of the best predictors of violence in an individual is a history of past violent behavior (7).

PREVENTION AND INTERVENTION

One of the most difficult problems with regards to youth gun violence is prevention and intervention. There are many programs and efforts that have been initiated with varying levels of success. The majority of these initiatives have been tailored to a certain population or geographic area to meet specific needs. There does not seem to be one strategy that is most effective and can be applied broadly. There are things that can be done by parents, school officials, the community, and medical providers that can help decrease the rates of violence in today's youth.

Parents have a large responsibility in gun violence prevention and intervention with their kids. It is essential that parents lock all guns that are inside the home to prevent easy access (9). Parents should monitor their children closely and should know the social circles in which they belong, the places that they are going, and their exposure to violent media (1). It is beneficial if parents are involved, supportive, and nurturing from a very early age and if they respond quickly and proactively to any signs of aggression that their child exhibits (7). Dealing with stress and conflict in a positive way needs to be modeled by parents in the home in order to teach children the best way to react in these situations (1).

School officials have a large responsibility to monitor kids closely in the school setting in order to help identify those kids at risk for violence, but also to provide resources to parents and students about violence and potential interventions. Bullying must be monitored and handled appropriately in order to prevent those victims from acting on their frustrations (11). School officials should foster a sense of safety for all children attending their school (1). Any individuals that present with threatening behavior should be addressed immediately by school officials, school law enforcement, and mental health providers in order to assess the situation appropriately and identify the resources that can be used to resolve the concern. In-school violence prevention programs need to be initiated and strongly supported in order for a positive difference to be made (9).

The community has a strong influence on the actions of the individuals living there, especially the youth. There are areas, especially urban areas of high poverty, where violence is accepted as the norm and the community tolerates this behavior. It is up to community leaders and residents to change that way of thinking and the beliefs of their area, which is extremely difficult to do in most cases, in order for positive change to occur (12). Community policing, which is where police are embedded in communities in order to form relationships and know the routines of an area, has been shown to be a positive influence on the individual satisfaction of residents and the community's trust in police. However, studies regarding community policing show no great decrease in overall crime rates due to these programs (13). A community deterrence strategy, called pulling levers, has been shown to be successful in crime reduction. These pulling levers campaigns target individuals or areas in need and increase the social services and community resources, police activity, and frequency of communication with known violent offenders in efforts to help reduce crime rates (14). Even those these interventions sound promising and show positive results, there is rarely sustainable funding to make these interventions a long-term solution.

Health care providers play a unique role in gun violence prevention. Since 1999, the American Academy of Pediatrics has endorsed routine screening of violence and gun safety in the child and adolescent population, but the actual number of providers performing these routine screens remains low (15). Literature reviews show that performing routine screenings in the primary care setting can help lower overall violence rates. There are many screening tools available for various patient settings. By identifying those at risk through routine screenings, social and mental health resources can be made available to the patient in order to help prevent future violence or victimization. It is essential to provide therapy to those kids exposed to gun violence, whether in the home or in the social setting (1). Mental health treatment may be one of the best interventions that we have to offer in the outpatient setting at this time (9). There have been numerous inpatient programs developed for identification and intervention on the inpatient side of care. Typically, patients are entered into these programs after being admitted to the hospital as a victim of gun violence. These programs provide different interventions while a victim is inpatient and some also have outpatient follow up. Inpatient violence prevention programs typically do show some benefit, but the programs need to be long-term in nature in order to significantly lower violent crime (16).

Due to the complexities of the gun violence problem at this time, more research is needed to explore various factors surrounding the issue in order to create better strategies for violence reduction. In the US, gun violence research has been controversial over the past two decades. In 1996, researchers at the Centers for Disease Control and Prevention (CDC) were banned from performing gun related research, which was thought to be due to the power of the American gun lobby and their influence on lawmakers (17). By looking into certain aspects of gun violence, such as gun laws, media violence, and family and school influences, the problem could be understood better and there could be research focused interventions to help reduce youth gun violence (7).

CONCLUSION

In conclusion, youth gun violence is a serious public health concern in today's society. This issue is affecting all parts of the globe and little is being done to help resolve the problem. To decrease the rates of gun violence among youth, it will take a collaborative effort from parents, school officials, community members, and health care providers. With better research performed on the topic, these key players would be better equipped to develop effective prevention and intervention programs. It is hoped that there will be new understanding in the near future and the rates of youth gun violence will begin to decline.

REFERENCES

[1] Garbarino J, Bradshaw CP, Vorrasi JA. Mitigating the effects of gun violence on children and youth. Future Child 2017;12:73-85.

[2] GunPolicy.org. Global impact of gun violence. URL: http://www.gunpolicy.org/firearms/region.

[3] Teen homicide, suicide and firearm deaths. Child Trends Databank, 2015. URL: https://www.childtrends.org/indicators/teen-homicide-suicide-and-firearm-deaths/.

[4] World Health Organization. Youth violence, 2016. URL: http://www.who.int/mediacentre/factsheets/fs356/en/.

[5] Centers for Disease Control and Prevention. Adolescent health, 2017. URL: https://www.cdc.gov/nchs/fastats/adolescent-health.htm.

[6] Centers for Disease Control and Prevention. Youth violence: Facts at a glance, 2017. URL: https://www.cdc.gov/violenceprevention/pdf/yv-datasheet.pdf.

[7] Bushman BJ, Calvert SL, Dredze M, Jablonski NG, Morrill C. Youth violence: What we know and what we need to know. Am Psychol 2016;71:17-39.

[8] Harding DJ. Living the drama: Community, conflict, and culture among inner-city boys. Chicago, IL: University of Chicago Press, 2010.

[9] American Psychological Association. Gun violence: Prediction, prevention, and policy, 2013. URL: http://www.apa.org/pubs/info/reports/gun-violence-prevention.aspx.

[10] Applbaum P. Public safety, mental disorders, and guns. JAMA Psychiatr 2013;70:565-6.

[11] Holt MK, Gini G. Complexities in the association between bullying victimization and weapon carrying. Pediatrics 2017;140:21-3.

[12] Hemenway D, Miller M. Public health approach to the prevention of gun violence. N Engl J Med 2013;368:2033-5.

[13] Gill C, Wiesburd D, Telep C, Vitter Z, Bennet T. Community-oriented policing to reduce crime, disorder and fear and increase satisfaction and legitimacy among citizens: A systematic review. J Exp Criminol 2014;10:399.

[14] Braga, AA. Pulling levers focused deterrence strategies and the prevention of gun homicide. J Crim Justice 2008;36:332-43.

[15] American Academy of Pediatrics. Policy statement: Role of the pediatrician in youth violence prevention. Pediatrics 2009;124:393-402.

[16] Loveland-Jones C, Ferrer L, Charles S, Ramsey F, van Zandt A. A prospective randomized study of the efficacy of “Turning point”: An inpatient violence intervention program. Trauma Acute Care Surg 2016;81:834-42.

[17] Frankel TC. Why gun violence research has been shut down for 20 years. Washington Post 2017 Oct 4.

In: Building Youth for the Future ISBN: 978-1-53613-768-2
Editors: H. A Omar and J. Merrick

Chapter 8

THE INTERNET AND SOCIAL MEDIA USE AMONG ADOLESCENTS: PITFALLS AND BENEFITS

John A Yozwiak*[1,*], *PhD and Douglas J Yozwiak*[2], *PA-C
[1]Kentucky Clinic, Division of Adolescent Medicine, Department of Pediatrics, University of Kentucky College of Medicine and [2]Department of General Surgery, University of Kentucky College of Medicine, Lexington, Kentucky, US

ABSTRACT

The internet and social media have become integrated into the fabric of daily life for adolescents, who use and rely on this technology for many functions. The internet and social media can provide adolescents with benefits, but it also has risks. Two pitfalls of the internet and social media will be presented. These pitfalls are the possible harmful effects of social media on psychological well-being and cyberbullying. In addition, the

* Correspondence: John A Yozwiak, PhD, Division of Adolescent Medicine, University of Kentucky College of Medicine, Kentucky Clinic, 740 South Limestone, Lexington, KY 40536, United States. Email: jayozw00@uky.edu.

controversy of internet addiction will be briefly reviewed. Three benefits of social media for adolescents will also be covered. These benefits are the effects of social media on peer affiliation, its effects on identity development, and its use in health care. Recommendations for adolescents, their parents, and health care providers are included.

INTRODUCTION

The internet and social media have become increasingly integrated into many aspects of adolescents' lives. Adolescents use the internet and social media for many educational, social, entertainment, and practical functions. Because of the widespread use of the internet and social media among adolescents, opportunities for them to encounter pitfalls exist. Two potential pitfalls are the harmful effects on personal well-being and cyberbullying. Adolescents can also derive benefits from their use of this technology. Benefits of social media include effects on peer affiliation, identity development, and its role in health care.

INTERNET, SOCIAL MEDIA, AND WELL-BEING

The use of social media has expanded greatly among adolescents in recent years. A nationally representative survey of American adolescents between 13 and 17 years of age conducted by the Pew Research Center in 2015 found that 92% of adolescents reported going online daily, including 24% who reported going online "almost constantly" (1). The authors pointed out that this frequency of use was due mostly to adolescents' access to mobile devices; 91% reported that they go online from mobile devices at least occasionally (1). Moreover, 73% have smartphones (1). The mean number of text messages sent per day was 67 (1). Of the various social media sites available to adolescents, Facebook was the most frequently used site, with 71% of adolescents accessing it, followed by Instagram (52%), Snapchat (41%), Twitter (33%), and Google+ (33%) (1). Forty-one percent of adolescents reported that Facebook is the site that they use most frequently, however 71% noted that they use more than one social media site (1).

The internet and social media are clearly a large part of most adolescents' lives, but it is not without is pitfalls and potential drawbacks. The manner in which adolescents use social media, and how this use interacts with other characteristics to affect well-being has been explored. Nesi and Prinstein (2) found that technology-based social comparison and seeking feedback were associated with depressive symptoms, with this finding particularly strong among females and adolescents who are low in popularity. These findings were found even when controlling for overall frequency of technology use, offline excessive reassurance-seeking, and prior depressive symptoms (2).

Lup, Trub, and Rosenthal (3) found that among a sample of older adolescents and young adult users of Instagram, more positive social comparison was related to less depressive symptoms. There were negative associations for those who follow more strangers, but positive outcomes for those who follow fewer strangers on this social media platform (3). At the lowest level of the number of strangers followed, more frequent use of Instagram was related to more positive social comparison, but at the highest level of the number of strangers followed, more frequent use was related to greater depressive symptoms (3). For those at higher levels of strangers followed a nonsignificant trend was found in which social comparison mediated the relationship between greater Instagram use and greater depressive symptoms, but for those at the lower levels of strangers followed a nonsignificant trend was found in which social comparison mediated the relationship between greater Instagram use and lower depressive symptoms (3).

CONTROVERSY ABOUT INTERNET ADDICTION

The negative effects of internet use have raised the issue of internet addiction being added to the diagnostic nomenclature as a way to capture the difficulties some individuals have with their use of this technology. For instance, in a sample of adolescents from Greece, maladaptive use of the internet was associated with poor academic functioning, as well as emotional and psychosocial maladjustment (4). Excessive internet use was also associated with a greater likelihood of conduct problems and hyperactivity (4). Whereas having an official, recognized psychiatric condition of internet addiction is not unique to adolescents, it is relevant to this population given their widespread use of social media and the internet. Arguments have been made in support of and against recognizing internet addiction as a psychiatric condition.

Arguments in favor of recognizing internet addiction as a psychiatric condition include the possibility that individuals who are struggling with their use of the internet might be motivated to seek help if this problem is considered a mental illness (5, 6). In addition, having internet addiction be a psychiatric condition might draw more attention to prevention, intervention, and research efforts about problematic use (5). Hinic (5) wondered if criteria for substance dependence can be applied to internet use, such as a desire or unsuccessful efforts to cut down or control the behavior; preoccupation with the behavior; a need for increased amounts of the behavior to achieve a desired effect, giving up important social, occupational, or recreational activities in order to engage in the behavior; impaired occupational, recreational, and academic functioning that result from the behavior; and persistent use despite having a physical or psychological problem caused by the behavior.

There are also arguments against recognizing internet addiction as a psychiatric condition. Griffiths (7) noted that internet use might not be the cause of an individual's difficulties, but the instrument through which other addictive behaviors are realized. For instance, with pathological gambling on the internet, treating an individual's computer use is not likely to ameliorate the fundamental problem behavior of gambling (8). In addition, physiological withdrawal and tolerance have not been established for the use of the internet as it has been with alcohol and other substances (6).

Grohol (9) pointed out that there might be some individuals who have difficulty moderating their use of the internet, but individuals have similar problems with work and hobbies, and those activities and behaviors are not labeled or considered a psychiatric condition. Pies (6) noted that internet addiction remains a label for a condition that likely represents multiple casual pathways and different manifestations. Instead of internet addiction being a psychiatric condition, excessive internet use might be a manifestation of other mental health problems (10).

Notwithstanding the controversy surrounding internet addiction, there likely are individuals who have difficulties moderating their use of the internet (6). Suggestions that have been provided for coping with internet addiction might be useful for these individuals, even though it is not a recognized psychiatric condition. For instance, using external stoppers as a reminder to end internet use, establishing new schedules to disrupt routine use, setting goals for the number of hours of internet use, arranging specific times for use, and abstaining from particular applications have been recommended (11). Individuals are also encouraged to keep sessions brief, but frequent to reduce cravings for internet use (11). Young (11) suggests that treatment be focused on controlling the use of the internet and learning to use it in moderation, rather than abstaining from its use altogether.

CYBERBULLYING

Another potential danger that adolescents might encounter with their use of the internet and social media is cyberbullying. According to Tokunaga (12), "cyberbullying is any behavior performed through electronic or digital media by individuals or groups that repeatedly communicates hostile or aggressive messages intended to inflict harm or discomfort on others" (12). An important feature of this definition is that the behavior is intended to inflict harm, which distinguishes cyberbullying from unintentional misdeeds. Forms of cyberbullying include flaming, harassment, denigration, exclusion, trickery, outing, cyberstalking, and impersonation (13).

Features of cyberbullying make it particularly distressing in comparison to traditional bullying. For instance, perpetrators of cyber-bullying can engage in this behavior anonymously, and the bullying can be spread quickly among others online (14). Unlike traditional bullying, which is limited to times when the victim and perpetrator are in each other's presence, cyberbullying can reach a victim at any time of the day (13). The perpetrators of cyberbullying do not typically see their victim's emotional reactions, and thus do not have cues about the effect of their behavior, which might otherwise inhibit their actions (13).

Findings from a variety of studies suggest that a sizeable percentage of youth might be victims of online harassment. In a sample of respondents under the age of 18 years (average age: 14.8), 32% of males and over 36% of females had been victims of cyberbullying (15). The Centers for Disease Control and Prevention found that 15.5% of high school students had been victims of electronic aggression in the previous 12 months (16). Rice et al. (17) found that 6.6% of middle school students reported being a victim of cyberbullying, 5.0% reported being a perpetrator of cyberbullying, and 4.3% reported being a victim and a perpetrator of cyberbullying during the past 12 months. Sexual-minority youth and youth who texted at least 50 times per day were more likely to report being a victim of cyberbullying, whereas girls were more likely to report being a perpetrator-victim of cyberbullying (17). In a survey of over 1,000 students at one university in the United States and two universities in Canada, 33.6% reported experiencing internet harassment in high school, and 8.6% reported experiencing such aggression in college (18). Some victims of cyberbullying are also victims of traditional bullying (19-21). Vazsonyi, Machackova, Sevcikova, Smahel, and Cerna (22) found associations between online and offline bullying behaviors in a sample of respondents from nine to 16 years of age in 25 European countries.

The effects of cyberbullying are broad and can affect victims and perpetrators. Being cyberbullied is associated with emotional and peer problems, headaches, sleep difficulties, recurrent abdominal pain, and not feeling safe at school (21). Hamm et al. (23) reviewed 36 studies that examined cyberbullying through social media among children and adolescents, and found a relationship between cyberbullying and depression. Hinduja and Patchin (24) reported that victims and perpetrators of cyberbullying had more thoughts of suicide and were more likely to attempt suicide than those who were not involved in this type of mistreatment. Perpetrating cyberbullying has been associated with conduct problems, hyperactivity, low prosocial behavior, frequent smoking and drunkenness, headaches, and not feeling safe at school (21). Sourander et al. (21) reported that individuals who tend to be the most troubled are those who are a victim and a perpetrator of cyberbullying.

The majority of the research on the effects of cyberbullying has used cross-sectional designs. Therefore, it is possible that problems and difficulties associated with cyberbullying could either be an antecedent, consequence, or both precede and follow this form of mistreatment, and it is not possible to determine if the correlates of this form of aggression play a role in its initiation, or are caused by it (12). Future research that uses longitudinal designs can more clearly determine the nature and direction of causality among these variables (12).

Given the association between cyberbullying and negative outcomes, finding ways to eliminate or reduce this form of mistreatment is imperative. Steps adolescents can take to reduce cyberbullying include keeping a log, journal, or other record of the bullying instances in the event that authorities become involved (25). Ignoring cyberbullying can be an option if the events are minor teasing (25) or are isolated instances (12). Adolescents can also employ technological coping strategies, such as using privacy settings (12). The effectiveness of using technological coping strategies to prevent cyberbullying is not known, but these techniques have been successful in cases of cyberstalking (12).

Adolescents are encouraged to consult with parents or another trusted adult to obtain ideas and assistance with regard to handling cyberbullying (26). Whereas adolescents are encouraged to manage the situation directly and by themselves, in some cases parental intervention might be necessary (26), and adolescents are encouraged to rely on trusted adults in these situations. Parents can find ways to block the cyberbully, report the behavior to the internet or website provider, and contact law enforcement if there are threats of violence or the use of sexually explicit images (27). Adolescents are encouraged to intervene in situations in which they are a bystander to cyberbullying (26). Having choices about how to respond to incidents of cyberbullying, and being flexible in using these approaches is recommended. Because the motives for cyberbullying likely vary, the solution and approach to each occasion of cyberbullying must also differ (28).

BENEFITS OF THE INTERNET AND SOCIAL MEDIA

In addition to the potential pitfalls and drawbacks of the internet and social media, there are many benefits that adolescents can derive from this technology. Some of these benefits are related to adolescents' interpersonal functioning. For instance, the internet can be used to broaden adolescents' social networks, provide opportunities to form meaningful relationships, improve self-confidence, and refine social abilities (29).

Spies Shapiro and Margolin (30) conducted a literature review on the impact of social networking sites on adolescents' social relationships and identity development. Based on a review of 13 studies that included adolescents, college students, and younger children, the authors concluded that the use of social networking sites generally seem to benefit adolescents' peer affiliations, but their social functioning offline might affect its impact (30). The authors pointed out that adolescents who have strong social skills offline seem to have more online connections (30). They also noted that adolescents who have limited social success offline might receive relationship satisfaction online, especially if they are more comfortable and at ease with online communication than offline communication (30). However, adolescents who post negative messages expose themselves to negative feedback from others (30).

In addition to the effect that social networking sites can have on adolescents' social relationships, their use might also affect identity development. Spies Shapiro and Margolin (30) reviewed 14 studies that explored the use of social networking sites and aspects of identity development. These studies consisted of samples of adolescents, adolescents and older participants, and college students. The authors concluded that social networking sites might permit adolescents to express themselves in a variety of ways and to receive feedback from others, which could hasten changes in their identity (30). Adolescents have the chance to join interest groups that represent different parts of their identity and what they might deem important, which can reaffirm and reassert their identity, as well as enable them to affiliate with others who share that interest (30).

Social networking sites might play an important role for ethnic, racial, and sexual minority youth. Adolescents from these groups use social networking sites to explore their identity, seek support, and establish connections with others (30), which might lead to greater feelings of inclusion and less social isolation. The use of social networking sites can also facilitate adolescents' attempts to interact and understand the experiences of others who are different from themselves, such as individuals with chronic illness, and those from different racial or ethnic backgrounds (30).

SOCIAL MEDIA AND HEALTH CARE

The Internet, and more specifically the information-sharing allowed by social media, have been shown to augment professional networking, patient education, and efforts to promote public health (31). There are efforts by some health care providers to use social media as a way of disseminating research discoveries, increasing case discussions among colleagues (e.g., crowd-sourcing), advertising their own practices, and taking part in health promotion (31). The widespread use and popularity of social media among adolescents has led to a consideration of how to use it to advance their health care. For instance, social media can complement information and care provided at routine office visits, and direct patients to websites with information on preventative topics and issues to be covered at an upcoming visit, such as sexual health and substance use (32). Social media can also be used to follow patients between visits to enhance adherence with treatment recommendations (32). A review of the use of social media in adolescents' health care found that social media is currently being used to assess aspects of risky health behaviors often missed during routine screening, such as alcohol use, substance use, and sexual behavior; provide important health information; engage in patient-provider communication to enhance continuity of care; and for recruitment in research studies (33). Adolescents can also use social media to interact with others with the same medical condition or disease, which can help them avoid stigma, improve social networks, learn about resources, and assist them in attempting to understand and manage the challenges associated with these medical conditions (34). Similarly, social media can promote social inclusion and interactions among those with the same medical condition who might otherwise feel isolated and excluded (34). Adolescents can use social media to explore stigmatized health topics anonymously and join online support groups and forums (32). If social media is used by adolescents to explore health topics, they are cautioned to be aware of misinformation and sites that promote unhealthy behaviors (34), and are encouraged to consult with a medical provider if they become concerned about their health. Utilizing social media in adolescents' health care is not without challenges. Wong, Merchant, and Moreno (32) noted that reimbursement for providers for health care delivered through social media, and integrating content from social media into medical records are issues of concern. Additional challenges include potentially inaccurate information on social media sites, as well as the risk of adolescents misinterpreting information on these sites; concerns about privacy and confidentiality; and the short-lived popularity of some social media sites, which can affect how many adolescents are reached if outdated social media platforms are used (32).

Recommendations

The internet and social media are powerful educational, social, entertainment, and practical tools, and their use among adolescents is widespread. Parents and health care providers can contribute to healthy online behavior, and reduce the chances that adolescents experience pitfalls from their online use. Parents are encouraged to know what social media sites their children are visiting; regularly discuss appropriate and inappropriate use; set clear consequences for inappropriate use and enforce these consequences when necessary; and model appropriate use of social media (27). It is recommended that parents educate their children about appropriate online behaviors, and maintain communication with them about their relationships and friendships (35).

The American Academy of Pediatrics Council on Communications and Media (36) provided several guidelines for successfully integrating media use into adolescents' lives. It is suggested that limits be placed on the number of hours per day adolescents use electronic media, as well as the types of media used, ensure that adolescents obtain adequate sleep, and receive about one hour of physical activity each day (36). Parents are encouraged to regularly discuss online citizenship and safety, such as avoiding cyberbullying; develop a network of adults who can interact with adolescents online and be a source of support if they encounter challenges; and communicate and share the guidelines that they establish with other caregivers to ensure that these guidelines are followed consistently (36).

Designating times and locations at home in which media is not used is recommended (36). Adolescents are encouraged to not sleep with electronic devices in their bedroom, and not use devices one hour before bedtime and during homework (36). Online tools such as the Media Time Calculator and the Family Media Use Plan (both tools are available at https://www.healthychildren.org/English/media/Pages/default.aspx#wizard) can be used by parents to inform their decisions and guidelines about their children's use of social media.

Clinicians can play a role in assessing and determining the role and impact of social media use in the lives of their adolescent patients, and intervene if problems are identified. Reid and Weigle (27) recommended that clinicians be informed about the technologies that adolescents use so that they can have productive conversations with them about social media use during clinic visits. Assessing social media use during the clinical interview, such as sites that are visited, the duration of time spent on these sites, and if the patient is involved in any risky online behavior is suggested (27). For patients who have unhealthy eating behaviors or engage in self-harm, it is important to determine if they visit sites that promote and encourage these behaviors (27). Clinicians can also explore possible underlying reasons for engaging in risky online behavior, such as interpersonal difficulties, depression, and anxiety; discuss appropriate use of social media with patients; provide information about possible academic, social, and legal consequences of inappropriate and high-risk use; and educate parents about risks online and encourage them to be aware of their child's online behavior (27).

In addition to assessing general online behavior, clinicians are encouraged to ask about cyberbullying (27). Inquiring about whether the patient is a victim of cyberbullying, a perpetrator of cyberbullying, or both is encouraged. If cyberbullying is identified, the effect that this mistreatment has on the adolescent's well-being can be assessed (27). Clinicians can play an active role in reducing cyberbullying by collaborating with parents, teachers, and school personnel (37). The guidelines and suggestions that clinicians discuss about media and privacy with their patients and their parents can be shared with school personnel, and included in programs that focus on digital citizenship (34).

The internet and social media are associated with benefits and drawbacks for adolescents. Additional research is needed to better understand the effect of this technology on adolescents' functioning. Longitudinal research is needed to explore the direction of causality among aspects of social media use and well-being, among excessive Internet use and associated difficulties, and between cyberbullying and related problems. Reid Chassiakos, Radesky, Moreno, and Cross (34) pointed out that the effects of social media use in children and adolescents depend on the characteristics of the individual, the type of media, the type of use, and the amount and extent of use. Research is needed to explore the effects of these factors.

CONCLUSION

The internet and social media are powerful tools. While there are possible pitfalls that can befall adolescents with their use of this technology, it is a valuable educational, social, entertainment, and practical resource when used appropriately, and has become almost indispensable in modern society. Education about the potential drawbacks of the internet and social media, along with involvement and collaborative discussions among adolescents, parents, and clinicians about adolescents' use and online behavior, can lessen the harmful effects of this technology. Facilitating and embracing the benefits of the internet and social media, being cognizant of potential pitfalls, and thoughtfully integrating it into one's life can allow adolescents to experience its benefits while minimizing or preventing its drawbacks.

REFERENCES

[1] Lenhart A, Pew Research Center. Teens, social media and technology overview, 2015. URL: http://www.pewinternet.org/2015/04/09/teens-social-media-technology-2015/.
[2] Nesi J, Prinstein MJ. Using social media for social comparison and feedback-seeking: Gender and popularity moderate associations with depressive symptoms. J Abnorm Child Psychol 2015;43:1427-38.
[3] Lup K, Trub L, Rosenthal L. Instagram #instasad?: Exploring associations among Instagram use, depressive symptoms, negative social comparison, and strangers followed. Cyberpsychol Behav Soc Netw 2015;18:247-52.
[4] Kormas G, Critselis E, Janikian M, Kafetzis D, Tsitsika A. Risk factors and psychosocial characteristics of potential problematic and problematic internet use among adolescents: a cross-sectional study. BMC Public Health 2011;11:595.
[5] Hinic D. Problems with 'Internet addiction' diagnosis and classification. Psychiatr Danub 2011;23:145-51.
[6] Pies R. Should DSM-V Designate "Internet Addiction" a Mental Disorder? Psychiatry (Edgmont) 2009;6:31-7.
[7] Griffiths MD. Internet addiction: Internet fuels other addictions. Student BMJ 1999;7:428-9.

[8] Sim T, Gentile DA, Bricolo F, Serpelloni G, Gulamoydeen F. A conceptual review of research on the pathological use of computers, video games, and the Internet. Int J Ment Health Addict 2012;10:748-69.

[9] Grohol JM. Why Internet addiction still doesn't exist, 2008. URL: https://psychcentral.com/blog/why-internet-addiction-still-doesnt-exist/.

[10] Lam LT, Peng ZW. Effect of pathological use of the internet on adolescent mental health: A prospective study. Arch Pediatr Adolesc Med 2010;164:901-6.

[11] Young KS. Internet addiction: Systems, evaluation, and treatment. URL: http://treatmentcenters.com/downloads/internet-addiction.pdf.

[12] Tokunaga RS. Following you home from school: a critical review and synthesis of research on cyberbullying victimization. Comput Human Behav 2010;26:277-87.

[13] Willard NE. Educators guide to cyberbullying and cyberthreats, 2005. URL: https://education.ohio.gov/getattachment/Topics/Other-Resources/School-Safety/Safe-and-Supportive-Learning/Anti-Harassment-Intimidation-and-Bullying-Resource/Educator-s-Guide-Cyber-Safety.pdf.aspx.

[14] Raskauskas J, Stoltz AD. Involvement in traditional and electronic bullying among adolescents. Dev Psychol 2007;43:564-75.

[15] Hinduja S, Patchin JW. Cyberbullying: An exploratory analysis of factors related to offending and victimization. Deviant Behav 2008;29:129-56.

[16] Kann L, McManus T, Harris WA, Shanklin SL, Flint KH, Hawkins J, et al. Youth Risk Behavior Surveillance, United States, 2015. URL: https://www.cdc.gov/healthyyouth/data/yrbs/pdf/2015/ss6506_updated.pdf.

[17] Rice E, Petering R, Rhoades H, Winetrobe H, Goldbach J, Plant A, et al. Cyberbullying perpetration and victimization among middle-school students. Am J Public Health 2015;105:e66-72.

[18] Beran TN, Rinaldi C, Bickham DS, Rich M. Evidence for the need to support adolescents dealing with harassment and cyber-harassment: prevalence, progression, and impact. Sch Psychol Int 2012;33:562-76.

[19] Dehue F, Bolman C, Vollink T. Cyberbullying: youngsters' experiences and parental perception. Cyberpsychol Behav 2008;11:217-23.

[20] Katzer C, Fetchenhauer D, Belschak F. Cyberbullying: Who are the victims? A comparison of victimization in Internet chatrooms and victimization in school. J Media Psychol 2009;21:25-36.

[21] Sourander A, Brunstein Klomek A, Ikonen M, Lindroos J, Luntamo T, Koskelainen M, et al. Psychosocial risk factors associated with cyberbullying among adolescents: a population-based study. Arch Gen Psychiatry 2010;67:720-8.

[22] Vazsonyi AT, Machackova H, Sevcikova A, Smahel D, Cerna A. Cyberbullying in context: Direct and indirect effects by low self-control across 25 European countries. Eur J Dev Psychol 2012;9:210-27.

[23] Hamm MP, Newton AS, Chisholm A, Shulhan J, Milne A, Sundar P, et al. Prevalence and Effect of cyberbullying on children and young people: A scoping review of social media studies. JAMA Pediatr 2015;169:770-7.

[24] Hinduja S, Patchin JW. Bullying, cyberbullying, and suicide. Arch Suicide Res 2010;14:206-21.
[25] Hinduja S, Patchin JW. Cyberbullying: Identification, prevention, and response, 2018. URL: https://cyberbullying.org/Cyberbullying-Identification-Prevention-Response-2018.pdf.
[26] CyberBully.org. A student's guide to cyber bullying, 2013-2018. URL: http://cyberbully.org/a-students-guide-to-cyber-bullying/.
[27] Reid D, Weigle P. Social media use among adolescents: Benefits and risks. Adolesc Psychiatry 2014;4:73-80.
[28] WiredSafety.org. Stop cyberbullying. URL: http://www.stopcyberbullying.org/why_do_kids_cyberbully_each_other.html.
[29] Weinstein A, Lejoyeux M. Internet addiction or excessive internet use. Am J Drug Alcohol Abuse 2010;36:277-83.
[30] Spies Shapiro LA, Margolin G. Growing up wired: social networking sites and adolescent psychosocial development. Clin Child Fam Psychol Rev 2014;17:1-18.
[31] Ventola CL. Social media and health care professionals: benefits, risks, and best practices. P T 2014;39(7):491-520.
[32] Wong CA, Merchant RM, Moreno MA. Using social media to engage adolescents and young adults with their health. Healthc (Amst) 2014;2:220-4.
[33] Yonker LM, Zan S, Scirica CV, Jethwani K, Kinane TB. "Friending" teens: Systematic review of social media in adolescent and young adult health care. J Med Internet Res 2015;17:e4.
[34] Reid Chassiakos YL, Radesky J, Christakis D, Moreno MA, Cross C, AAP Council On Communications and Media. Children and adolescents and digital media. Pediatrics 2016;138:e1-e18.
[35] Moreno MA. Cyberbullying. JAMA Pediatr 2014;168(5):500.
[36] AAP Council On Communications and Media. Media use in school-aged children and adolescents. Pediatrics 2016;138:1-6.
[37] David-Ferdon C, Hertz MF. Electronic media, violence, and adolescents: An emerging public health problem. J Adolesc Health 2007;41:S1-5.

In: Building Youth for the Future
Editors: H. A Omar and J. Merrick
ISBN: 978-1-53613-768-2

Chapter 9

Gender Identity in Adolescents

Mandakini Sadhir*, MD and Robyn Morris, LCSW
Division of Adolescent Medicine, Department of Pediatrics,
University of Kentucky, Lexington, Kentucky, US

Abstract

During adolescence, understanding and expressing gender and sexual orientation are typical developmental tasks. For most adolescents, gender identity is consistent with their biologic sex. But for some their gender identity, role or expression differs from the cultural norms of a particular sex. The chapter describes gender dysphoria, mental health, and risk taking behaviors and guidelines on providing care to transgender youth.

Keywords: transgender, gender dysphoria, adolescent

Introduction

Adolescence is an important time period for identity development. One of the typical developmental tasks is to understand and express gender and

* Correspondence: Mandakini Sadhir, MD, Division of Adolescent Medicine, Department of Pediatrics, University of Kentucky, Lexington, KY 40536-0284, United States. Email: m.sadhir@uky.edu.

sexual orientation. This process is not a one-time event. It varies across individuals and influenced by personal, cultural, and social factors (1). According to American psychological association, sex is defined as a biological status categorized as male, female or inters sex based on factors such as chromosomes, gonads, genitalia. Gender is a psychological status and represents attitudes, feelings, and behaviors associated with being feminine or masculine (2). Research has shown that gender identity is not simply psychosocial construct but it is a complex interplay of biologic, environmental, cultural factors. There may be a genetic, hormonal, and neuroanatomical influence on gender identity development (3). A child, around age 2 years internalizes and identifies with their gender as either male or female. Around the age of 3 years, the child begins to learn that the genitals are what make a person a male or female (4). By age 4 or 5 years, children have learned a wide array of social stereotypes about how boys and girls should behave. Consequently, they tend to react approvingly or disapprovingly toward each other according to their choice of sex-appropriate play patterns and toys (4). Majority of children and adolescents have gender identity aligned according to their sex (cisgender). Some of them may have a gender identity, role, or expression which is different from the cultural norms prescribed for people of a particular sex (gender diverse) (5, 6). They may identify as opposite sex (transgender male, transgender female); identify as both (bi gender, androgyn); identify as none (agender, gender neutral) or move between genders (gender fluid) (5).

GENDER DYSPHORIA IN CHILDREN AND ADOLESCENTS

Children and adolescents who identify differently from their sex assigned at birth and experience distress are diagnosed with gender dysphoria (7). Diagnosis of gender dysphoria has replaced the previous diagnosis of gender identity disorder (8). According to "Diagnostic and statistical manual" (DSM V), in order to meet criteria for gender dysphoria, a cluster of traits (listed in Table 1) must be present and traits must be "consistent, persistent, and insistent" (8).

Table 1. Criteria for gender dysphoria

Children	**Adolescents**
A. A marked incongruence of at least six month's duration, manifested by at least *six* of the following: • Strong desire to be of the other or an alternative gender. • In boys, strong desire to cross dress; in females, strong desire for wearing masculine clothing. • Strong preference for cross-gender roles in play. • Strong preference for toys, games, etc. used by other gender. • Strong preference for playmates of other gender. • Boys reject masculine toys, avoid rough and tumble play; Girls reject feminine toys. • Strong dislike of one's sexual anatomy. • Strong desire for primary/secondary sex characteristics that match experienced gender B. Condition associated with clinically significant distress/impairment in social, school, or other important areas of functioning.	A. A marked incongruence between one's experienced/expressed gender and assigned gender, of at least 6 months' duration, as manifested by at least two of the following: • A marked incongruence between one's experienced/expressed gender and primary and/or secondary sex characteristics (or in young adolescents, the anticipated secondary sex characteristics). • A strong desire to be rid of one's primary and/or secondary sex characteristics because of a marked incongruence with one's experienced/expressed gender (or in young adolescents, a desire to prevent the development of the anticipated secondary sex characteristics). • A strong desire for the primary and/or secondary sex characteristics of the other gender. • A strong desire to be of the other gender (or some alternative gender different from one's assigned gender). • A strong desire to be treated as the other gender (or some alternative gender different from one's assigned gender). • A strong conviction that one has the typical feelings and reactions of the other gender (or some alternative gender different from one's assigned gender). B. The condition is associated with clinically significant distress or impairment in social, occupational, or other important areas of functioning.

Source: American Psychiatric Association. *Gender Dysphoria. Diagnostic and statistical manual of mental disorders* 5th ed. Arlington, VA. American Psychiatric Association, 2013.

Traits must also cause impairment or distress and be distinguished from prejudice or stigma (8). Criteria for children are more concrete, and behavioral. Young children are less likely to express extreme anatomic dysphoria. Adolescents and adults have more incongruence between their gender identity and somatic sex (1, 3). Factors related to distress and impairment varies with age. Longitudinal studies have shown that many pre-pubertal children may no longer fulfill criteria for gender dysphoria with the onset of puberty (3). Children who are persistent report greater magnitude of gender dysphoria and have often undergone social transition during childhood (3, 6). They "believed" that they were affirmed gender. Children who "wished they were" the other sex tend to desist. Gender dysphoria typically persists when presenting in adolescence. Distress is often exacerbated with the onset of puberty (6, 10).

In past decade, specialty clinics have reported increasing numbers of pediatric patients with gender dysphoria. According to recent estimates, 150,000 youth (0.7%) ages 13 to 17 years identify as transgender in the US. About 0.7 percent of young adults ages 18 to 24 years, 0.6 percent of adults ages 25 to 64 years, 0.5 percent of adults ages 65 years and older identify as transgender (9). Sex differences in the rate of referrals to specialty clinics vary by age group. In children under age 12 years, the male/female ratio ranges from 6:1 to 3:1 as compared to adolescents older than age 12 years, the male/female ratio is close to 1:1(11).

MENTAL HEALTH AND RISK-TAKING BEHAVIORS IN TRANSGENDER YOUTH

Adolescents with gender dysphoria are a vulnerable population. They experience significant stigmatization, isolation, harassment in family, school, and communities. According to GLSEN survey, transgender, genderqueer, and other non-cisgender youth faced more hostile school climates and felt unsafe (12). Restroom use is often a huge concern.

Transgender youth are at a higher risk than their non-transgender peers for negative health outcomes and health risk behaviors, including substance use, depression, suicidality, anxiety, sexual/physical abuse, STDs, social isolation, homelessness(6). A recent retrospective cohort study of female to male transgender (n=106) and male to female transgender (n=74) adolescents aged 12-29 years showed that transgender youth had twofold to threefold increased risk of depression, anxiety disorder, suicidal ideation, suicide attempt, self-harm without lethal intent, and both inpatient and outpatient mental health treatment in comparison with cisgender controls (13). There were no statistically significant differences in mental health outcomes when comparing female to male transgender and male to female youth, adjusting for age, race/ethnicity, and hormone use (13). In various clinical samples, a high percentage of gender non-conforming, transgender youth report depression, suicidal ideation, self-harm, suicidal attempts (14, 15). Gender minority youth were more likely to report alcohol use, marijuana use, and other illicit drug use in past month as compared to cisgender peers. In addition, bullying and harassment in past one year were associated with increased odds of the substance use (16). In another survey among middle and high school students in California, transgender adolescents were 2 to 3 times more likely to use cigarettes in school and use cocaine/methamphetamine in their lifetime. They were more than twice as likely to report past 30-day inhalant and prescription pain medication use (17).

Transgender adolescents also engage in high-risk sexual behaviors. Transgender adolescents were reported to have sex with two or more partners, not using condoms at last sex, no birth control use and were intoxicated at last sex as compared to cisgender youth (18). Transgender adolescents also have increased rates of eating disorder diagnosis compared to cisgender heterosexual women, past-month diet pill use and past-month vomiting or laxative use (14). In addition, higher rates of harassment and discrimination were linked to higher odds of reported past year binge eating and fasting or vomiting to lose weight in transgender youth (19).

PROVIDING CARE TO TRANSGENDER YOUTH

There are significant barriers for health care access including fear of experiencing transphobia, lack of provider and staff knowledge and cultural competence, few accessible providers trained in gender-affirming health care for youth and insurance exclusions (20). In previous years, gender concerns were considered as mental health disorder and conversion therapy was practiced. The focus of the conversion therapy was to eliminate transgender identity or gender-expansive traits (21). Transition was never considered appropriate and the child was expected to live in gender assigned at birth (21). Over the years, research shows that it has no proven benefit and causes lasting damage to children (21, 22). Various professional organizations such as American college of physicians, the American Academy of Pediatrics, the American Psychoanalytic Association, etc. have all condemned and rejected conversion therapy (21, 22).

Providing gender affirmative care is now a widely accepted approach (3, 6, 11, 21, 22). Gender affirmative model of care identifies gender identity as fluid and not binary. It emphasizes that individual psychological problems are often secondary to negative interpersonal and cultural reactions to a child. Transition to affirmed gender is thus supported at developmentally appropriate age (11, 21, 22).

Transgender children and adolescents have unique health care needs. Their care involves a multidisciplinary approach with involvement of primary care medical providers, specialists in adolescent medicine, endocrine, gynecology, surgeons, mental health professionals. Support from families, school and, community is imperative (22). Gender transition is a stepwise approach and often individualized. This includes social transition, use of puberty blockers, gender-affirming hormone therapy and surgery and legal transition (22). WPATH (World professional association on transgender health) and Endocrine society guidelines are widely utilized for transition process (11, 28). Legal transition involves changing gender and name recorded on birth certificates, school records, and other documents. State law may vary for legal transition (22).

Social transition allows child or adolescent to choose how they express their gender. It can be done at any age and is reversible. During the social transition, a child wears clothing; adopts a hairstyle that affirms their gender. They may also choose a name or use pronouns (such as "he" or "she" or "they"); may use bathrooms and other facilities that match their gender identity (22). A recent study found that depression and self-worth in socially transitioned transgender children aged 6-14 year did not differ from their control or sibling peers (23).They were however found to have slightly increased anxiety. Parents also reported slightly elevated anxiety in their socially transitioned children but no increase in depression as compared to control groups (24). These findings are different than previous studies which showed children who had not socially transitioned had higher rates of depression, anxiety and lower self-worth (25, 26).

Transgender children and adolescents experience significant distress with puberty as new secondary sex characteristics develop. Changes can either trigger their gender dysphoria or make it worse (27). Adolescents can develop significant depression and anxiety that can also lead to a mental health crisis and suicidality (27). Current guidelines recommend using reversible medication such GnRH inhibitors commonly known as puberty blockers to stop the progression of puberty, thus preventing the consequences of going through physical changes that doesn't match a transgender child's identity (11, 28). Use of puberty blocker is a reversible treatment and provides time for the adolescent to further explore their identity. It is important to continue to seek help from medical and mental health professional to monitor progress and side effects of treatment (11, 22, 28). Next step in gender transition is use of gender affirming hormones such as testosterone for transgender males and estrogen for transgender females. This phase of transition is partially reversible and thus it is important for families and adolescents to make an informed decision (11, 28). During this treatment, adolescents are closely monitored for progression of changes and side effects associated with it. Discussion about fertility preservation before and during treatment is recommended (11, 28). Once, adolescents become adults, they may choose to undergo irreversible gender-affirming surgery. Surgery typically includes "top" surgery (to enhance breasts or create male typical chest shape), "bottom" surgery (surgery on genitals or reproductive organs), facial feminization surgeries (11, 22).

While research in adolescents is limited, preliminary studies have shown promising results. A study investigated gender dysphoria, body image, depression, anxiety, emotional and behavioral problems, and social and educational/professional functioning as well as subjective well-being among transgender youth. In the study, there were 22 transgender females and 33 transgender males who underwent puberty suppression at 12 years, gender-affirming hormone treatment at 16 years and surgery at 18 years. Gender dysphoria was largely resolved in this population following gender affirming hormone treatment and genital surgery. Overall functioning and their well-being was comparable to peers. None regretted the treatment. Limitations of the study were its small size and lack of long-term (10 to 20 years) outcomes.

Conclusion

Gender diverse youth have unique social-emotional and health care needs. It is important to identify gender dysphoria and seek appropriate intervention under expert guidance. Family, school and community support is crucial for their overall health and well-being. Further research is needed to measure long term outcomes and guide best practices to address health care needs.

References

[1] Steensma TD, Kreukels BP, de Vries AL, Cohen-Kettenis PT. Gender identity development in adolescence. Horm Behav 2013;64(2):288-97.

[2] American psychological association. Definitions related to sexual orientation and gender diversity in APA Documents. American Psychological Association. URL: https://www.apa.org/pi/lgbt/resources/sexuality-definitions.pdf.

[3] Rosenthal SM. Transgender youth: current concepts. Ann Pediatr Endocrinol Metab 2016;21(4):185-92.

[4] Yarber WL, Sayad BW, Strong B. Human sexuality: Diversity in contemporary America, 9th edition. New York: McGraw Hill Education, 2016.

[5] National LGBT Health Education Center. Glossary of LGBT terms for health care teams, 2016. URL: https://www.lgbthealtheducation.org/wp-content/uploads/LGBT-Glossary_March2016.pdf.

[6] Vance SR jr, Ehrensaft D, Rosenthal SM. Psychological and medical care of gender nonconforming youth. Pediatrics 2014;134:1184-92.

[7] American Psychiatric Association. What is gender dysphoria? URL: https://www.psychiatry.org/patients-families/gender-dysphoria/what-is-gender-dysphoria.

[8] American Psychiatric Association. Gender Dysphoria. Diagnostic and statistical manual of mental disorders, 5th edition. Arlington, VA: APA, 2013.

[9] Herman, JL, Flores AR., Brown TNT, Wilson, BDM, Conron KJ. Age of individuals who identify as transgender in the United States. Los Angeles, CA: Williams Institute, 2017. https://williamsinstitute.law.ucla.edu/wpcontent/uploads/TransAgeReport.pdf.

[10] Rosenthal SM. Approach to the patient. Transgender youth: Endocrine considerations. J Clin Endocrinol Metab 2014;99(12):4379-89.

[11] The World Professional Association for Transgender Health. Standards of care for the health of transsexual, transgender, and gender nonconforming people, 7th version. URL: http://www.wpath.org.

[12] Kosciw JG, Greytak EA, Giga NM, Villenas C, Danischewski DJ. The experiences of lesbian, gay, bisexual, transgender, and queer youth in our nation's schools. The 2015 National School Climate Survey, 2016. URL: https://www.glsen.org.

[13] Reisner SL, Vetters R, Leclerc M, Zaslow S, Wolfrum S, Shumer D, et al. Mental health of transgender youth in care at an adolescent urban community health center: A matched retrospective cohort study. J Adolesc Health 2015;56(3):274-9.

[14] Connolly MD, Zervos MJ, Barone CJ. The mental health of transgender youth: Advances in understanding. J Adolesc Health 2016;59(5):489-95.

[15] Peterson CM, Matthews A, Copps-Smith E, Conard LA. Suicidality, self-harm, and body dissatisfaction in transgender adolescents and emerging adults with gender dysphoria. Suicide Life Threat Behav 2017;47(4):475-82.

[16] Reisner SL, Greytak EA, Parsons JT, Ybarra ML. Gender minority social stress in adolescence: disparities in adolescent bullying and substance use by gender identity J Sex Res 2015;52(3):243-56.

[17] De Pedro KT, Gilreath TD, Jackson C, Esqueda MC. Substance use among transgender students in California public middle and high schools. J Sch Health 2017;87(5):303-9.

[18] Eisenberg ME, Gower AL, McMorris BJ, Rider GN, Shea G, Coleman E. Risk and protective factors in the lives of transgender/gender nonconforming adolescents. J Adolesc Health 2017;61(4):521-6.

[19] Watson RJ, Veale JF, Saewyc EM Disordered eating behaviors among transgender youth: probability profiles from risk and protective factors. Int J Eat Disord 2017;50(5):515-22.

[20] Gridley SJ, Crouch JM, Evans Y, Eng W, Antoon E, Lyapustina M, et al. Youth and caregiver perspectives on barriers to gender-affirming health care for transgender youth. J Adolesc Health 2016;59(3):254-61.

[21] Ehrensaft D. Gender nonconforming youth: Current perspectives. Adolesc Health Med Ther 2017;25(8):57-67.

[22] Murchison G, Adkins D, Conard LA, Ehrensaft D, Elliot T, Hawkins LA, et al. Supporting and caring for transgender children. Human Rights campaign, 2016. URL: http://hrc.im/supportingtranschildren.

[23] Olson KR, Durwood L, DeMeules M, McLaughlin KA. Mental health of transgender children who are supported in their identities. Pediatrics 2016;137(3). doi: 10.1542/peds.2015-3223.

[24] Durwood L, McLaughlin KA, Olson KR. Mental health and self-worth in socially transitioned transgender youth. J Am Acad Child Adolesc Psychiatry 2017;56(2):116-23.

[25] Balleur-van Rijn A, Steensma TD, Kreukels BP, Cohen-Kettenis PT. Self-perception in a clinical sample of gender variant children. Clin Child Psychol Psychiatry 2013;18:464–74.

[26] Cohen-Kettenis PT, Owen A, Kaijser VG, Bradley SJ, Zucker KJ. Demographic characteristics, social competence, and behavior problems in children with gender identity disorder: A cross-national, cross-clinic comparative analysis. J Abnorm Child Psychol 2003;31:41–53.

[27] Lopez X, Stewart S, Jacobson-Dickman E. Approach to children and adolescents with gender dysphoria. Pediatr Rev 2016;37(3):89-96.

[28] Hembree WC, Cohen-Kettenis PT, Gooren L, Hannema SE, Meyer WJ, Murad MH, et al. Endocrine treatment of gender-dysphoric/gender-incongruent Persons: An endocrine society clinical practice guideline. J Clin Endocrinol Metab 2017;102(11):3869-3903.

[29] de Vries AL, McGuire JK, Steensma TD, Wagenaar EC, Doreleijers TA, Cohen-Kettenis PT. Young adult psychological outcome after puberty suppression and gender reassignment. Pediatrics 2014;134(4):696-704.

In: Building Youth for the Future ISBN: 978-1-53613-768-2
Editors: H. A Omar and J. Merrick

Chapter 10

SELF-HARM

Stephanie Stockburger*, MD and Jennifer Perry, LCSW
Department of Pediatrics, Division of Adolescent Medicine,
University of Kentucky, Lexington, Kentucky, US

ABSTRACT

Non-suicidal self-injury (NSSI) is relatively common in the adolescent population. It is typically a signal of underlying distress. There is an important relationship between NSSI and suicide. It is important to be comfortable asking youth about self-harm behaviors and also to respond appropriately if a youth discloses this behavior. There are a number of therapies available to help youth who have self-harm behavior.

INTRODUCTION

Non-suicidal self-injury (NSSI), also known as self-harm, self-mutilation, self-abuse, or para-suicide occurs when someone intentionally and

* Correspondence: Stephanie Stockburger, MD, Assistant Professor of Pediatrics, Department of Pediatrics, Division of Adolescent Medicine, 740 S Limestone, Lexington, KY 40536-0284, United States. Email: Sjstoc2@uky.edu.

repeatedly harms herself/himself in a way that is impulsive and not intended to be lethal. It can feel to other people that these things are done calmly and deliberately – almost cynically. But we know that someone who self-harms is usually in a state of high emotion, distress and unbearable inner turmoil. Some people plan it in advance, for others, it happens on the spur of the moment. Some people self-harm only once or twice, but others do it regularly - it can be hard to stop.

Karl Menninger, MD (1893-1990) was the first to propose self-injury as a way to soothe oneself, an act of "self-destruction—a partial suicide to avert total suicide" (1). In the late 19th century, two American doctors--George Gould and Walter Pyle--documented something they saw as a strange medical phenomenon. They reported that women all over Europe were puncturing themselves with sewing needles. In fact, this practice was common enough that European doctors had developed a name for the supposedly hysterical women who practiced this form of self-torture. They were called needle girls (2). Favazza, who works at the University of Missouri, ancient Greece excerpt from the work of the famous Greek historian Herodotus, who wrote of a Spartan leader who was thrown into the stocks after exhibiting strange behavior and as he was lying there, fast bound, he noticed that all the guards had left him, except one, and he asked the man, who was his serf, to lend him his knife. As soon as the knife was in his hands, he began to mutilate himself, beginning on his shins (2).

COMMON FORMS OF SELF-HARM

Most common forms of self-harm are cutting the skin (may carve words or symbols), banging or punching objects or oneself to the point of injury, then burning the skin. Other forms can include: scratching or pinching with fingernails on the skin, biting and leaving marks, pulling out hair, eyelashes, or eyebrows with intention of hurting oneself, or intentionally preventing would healing, taking pills to overdose, sticking things in your body, and swallowing things (3). Forms of self-harm are considered not socially sanctioned. In other words, tattooing and piercing are considered social acceptable and would not be considered self-harm. However, excessive tattooing and piercing may be seen as harmful and may be undertaken with the same intentions.

The research probably under-estimates how common self-harm is. It is usually based on surveys of people who go to hospital or their general practitioner after harming themselves. However, we know that a lot of people do not seek help after self-harm. Some types of self-harm, like cutting, may be more secret and so less likely to be noticed. In general, studies suggest that about 13-25% of adolescents and young adults surveyed in schools have some history of self-injury (3). However, many of these youth engage in the self-harm behavior once or twice and then stop. Other youth go on to become chronic self-injurers. Studies of college students show that approximately 6% are actively and chronically self-injuring (3). The middle school population may have a somewhat higher prevalence since that is the age at which most individuals initiate self-harm behaviors (3). It has been reported that 70% of teens engaging in self-injury behavior have made at least one suicide attempt. Fifty-five percent had multiple suicide attempts (4).

Self-injury is an individual's way to cope with or relieve painful or hard-to-express feelings, and is generally not a suicide attempt. Relief is temporary, and a self-destructive cycle often develops without proper treatment. The act of self-injury can also be a way to have control over your body when you can't control anything else in your life. A lot of people who cut themselves also have an eating disorder. People who self-injure commonly report they feel empty inside, over or under stimulated, unable to express their feelings, lonely, not understood by others and fearful of intimate relationships and adult responsibilities. Research has shown that many people who harm themselves are struggling with intolerable distress or unbearable situations. A person will often struggle with difficulties for some time before they self-harm. Common problems include: physical or sexual abuse, feeling depressed, feeling bad about yourself, relationship problems with partners, friends, and family, being unemployed, or having difficulties at work. You may be more likely to harm yourself if you feel: that people don't listen to you, hopeless, isolated, alone, out of control, powerless – it feels as though there's nothing you can do to change anything. It's more likely to happen if you are using alcohol or drugs – it may feel that these are as out of control as the rest of your life.

SELF-HARM VERSUS SUICIDE

It is very common for people who are not familiar with self-injury to assume that it is a suicide attempt. However, the intent is typically the opposite. Individuals who self-injure are usually aiming to feel better, not end life. In fact, NSSI is typically undertaken with the intention of self-integrating and preserving life. However, individuals who self-injure are at higher risk for suicidality. If someone is practicing self-harm, an assessment for suicidality should be undertaken. One study found that individuals who reported NSSI were nine times more likely to report having made a suicide attempt at some point in their life (5). Both behaviors indicate underlying distress. The distress may or may not be successfully mitigated through NSSI or other self-medicating or soothing behaviors. Someone may be practicing NSSI and may also be suicidal. Another study found that even individuals who have stopped practicing NSSI may be at increased risk for suicidality at a later point in their life (5).

RED FLAGS

How can you tell if someone is self-injuring? A person often takes steps to hide the injuries. It is important to remember that not all individuals who self-harm will become emotionally withdrawn. There are a significant number of individuals that are highly functional and socially engaged who self-injure (6).

Red flags for self-harm include unexplained or clustered scars or marks, fresh cuts, bruises, burns, or other signs of bodily damage, bandages worn frequently, inappropriate dress for the season (long pants in summer), unwillingness to participate in events that require less body coverage (i.e., swimming), constant use of wrist bands, physical or emotional absence, preoccupation, distance, social withdrawal, sensitivity to rejection, difficulty handling anger, compulsiveness, expressions of self-loathing, shame, and/or worthlessness. It is important to remember that not all youth who are self-harming become emotionally withdrawn (3). Also, individuals may have some of the signs listed above and may not necessarily be engaging in self-harm behavior.

When you encounter someone who is self-injuring, you may feel uncomfortable. The more you know about self-harm, the more support you will be able to provide. Search out resources and arm yourself with knowledge. If you don't know how to react to self-harm, don't react at all. No reaction is better than a negative reaction. It can help to talk with someone you trust. Especially if you are angry or have intense emotions about the situation. This may help to keep you emotionally balanced when you do directly raise the issue with a person who self-injures.

CONTAGIOUS?

Is self-injury contagious? The seemingly rapid spread of self-injury among community populations of youth suggests that there may be a social contagion factor at work. Indeed, self-injury has been shown repeatedly to follow epidemic-like patterns in institutional settings such as hospitals and detention facilities. For many, self-injury is a very private, hidden act. However, anecdotal reports from adults working with youth in school settings report a fad quality to the behavior similar to that which occurs with eating disorders. Causes for the spread of the behavior in non-clinical populations have left many wondering what larger contextual factors might be at work. Some research suggests that the Internet and the increasing prevalence of self-injury in popular media, such as movies, books, and news reports, may play a role in the spread of self-injury.

Your initial response is critical in the individual's future help-seeking behavior and participation in intervention. It is extremely important to build supportive and trusting relationship with youth. It is not recommended to express shock, revulsion, or discomfort when self-harm is disclosed. Ask directly: "I notice that you have wounds or scars on your arms and know that this can be a sign of self-injury/cutting. Are you injuring yourself?" If they evade the question or deny self-injury, do not push. If they deny self-injury, just keep the door open: "If you ever want to talk about anything, I am available." Continue to look for further opportunities to ask (3). If someone relays to you that they have self-injured, first assess the severity of the injury. Do you need to help them get to a medical provider or to a local emergency department for further evaluation of the wound?

HIGH RISK

Individuals should be assessed for immediate risk of suicide and other mental health issues. High risk patients include adolescents that are at risk for suicide. Experiencing comorbid mental health problems is common. There may be a history of abuse or trauma, substance use, and/or an eating disorder. Response to self-harm depends on an organization's ethical and legal guidelines. While working with high risk adolescents, confidentiality must be broken and parents contacted immediately if individual is suicidal or homicidal. If severe tissue damage or infection, medical attention must be sought immediately. If a patient is found to be low risk continue to assess bi-weekly for risk, provide appropriate interventions, and follow protocol with your agencies recommendations for parent involvement.

Next, it is recommended to engage the young person directly in assessment of the behavior, consequences, and next steps. If you are a friend or parent: engage others who are in a position to offer support, guidance, and advice for both the young person and yourself. Help the youth who is self-injuring to understand the risks of contagion, the risks of avoiding a behavior that could hurt a friend. Become aware of local resources for referring a self-injurious youth.

INTERVENTIONS AND THERAPY

Interventions can be helpful to put in place include communication skill building, encouraging the individual to use communication to express emotions. Teaching use of journals to express emotions through writing. A trigger log can also be effective in which an individual tracks each time they engage in self-harm and the events leading up to it. Some behavioral interventions for stress management include tension release through diaphragmatic and controlled breathing, meditation, visualization and aerobic exercise.

There are different types of therapy that can be beneficial to those self-harming. One recommended therapy is counseling groups that focus on developing problem-solving techniques, adaptive coping strategies, self-esteem building, communication and social skills. Groups should NOT focus on self-harm behavior due to contagion effect. Solution Focused Therapy is a good option for teens as well as Selekman's Stress Busters' Leadership Program – designed to work with self-harming adolescents in a group setting. Family Therapy can provide the adolescent with family support. Family therapy also allows the family to learn about self-injury and often helps the entire family with coping strategies. Other theories that can be helpful are Cognitive Behavior Therapy (CBT) which is based on the premise that cognitions influence mood and behavior and targets both the faulty cognitions of the adolescent and the maladaptive behaviors that result. Dialectical Behavior Therapy (DBT) goal is to reduce self-destructive behavior, learn adaptive coping and problem-solving skills, and to accept self while changing. Lastly, Manual Assisted Cognitive Behavior Therapy (MCAT) is a short-term problem-solving intervention that teaches how to manage negative thoughts and emotions.

Conclusion

Self-harm is relatively common in the adolescent population. Research suggests that individuals who have ever self-harmed are at risk for suicide. It is important to respond appropriately to a disclosure of self-harm and also to inquire about self-harm when there are risk factors. The act of self-harm is a sign of underlying distress which should be taken seriously. Multiple therapies are available for adolescents and youth with self-harm behaviors. It is important to develop high quality trusting relationships with adolescents and pay attention to changes in their behavior and any cries for help.

References

[1] Shafer KC. Understanding the cutting edge: Self-mutilation. Limitless Potentials, Inc. URL: http://www.funtherapist.com/pdf/self_mutiliation.pdf.
[2] Spiegel A, Favazza A. The history and mentality of self-mutilation [Internet]. National Public Radio 2005. URL: https://www.npr.org/templates/story/story.php?StoryId=4697319.
[3] Whitlock J. The cutting edge: Non-suicidal self-injury in adolescents [Internet]. ACT for Youth Center of Excellence 2009. URL: http://www.actforyouth.net/resources/rf/rf_nssi_1209.cfm.
[4] TeenHelp.com. Cutting statistics and self-injury treatment [Internet]. TeenHelp.com, 2016. URL: https://www.teenhelp.com/physical-health/cutting-statistics-and-self-injury-treatment/
[5] Whitlock J, Knox K. The relationship between suicide and self-injury in a young adult population. Arch Pediatr Adolesc Med 2007;161:634-40.
[6] Whitlock J, Eckenrode J, Silverman D. Self-injurious behaviors in a college population. Pediatrics 2006;117:1939-48.

In: Building Youth for the Future ISBN: 978-1-53613-768-2
Editors: H. A Omar and J. Merrick

Chapter 11

ANXIETY AND DEPRESSION IN YOUNG ATHLETES

Dilip R Patel[1,*], MD, MBA, MPH, Hatim A Omar[2], MD and Joav Merrick[2-5], MD, MMedSci, DMSc

[1]Department of Pediatric and Adolescent Medicine, Western Michigan University Homer Stryker MD School of Medicine, Kalamazoo, Michigan, US

[2]Division of Adolescent Medicine, KY Children's Hospital, Department of Pediatrics, Lexington, Kentucky, US

[3]National Institute of Child Health and Human Development, Jerusalem, Israel

[4]Division of Pediatrics, Hadassah Hebrew University Medical Centers, Mt Scopus Campus, Jerusalem, Israel

[5]School of Public Health, Georgia State University, Atlanta, Georgia, US

[*] Correspondence: Dilip R Patel, MD, MBA, MPH, Professor and Chair, Department of Pediatric and Adolescent Medicine, Western Michigan University Homer Stryker MD School of Medicine, 1000 Oakland Drive, Kalamazoo, Michigan 49024, United States. Email: Dilip.patel@med.wmich.edu.

ABSTRACT

The prevalence of anxiety disorders in adolescents range from 6-20%, and it is much higher for anxiety symptoms not meeting criteria for a specific anxiety disorder. The prevalence is much higher in females. Athletes participating in sports experience different levels of stress from competitive sports. For most young athletes (generally 13 to 24 years old, i.e., high-school and college age group) sport participation is reported to be no more stressful than many other activities of daily student or work life in general where competition is involved and performance is measured. Some level of sport-related performance anxiety is considered to be normal and healthy; however, extreme anxiety in athletes can be detrimental in these performance situations. A number of factors may contribute to the development, severity, and persistence of performance anxiety related to sport participation. The exact prevalence of depression in young athletes is not known. Sports injuries and concussion have been most studied in relation to depression. Several behavioral approaches, combined in some cases with pharmacotherapy are the mainstay for treatment of anxiety and depression in young athletes.

INTRODUCTION

In the context of sport participation, competitive anxiety is defined as "a tendency to perceive competitive situations as threatening and to respond to these situations with feelings of apprehension and tension (1)." Anxiety symptoms are related to the stress of participation in sports. Stress results from an imbalance between perceived environmental demands and the perceived response capability of the athlete (1). Anxiety is an apprehensive anticipation or fear by the individual of some dangerous occurrence in the future (2). Anxiety is usually accompanied by unpleasant feelings, stress or tension, and somatic symptoms and signs. Sport-related anxiety symptoms may or may not be indicative of an anxiety disorder. The "Diagnostic and statistical manual of mental disorders, 4th edition, Text revision" (DSM-IV-TR), defines anxiety disorder as persistent fear or worry that causes significant distress and impairment of age-appropriate functioning such as school work, play, occupation, and interpersonal relations (2). The symptoms in anxiety disorder take up a significant amount of daily time of the individual and can last over a period of several months, typically six or more months. Types of specific anxiety disorders as classified in the DSM-IV-TR are listed in Table 1 (2). Various types of sport-related anxiety are summarized in Table 2 (1, 3-10).

Table 1. Classification of anxiety disorders

Panic disorder without agoraphobia
Agoraphobia without history of panic disorder
Specific phobia
Social phobia
Obsessive-compulsive disorder
Posttraumatic stress disorder
Acute stress disorder
Generalized anxiety disorder
Anxiety disorder due to a general medical condition
Substance-induced anxiety disorder
Anxiety disorder not otherwise specified
Separation anxiety disorder

Partly based on data from DSM-5.

Table 2. Terms used to describe types of sport-related anxiety states

Competitive state anxiety	Anxiety induced by a specified competitive situation such as a team game that required performance. May encompass worry about failure, others' expectations, social critique, and parental pressure.
Competitive trait anxiety	Anxiety that is an enduring characteristic of a person's personality which influences one's perception of a competitive situation.
Somatic anxiety	Physiological expression of anxiety (e.g., sweat, tremor, tachycardia).
Cognitive anxiety	Psychological expression of anxiety (e.g., negative thoughts about performance, worry, inability to concentrate, and inattention).
Behavioral anxiety	Behavioral expression of anxiety (e.g., body language, communication patterns, restlessness).
Performance anxiety	Anxiety or fear which negatively affects the attempted activity, also known as Stage Fright.

Table 2. (Continued)

Debilitative anxiety	Anxiety that results in worsened performance.
Facilitative anxiety	Anxiety that results in improved performance.
Precompetition anxiety	Anxiety prior to the onset of competition which is reflective of the objective and perceived requirements of the individual or team to participate in the contest. May be influenced by the type of sport, importance of the contest, amount of time before the competition starts, and personality of the athlete.
Competition Anxiety	Anxiety that occurs during a competition. May be influenced by the importance of the contest, current situation, previous performance, and personality of the athlete.
Postcompetition anxiety	Anxiety after the completion of the competition. May be influenced by perceived performance, win or loss, and sense of enjoyment during the competition.

EPIDEMIOLOGY OF SPORT-RELATED ANXIETY

The exact prevalence of sport-related anxiety symptoms is difficult to ascertain because of difference in severity, definitions, and assessment tools applied. Numerous studies report a range of sport-related performance anxiety symptoms in team and individual sports; however, large scale epidemiological data are not available (8, 11-32). Many factors have been identified that influence the development, severity, and persistence of sport-related performance anxiety (33-65) (see Table 3).

Prevalence of anxiety disorders that meet the DSM 5 criteria in adolescents is estimated to be 6-20%; however, a higher percentage may have anxiety symptoms that do not meet the criteria for a specific disorder (2, 3, 8). An estimated 2% of individuals are affected by debilitating performance anxiety (22). Worry about performing poorly in sports is reported to be greater in female athletes and older athletes, whereas male athletes report higher levels of concentration disruption in competitive sport situations (22). Vardar et al. (29)investigated the prevalence rate of disordered eating behaviors in young female athletes and compared the anxiety levels of the athletes with or without disordered eating behaviors; athletes with disordered eating behaviors were found to have higher state and trait anxiety scores (29).

Development of anxiety and how it affects sport performance has been studied extensively. In the context of sport participation, arousal refers to a continuous scale of mental and physical attentiveness, ranging from heavy sleep to intense excitement (1). The main theories of arousal, related anxiety symptoms, and their relationship to sport performance are summarized in Table 4 (66-77).

Table 3. Factors that influence development, severity and persistence of anxiety symptoms

Achievement goals
Career maturity
Clarity of completion goal
Coaching behaviors and style
Commitment to sport
Coping skills
Difficulty of sport routine
Expectations of performance
Experience
Fear of failure
Game location
Gender
Intensity of the sport
Level of competition
Motivational climate
Perceived abilities
Performance setting
Pre-competition mood state
Self-confidence
Significance of win or loss
Social support
Sports contact
Team cohesion
Team goal
Underlying anxiety traits

Table 4. Theories of arousal-athletic performance relationship

Theory	Comments
Drive theory (70)	Motivation to compete creates a state of heightened arousal which allows an athlete to perform at his or her highest skill level during the competition in order to fulfill the motivation and achieve subjective relaxation at the end of the competition.
Inverted-U hypothesis (76)	Describes a continuous relationship between performance and arousal. The best performance occurs at the midpoint of arousal. Either increased or decreased arousal relative to the peak causes decreased performance.
Multi-dimensional anxiety theory (1)	Explores 2 components of anxiety: (1) Cognitive anxiety (negative thoughts, concerns about performance, disrupted concentration) that originates from a fear of evaluation, and (2) Somatic anxiety (classically-conditioned physical reactions to competition including sweating, increased heart rate, tremor, unsettled stomach).
Individual zone of optimal function theory (71)	Hypothesizes that athletes are able to interpret emotions within a predetermined construct and regulate their psychological state to facilitate optimal performance.
Reversal theory (74)	Postulates that an athlete can selectively perceive his or her level of arousal and physical reactions as either positive or negative and subsequently perform well or poor, respectfully.
Catastrophe theory (72)	Suggests that as an athlete becomes aroused above the peak level required for optimal performance, there is a sudden and severe drop-off in performance.

CLINICAL PRESENTATION AND ANXIETY

Athletes who experience sport-related performance anxiety may present with a wide spectrum of symptoms and signs ranging from mild to debilitating (4, 6, 8, 78-80). Athletes often seek help because their anxiety before and during an event causes them to perform at a level well below their demonstrated capabilities (22). Deterioration of performance may be sudden or insidious, lasting over several weeks or months, referred to by some as a "slump (80)." Anxiety symptoms may occur before, during, or after the event and include cognitive, behavioral and physiological symptoms and signs (4, 8, 18, 19, 79). Cognitive signs and symptoms include indecision, a sense of confusion, negative thoughts, poor concentration, irritability, fear, forgetfulness, a lack of confidence, images of failure, negative self-talk, feeling weak, inability to follow instructions, and thoughts of avoiding participation. Somatic signs and symptoms include increased blood pressure, racing heart, fast breathing, sweating, cold and clammy hands and feet, butterflies in the stomach, dry mouth, need to urinate, muscular tension, tightness in neck and shoulders, trembling, blushing, pacing up and down, distorted vision, twitching, yawning, nausea, vomiting, diarrhea, loss of appetite, and loss of sleep. Behavioral signs and symptoms include biting fingernails, defensive mannerisms, inhibited posture, repetitive movements, withdrawal, aggressive outbursts, fidgeting, avoiding eye contact, and covering face with hands. Some athletes may "choke" or be debilitated to the point of being unable to participate in sports.

Sport-related performance anxiety in principle is similar to social phobia; however, there are subtle differences between the two, especially when it is debilitating. Social phobia is related to exposure to or anticipation of certain social or performance situations in which evaluation or scrutiny by others is likely. In social phobia, the overall impairment is more pervasive, focus of fears is most interactions with others, expectations of self are low, fear of scrutiny by others is primary, anticipatory anxiety is high, and the commitment to feared task is low (22). In debilitating sport-related performance anxiety, the impairment is limited to sport participation, focus of fears is limited to specific performance situation, expectations of self are high, fear of scrutiny by others is secondary, anticipatory anxiety is variable, and commitment to sports is very high (22).

EVALUATION OF ANXIETY

The diagnosis of sport-related performance anxiety is apparent in most cases based on the presenting history. In few cases, criteria for a specific anxiety disorder may be met. A detailed history is the mainstay of evaluation. Many athletes may not recognize the significance of their symptoms and so never seek appropriate professional advice. Physicians need to be aware of psychosocial issues related to sport participation by young athletes and a thorough psychosocial history should be obtained. Mann et al. reported results of their survey of sports medicine physicians regarding psychological issues in patient-athletes (7).

Table 5. Differential diagnosis of anxiety symptoms and disorders

Mental health conditions
Agoraphobia
Acute stress disorder
Adjustment disorder with anxious mood
Competitive anxiety in athletes
Generalized anxiety disorder
Hypochondriasis
Obsessive-compulsive disorder
Panic attacks and panic disorder
Posttraumatic stress disorder
Separation anxiety disorder
Social phobia
Somatization disorder
Specific phobia
Substance abuse
Medical conditions
Asthma
Epilepsy
Hyperthyroidism
Hyperparathyroidism
Hyperadrenocorticism
Hyperventilation syndrome
Hypoglycemia
Mitral valve prolapse
Pheochromocytoma
Porphyria
Vestibular dysfunction
Vocal cord dysfunction

Table 6. Instruments used in assessing anxiety in athletes

Sport Anxiety Scale (86)	Widely used by researchers. Twenty-one items, ranking short statements on a four-point scale, ranging from, "not at all" to "very much so," Three dimensional measure of anxiety including somatic, cognitive, and concentration-disruption components.
Cognitive Appraisal Scale in Sport Competition – Threat Perception (89)	Original version in Portuguese. Eight-item assessment of an athlete's perception of the demands of a competition that cause the athlete to feel anxious.
COPE Inventory (82)	Sixty item quantitative measure to categorize an athlete's response to a stressful event. The 4-point scale ranges from "I usually don't do this at all," to "I usually do this a lot."
Brief COPE Inventory (83)	Widely used by researchers. Twenty-eight item revised edition of the COPE Inventory.
Competitive State Anxiety Inventory – 2 (1)	Widely used by researchers. Twenty-seven item questionnaire with responses on a 4-point scale, ranging from "not at all" to "very much so." Differentiates cognitive anxiety, somatic anxiety, and self-confidence sub-scales.
Competitive State Anxiety Inventory – Children (1,84)	Same as above, except modified for children rather than adults.
State-Trait Anxiety Inventory (87)	Assessment of anxiety in adults and adolescents. Forty items total, ranked on a 4-point scale. The state, or S-anxiety component asks the participants to rank their current subjective emotional state, from "not at all" to "very much so." The trait, or T-anxiety component requires the participants to rank the frequency with which they generally tend to feel, from "almost never" to "almost always."
State Anxiety Inventory for Children (88)	Adapted version of the State-Trait Anxiety Inventory as above. Forty items total, ranked on a three-point scale.
Sport Competition Anxiety Test (84)	Ten-item measurement of competitive trait anxiety, ranked on a three-point scale: "often," "sometimes," and "hardly ever."
Cognitive-Somatic Anxiety Questionnaire (75)	Fourteen-item questionnaire ranking from one, meaning "not at all," to five, "very much so," the symptoms that the participant experiences when feeling anxious. Differentiates both cognitive and somatic divisions of trait anxiety.

The extent to which physicians discussed psychological issues with athletes varied by subspecialty and by specific issues assessed. The three most frequent injury-related topics discussed were fears about reinjury, fears related to surgery, and lack of patience with recovery or rehabilitation. The three most common non-injury-related topics discussed were stress or pressure, anxiety, and burnout. Interestingly, family physicians were more likely to discuss injury-related issues than orthopedic surgeons.

Although most cases of sport-related anxiety are straightforward, physicians should consider other conditions that can present with anxiety symptoms (see Table 4) (2, 9). Asthma and vocal cord dysfunction are the most common medical conditions confused with anxiety disorders in athletes. Some of these athletes are initially referred to pulmonologists and often get a diagnostic work-up for asthma and vocal cord dysfunction. Conditions comorbid with anxiety disorders include mood disorders, learning disorders, and attention deficit hyperactivity disorder (2) (see Table 5).

Based on the initial clinical evaluation, some athletes may need additional or formal psychological assessment by a clinical psychologist with experience in sport psychology. Several standardized instruments that are used to evaluate athletes who experience anxiety symptoms related to their participation in sports are summarized in Table 6 (81-88).

Management of anxiety symptoms

Athletes employ different strategies to cope with anxiety symptoms (89-91). Athletes who experience sport-related anxiety should be managed in consultation with clinical psychologist or other similarly qualified clinicians. Major behavioral approaches for management of sport-related anxiety are listed in Table 7. In some cases, pharmacotherapy is indicated. Selective serotonin re-uptake inhibitors are the drugs of choice for the treatment of anxiety and depression in adolescents.

Table 7. Selected behavioral and psychological approaches to treating sport-related anxiety

Biofeedback
Relaxation techniques
Cognitive behavior therapy
Stress management training
Meditation
Mental toughness training
Environmental manipulation

DEPRESSION IN ATHLETES

The prevalence of depression in college age athletes has been reported to be 15%-20% (93-97). Some of these studies reported that being an athlete was not a significant predictor of depression when compared with other variables, including gender, self-esteem levels, social connectedness or rested sleep. Others showed that social network and team sport participation were protective factors for depression. The relationship between sport injury and depression is the most studied aspect of sport-related depression. It was found that, 80% of the time, athletes who sought medical care for an injury also discussed psychological issues related to injury. Sport-related injury is the most widely studied risk factor for psychological distress among athletes. Psychological responses to an injury vary depending up on multiple factors. Type of injury is an important such variable. For example, athletes with an anterior cruciate ligament tear had more severe levels of depression and longer duration of depression compared with those athletes with concussion. Emotional responses of athletes to sport-related injury include, sadness, isolation, irritation, lack of motivation, anger, frustration, changes in appetite, sleep disturbance and disengagement. Problematic emotional reactions to an injury are listed in Table 8. Whether an athlete seeks medical attention for sport-injury related emotional symptoms depends on multiple factors; some of the barriers and facilitators to seeking care are listed in Table 9.

Table 8. Problematic emotional reactions to injury

Persistent symptoms	• Alterations of appetite • Sleep disturbance • Irritability
Worsening symptoms	• Alterations of appetite leading to disordered eating • Sadness leading to depression • Lack of motivation leading to apathy • Disengagement leading to alienation
Excessive symptoms	• Pain behaviors • Excessive anger or rage • Frequent crying or emotional outbursts • Substance abuse

Table 9. Barriers and facilitators to help seeking following an injury

Barriers	**Facilitators**
• Stigma • Lack of problem awareness • Difficulty in or not willing to express emotion • Lack of time • Denial of problem • Not sure who to ask for help • Fear of what might happen • Worried about affecting ability to play or train • Belief that it would not help • Not accessible	• Education and awareness of mental health issues and or services or both • Social support • Encouragement from others • Accessibility • Positive relationship with service staff • Confidentiality • Time • Integration into athlete life • Positive past experiences • Ease of expressing emotion and openness

The relationship between depression and performance in sport is bidirectional. Athletes may be prone to experience depression when they face decline in sport-performance. On the other hand, declining sport performance may result in lack of external reinforcement, behavioral de-activation, negative self-perception and evaluation, and feeling of helplessness or hopelessness.

Sport-related concussions have been shown to result in long term behavioral symptoms. Multiple behavioral symptoms may persist long after resolution of other symptoms and signs. Depression may be one of the behavioral consequences of sport-related concussion. Long-term adverse impact of traumatic brain injury has been well documented. In a systematic review Yrondi et al. (97), reported symptoms of depression can appear shortly following a concussion or may be associated with symptoms of concussion. Repeated concussions may result in late onset chronic depression.

In general, the management of depression follows similar behavioral and pharmacological approaches to that of management of anxiety disorders.

CONCLUSION

Anxiety and depression are often associated with sport participation. Sport-associated anxiety symptoms are common and may or may not indicate an anxiety disorder. Specific anxiety provoking stimuli within the sport environment should be recognized. The relationship between depression and sport participation in not clearly established. Symptoms suggestive of depression have been reported specifically in association with musculoskeletal injuries that limit further sport participation. Also, some association has been reported between concussion and development of depression. Overall, the general principles of management of both anxiety and depression in athlete are similar and apply various behavioral techniques and judicious and limited use of pharmacotherapy.

Acknowledgments

The section on anxiety is partly adapted with permission from previous work: Patel DR, Omar HA, Terry M. Sport-related performance anxiety in youth female athletes, J Pediatr Adolesc Gynecol 2010;23:325-335. We thank Jody Pyne for technical assistance with manuscript.

References

[1] Martens R, Vealey RS, Burton D. Competitive anxiety in sports. Champaign, IL: Human Kinetic Books, 1990.

[2] American Psychiatric Association. Diagnostic and statistical manual of mental disorders, DSM 5. Washington, DC: APA, 2013:155-234.

[3] Spielberger CD, Sarason IG, eds. Stress and emotion: Anxiety, anger, and curiosity, Vol 17. New York: Routledge, 2017.

[4] Small FL, Smith RE. Competitive anxiety: Sources, consequences and intervention strategies. In: Small FL, Smith RE, eds. Children and youth in sport: A biopsychosocial perspective. New York: McGraw Hill, 1996:359-80.

[5] Gould D, Krane V. The arousal-athletic performance relationship: current status and future directions. In: Hom TS, ed. Advances in sport psychology. Champaign, IL: Human Kinetics, 1992:119-42.

[6] Maffulli N, Helms P. Controversies about intensive training in young athletes. Arch Dis Child 1988;63:1405-7.

[7] Mann BJ, Grana WA, Indelicato PA, O'Neill DF, George SZ. A survey of sports medicine physicians regarding psychological issues in patient-athletes. Am J Sports Med 2007;35(12):2140-7.

[8] Raglin JS. Anxiety and sport performance. Exerc Sport Sci Rev 1992; 20:243-74.

[9] Varley CK, Smith CJ. Anxiety disorders in the child and teen. Pediatr Clin North Am 2003;50:1107-38.

[10] Connolly SD, Bernstein GA, Work Group on Quality Issues. Practice parameter for the assessment and treatment of children and adolescents with anxiety disorders. J Am Acad Child Adolesc Psychiatry 2007; 46(2):267-83.

[11] DeMoja CA, DeMoja G. State-trait anxiety and motocross performance. Percept Mot Skills 1986;62(1):107-10.

[12] Filaire E, Sagnol M, Ferrand C, Maso F, Lac G. Psychophysiological stress in judo athletes during competitions. Sports Med Phys Fitness 2001;41(2):263-8.

[13] Finkenberg ME, DiNucci JM, McCune ED, McCune SL. Analysis of the effect of competitive trait anxiety on performance in Taekwondo competition. Percept Mot Skills 1992;75(1):239-43.
[14] Haase AM, Prapavessis H. Social physique anxiety and eating attitudes in female athletic and non-athletic groups. J Sci Med Sport 2001;4(4):396-405.
[15] Hale BS, Koch KR, Raglin JS. State anxiety responses to 60 minutes of cross training. Br J Sports Med 2002;36(2):105-7.
[16] Hammer WM. A comparison of differences in manifest anxiety in university athletes and non-athletes. J Sports Med Phys Fitness 1967;7(1):31-4.
[17] Hanna EA. Potential sources of anxiety and depression associated with athletic competition. Can J Appl Sport Sci 1979;4(3):199-204.
[18] Hannon B, Fitzgerald P. Anxiety and performance in elite non-professional athletes. Ir Med J 2006;99(8):238-40.
[19] Kirkby RJ, Liu J. Precompetition anxiety in Chinese athletes. Percept Mot Skills 1999;88(1):297-303.
[20] McKelvie SJ, Huband DE. Locus of control and anxiety in college athletes and non-athletes. Percept Mot Skills 1980;50(3 Pt 1):819-22.
[21] Miller TW, Vaughn MP, Miller JM. Clinical issues and treatment strategies in stress-oriented athletes. Sports Med 1990;9(6):370-9.
[22] Powell DH. Treating individuals with debilitating performance anxiety: An introduction. Clin Psychol 2004;60(8):801-8.
[23] Pratt HD. Principles of psychological management. In: Greydanus DE, Calles JL Jr, Pratt HD, eds. Pediatric and adolescent psychopharmacology. New York, Cambridge University Press, 2008:1-24.
[24] Psychountaki M, Zervas Y. Competitive worries, sport confidence, and performance ratings for young swimmers. Percept Mot Skills 2000;91(1):87-04.
[25] Rouveix M, Bouget M, Pannafieux C, Champely S, Filaire E. Eating attitudes, body esteem, perfectionism and anxiety of judo athletes and nonathletes. Int J Sports Med 2007;28(4):340-5.
[26] Sanderson FH, Reilly T. Trait and state anxiety in male and female cross-country runners. Br J Sports Med 1983;17(1):24-6.
[27] Tenenbaum G, Milgram RM. Trait and state anxiety in Israeli student athletes. J Clin Psychol 1978;34(3):691-3.
[28] Thirer J, O'Donnell LA. Female intercollegiate athletes' trait-anxiety level and performance in a game. Percept Mot Skills 1980;50(1):18.
[29] Vardar E, Vardar SA, Kurt C. Anxiety of young female athletes with disordered eating behaviors. Eat Behav 2007;8(2):143-7.
[30] Wadey R, Hanton S. Basic psychological skills usage and competitive anxiety responses: Perceived underlying mechanisms. Res Q Exerc Sport 2008;79(3): 363-73.
[31] Wiggins MS, Lai C, Deiters JA. Anxiety and burnout in female collegiate ice hockey and soccer athletes. Percept Mot Skills 2005; 101(2):519-24.

[32] Wilson GS, Raglin JS. Optimal and predicted anxiety in 9-12-year-old track and field athletes. Scand J Med Sci Sports 1997;74):253-8.

[33] Wong EH, Lox CL, Clark SE. Relation between sports context, competitive trait anxiety, perceived ability, and self-presentation confidence. Percept Mot Skills 1993;76(3 Pt 1):847-50.

[34] Abrahamsen FE, Roberts GC, Pensgaard AM, Ronglan LT. Perceived ability and social support as mediators of achievement motivation and performance anxiety. Scand J Med Sci Sports 2008;18(6):810-21.

[35] Baker J, Cote J, Hawes R. The relationship between coaching behaviours and sport anxiety in athletes. J Sci Med Sport 2000;3(2):110-9.

[36] Bekiari A, Patsiaouras A, Kokaridas D, Sakellariou K. Verbal aggressiveness and state anxiety of volleyball players and coaches. Psychol Rep 2006;99(2):630-4.

[37] Cerin E, Szabo A, Hunt N, Williams C. Temporal patterning of competitive emotions: a critical review. J Sports Sci 2000;18(8):605-26.

[38] Cox LM, Lantz CD, Mayhew JL. The role of social physique anxiety and other variables in predicting eating behaviors in college students. Int J Sport Nutr 1997;7(4):310-7.

[39] Cresswell S, Hodge K. Coping skills: Role of trait sport confidence and trait anxiety. Percept Mot Skills 2004;98(2):433-8.

[40] Finkenberg ME, DiNucci JM, McCune SL, Chenette T, McCoy P. Commitment to physical activity and anxiety about physique among college women. Percept Mot Skills 1998;87(3 Pt 2):1393-4.

[41] Hanton S, Cropley B, Lee S. Reflective practice, experience, and the interpretation of anxiety symptoms. J Sports Sci 2009;27(5):517-33.

[42] Hassmen P, Koivula N, Hansson T. Precompetitive mood states and performance of elite male golfers: do trait characteristics make a difference? Percept Mot Skills 1998;86(3 Pt 2):1443-57.

[43] Kjormo O, Halvari H. Two ways related to performance in elite sport: the path of self-confidence and competitive anxiety and the path of group cohesion and group goal- clarity. Percept Mot Skills 2002;94(3 Pt 1):950-66.

[44] Lorimer R, Westbury T. Physical self-presentation and competitive anxiety in male master divers. Psychol Rep 2006;99(3):773-80.

[45] Martinent G, Ferrand C. A cluster analysis of perfectionism among competitive athletes. Psychol Rep 2006;99(3):723-38.

[46] Matheson H, Mathes S. Influence of performance setting, experience and difficulty of routine on precompetition anxiety and self-confidence of high school female gymnasts. Percept Mot Skills 1991;72(3 Pt 2):1099-105.

[47] Mellalieu SD, Neil R, Hanton S. Self-confidence as a mediator of the relationship between competitive anxiety intensity and interpretation. Res Q Exerc Sport 2006;77(2):263-70.

[48] Mullen R, Lane A, Hanton S. Anxiety symptom interpretation in high-anxious, defensive high-anxious, low-anxious and repressor sport performers. Anxiety Stress Coping 2009;22(1):91-100.
[49] Ntoumanis N, Biddle S. The relationship between competitive anxiety, achievement goals, and motivational climates. Res Q Exerc Sport 1998;69(2):176-87.
[50] O'Brien M, Hanton S, Mellalieu SD. Intensity and direction of competitive anxiety as a function of goal attainment expectation and competition goal generation. J Sci Med Sport 2005;8(4):423-32.
[51] Ommundsen Y, Pedersen BH. The role of achievement goal orientations and perceived ability upon somatic and cognitive indices of sport competition trait anxiety. A study of young athletes. Scand J Med Sci Sports 1999;9(6):333-43.
[52] Peng H, Johanson RE. Career maturity and state anxiety of Taiwanese college student athletes given cognitive career-oriented group counseling. Psychol Rep 2006;99(3):805-12.
[53] Raglin JS. Psychological factors in sport performance: The Mental Health Model revisited. Sports Med 2001;31(12):875-90.
[54] Robazza C, Bortoli L. Intensity, idiosyncratic content and functional impact of performance-related emotions in athletes. J Sports Sci 2003;21(3):171-89.
[55] Robazza C, Pellizzari M, Bertollo M, Hanin YL. Functional impact of emotions on athletic performance: Comparing the IZOF model and the directional perception approach. J Sports Sci 2008;26(10):1033-47.
[56] Ryska TA. The relationship between trait and precompetitive state anxiety among high school athletes. Percept Mot Skills 1993;762):413-4.
[57] Smith AM, Sim FH, Smith HC, Stuart MJ, Laskowski ER. Psychologic, situational, and physiologic variables and on-ice performance of youth hockey goalkeepers. Mayo Clin Proc 1998;73(1):17-27.
[58] Smith RE, Smoll FL, Cumming SP. Effects of a motivational climate intervention for coaches on young athletes' sport performance anxiety. J Sport Exerc Psychol 2007;29(1):39-59.
[59] Storch EA, Storch JB, Adams BG. Intrinsic religiosity and social anxiety of intercollegiate athletes. Psychol Rep 2002;91(1):186.
[60] Swain A, Jones G. Intensity and frequency dimensions of competitive state anxiety. J Sports Sci 1993;11(6):533-42.
[61] Terry PC, Walrond N, Carron AV. The influence of game location on athletes' psychological states. J Sci Med Sport 1998;1(1):29-37.
[62] Turner PE, Raglin JS. Variability in precompetition anxiety and performance in college track and field athletes. Med Sci Sports Exerc 1996;28(3):378-85.
[63] Wang J, Marchant D, Morris T, Gibbs P. Self-consciousness and trait anxiety as predictors of choking in sport. J Sci Med Sport 2004;7(2):174-85.
[64] Wiggins MS, Brustad RJ. Perception of anxiety and expectations of performance. Percept Mot Skills 1996;83(3 Pt 1):1071-4.

[65] Wiggins MS, Cremades JG, Lai C, Lee J, Erdmann JB. Multidimensional comparison of anxiety direction and burnout over time. Percept Mot Skills 2006;102(3):788-90.
[66] Jokela M, Hanin YL. Does the individual zones of optimal functioning model discriminate between successful and less successful athletes? A meta-analysis. J Sports Sci 1999;17(11):873-87.
[67] Pons D, Balaguer I, Garcia-Merita ML. Is the breadth of individualized ranges of optimal anxiety (IZOF) equal for all athletes? A graphical method for establishing IZOF. Span J Psychol 2001;4(1):3-10.
[68] Prapavessis H, Cox H, Brooks L. A test of Martens, Vealey and Burton's theory of competitive anxiety. Aust J Sci Med Sport 1996;28(1):24-9.
[69] Raglin JS, Morris MJ. Precompetition anxiety in women volleyball players: a test of ZOF theory in a team sport. Br J Sports Med 1994; 28(1):47-51.
[70] Hull C. Principles of behavior. New York: Appleton- Century-Crofts, 1943.
[71] Hanin Y. Emotions in sport. Champaign, IL: Human Kinetics, 2000.
[72] Hardy L, Parfitt G. A catastrophe model of anxiety and performance. Br J Psychol 1991;82(Pt2):163-78.
[73] Kerr JH. Motivations and emotions in sport: Research theory. Hove, East Sussex: Psychology Press, 1997.
[74] Kerr JH. Structural phenomenology and performance. J Human Mov Studies 1987;13(5):211-29.
[75] Schwartz GE, Davidson RJ, Goleman DJ. Patterning of cognitive and somatic processes in the self-regulation of anxiety: Effects of meditation versus exercise. Psychosom Med 1978;40(4):321-8.
[76] Yerkes RM, Dodson JD. The relation of strength of stimulus to rapidity of habit formation. J Comp Neural Psych 1908;18:459-82.
[77] McNally IM. Contrasting concepts of competitive state anxiety in sport: multidimensional anxiety and catastrophe theories. Athletic Insight 2002;4(2):10-22.
[78] Patel DR, Greydanus DE, Pratt HD. Psychosocial aspects of youth sports. In: Patel DR, Greydanus DE, Baker RJ, eds. Pediatric practice: Sports medicine. New York: McGraw Hill Medical, 2009.
[79] Grossbard JR, Smith RE, Smol FL, Cumming SP. Competitive anxiety in young athletes: Differentiating somatic anxiety, worry, and concentration disruption. Anxiety Stress Coping 2009;22(2):153-66.
[80] Grove JR, Eklund RC, Heard NP. Coping with performance slumps: factor analysis of the Ways of Coping in Sport Scale. Aust J Sci Med Sport 1997;29(4):99-105.
[81] Abrahamsen FE, Roberts GC, Pensgaard AM. An examination of the factorial structure of the Norwegian version of the sport anxiety scale. Scand J Med Sci Sports 2006;16(5):358-63.
[82] Carver CS, Scheier MF, Weintraub JK. Assessing coping strategies: a theoretically based approach. J Pers Soc Psychol 1989;56(2):267-83.

[83] Carver CS. You want to measure coping but your protocol is too long: consider the brief COPE. Int J Behav Med 1997;4(1):92-100.
[84] Martens R. Sport Competitive Anxiety Test. Champaign, IL: Human Kinetics, 1977.
[85] Wilson GS, Raglin JS, Harger GJ. A comparison of the STAI and CSAI-2 in five-day recalls of precompetition anxiety in collegiate track and field athletes. Scand J Med Sci Sports 2000;10(1):51-4.
[86] Smith RE, Small FL, Schutz RW. Measurement and correlates of sport-specific cognitive and somatic trait anxiety: The sport anxiety scale. Anxiety Res 1990;2(4):263-80.
[87] Spielberger CD, Gorsuch RL, Lushene RE. Manual for the State-trait Anxiety Inventory. Palo Alto, CA: Consulting Psychologists Press, 1970.
[88] Spielberger CD. Preliminary Manual for the State-Trait Anxiety Inventory for Children: "How I feel questionnaire." Palo Alto, CA: Consulting Psychologists Press, 1973.
[89] Dias C, Cruz JF, Fonseca AM. Anxiety and coping strategies in sport contexts: a look at the psychometric properties of Portuguese instruments for their assessment. Span J Psychol 2009;12(1):338-48.
[90] Johnson U. Coping strategies among long-term injured competitive athletes. A study of 81 men and women in team and individual sports. Scan J Med Sci Sport 1997;7(6):367-72.
[91] Partridge JA, Wiggins MS. Coping styles for trait shame and anxiety intensity and direction in competitive athletes. Psychol Rep 2008;103(3):703-12.
[92] Wilks B. Stress management for athletes. Sport Med 1991;11:289-99.
[93] Wolanin A, Gross MA, Hong E. Depression in athletes: Prevalence and risk factors. Curr Sport Med Rep 2015;14(1):56-60.
[94] Putukian M. The psychological response to injury in student athletes: a narrative review with a focus on mental health. Br J Sport Med 2016;50:145-8.
[95] Portugal EMM, Cevada T, Moteiro-Junior RS, Guimaraes TT, Rubini EC, Lattari E, et al. Neuroscience of exercise: From neurobiology mechanisms to mental health. Neuropsychobiology 2012;68:1-14.
[96] Evans MB, Allan V, Erickson K, Martin LJ, Budziszewski R, Cote J. Are all sport activities equal? A systematic review of how youth psychosocial experiences vary across differing sport activities. Br J Sports Medicine 2017;51:169-76.
[97] Yrondi A, Brauge D, LeMen J, Arbus C, Pariente J. Depression and sport-related concussion: A systematic review. Presse Med 2017;46(10):890-902.

In: Building Youth for the Future ISBN: 978-1-53613-768-2
Editors: H. A Omar and J. Merrick

Chapter 12

SUPPORTING ADOLESCENTS WHO HAVE EXPERIENCED TRAUMA

Cori Morgan*[*]*, MSN, APRN, FNP-C
KY Clinic, Division of Adolescent Medicine, Department of Pediatrics, Kentucky Children's Hospital, University of Kentucky College of Medicine, Lexington, Kentucky, US

ABSTRACT

Adverse childhood experiences (ACEs) have a profound effect on our population and are associated with a wide range of negative health outcomes. ACEs cause a significant dysregulation of neuroendocrine coordination and development leading to alterations in several body systems. ACEs are highly prevalent and associated with risky health behaviors, chronic health conditions, and early death. As the number of adverse childhood experiences increases so does the risk for these negative health outcomes in an adult life. It is vital to address and prevent adversity in childhood and adulthood to promote the health and well-being of our population. ACEs prevention and intervention efforts may

[*] Correspondence: Cori Morgan, MSN, APRN, FNP-C, Division of Adolescent Medicine, University of Kentucky College of Medicine, 740 S Limestone, Lexington, KY 40536, United States. Email: cearen2@uky.edu.

aid in reducing exposure and the severity of negative effects of adversity in childhood.

INTRODUCTION

Traumatic experiences can potentially strip a child of healthy development and future wellness. The Substance Abuse and Mental Health Services Administration defines individual trauma resulting from "an event, series of events, or set of circumstances that is experienced by an individual as physically or emotionally harmful or life threatening and that has lasting adverse effects on the individual's functioning and mental, physical, social, emotional, or spiritual well-being" (1). Evolving research suggests that the definition of trauma is more complex than a single negative event in time. Chronic negative events experienced by developing children have the potential to have everlasting detrimental effects (2). Two decades ago, researchers linked childhood toxic stress and negative health outcomes across the lifespan (3). The response of such events may not meet the criteria to diagnose trauma related complications such as post-traumatic stress disorder or acute stress disorder (2). Nevertheless, childhood adversity is prevalent and its impact is significant.

DEFINING ADVERSE CHILDHOOD EXPERIENCES (ACES)

The Centers for Disease Control (CDC) and Kaiser Permanente began investigating adverse childhood experiences (ACEs) between the years 1995 and 1997. The CDC continues to conducted research nationally on ACEs and associated consequences on morbidity and mortality in the United States (4). Researchers collected two waves of health data on middle class adults who obtained health insurance in California during that time frame (3). Subjects underwent extensive physical exams and completed health histories in addition completing adverse childhood experience surveys. Data found an undeniable impact of adversity in childhood on health throughout the lifecycle (3). Significant findings of this group included that ACEs are prevalent, they cluster, and that they are dose-dependent (4). Two thirds of respondents had at least one ACE. If one ACE category experience was present, there was an 84% likelihood that respondents had additional categories present (3). As subject's numerical value of ACEs increased, so did their risk for negative health impacts in adult years (3). ACEs are categorized into childhood abuse, childhood neglect, and family household dysfunction (3). Significant adversity in childhood disrupts a child's neuro-development, resulting in social, emotional, and cognitive impairments (5). These impairments increase individual's risk for adopting unhealthy behaviors leading to disease, disability, social problems, and early death. Negative health outcomes from toxic stress include but are not limited to chronic bronchitis, stroke, diabetes, alcoholism, obesity, illicit drug use, injection of illegal drugs, attempted suicides, and high risk sexual activity (3).

Toxic effects of stress

Human stress response is categorized into positive, tolerable, and toxic (5). Positive stress is normal and healthy. This positive stress involves physiologic response of an elevated heart rate and blood pressure that shuts down through a negative feedback system built on protection and coping (5). Such a response consistently exists in the midst of caring relationships allowing individuals to grow and thrive after stressful experiences (5). Toxic stress exists in response to consistent and significant adversity. Examples of adverse childhood experiences include parental divorce, chronic neglect, parental incarceration, caregiver substance abuse or mental illness, exposure to violence, homelessness, inadequate adult support, and emotional, physical, and sexual abuse (3).

Advances in the studies of the biological sciences have heightened understanding of the negative impact of ACEs, especially in the fields of neuroscinence and epigentics (4). Toxic stress in children is detrimental to developing brain architecture. The field of epigenitics looks beyond gentic predisposition to investigate the implications of altered gene expression due to human environment (4). Toxic stress is associated to prolonged activation of the body's stress response systems and negatively affects the structure and function of the neurologic, endocrine, cardiovascular, and immunologic systems (5, 6). Altered neurodevelopment and neurotransmitter function result in behavioral impulsivity, increased anxiety, increased startle response, and sleep abnormalities (2, 6). Ramification of such function may hinder one's ability in forming future positive relationships (2). They are more likely to have a poor sense of self, low self-esteem, lack of trust and security in others, and an expectation of poor treatment by others (2, 6). Such social, cognitive, and biological changes are associated with vulnerability of substance abuse, risky sexual behavior, and criminal activity (6).

Adverse childhood experiences are highly associated with poor mental and emotional health. Research indicates that neglect and childhood maltreatment are well-documented risks factors in suicidality (7). A powerful relationship exists between the ACEs and suicidality (8). Evidence estimates that those exposed to 4 ACEs are twelve times more likes to attempt a suicide comparison to an individual with no history of ACEs (8). Exposure to seven ACEs in adulthood increases the risk of suicide attempts 30-fold, and in children and adolescents, increases risk to an astounding 51-fold (8). Consideration of ACEs screenings for assessment of suicide risk may be beneficial due to the high dose-response relationship of ACEs and attempted suicides.

Intervention and prevention

Strategies to reduce the exposure to ACEs include assuring that families have access to safe, stable, and nurturing environments (5, 9). Resilience is necessary where adversity is highly prevalent in today's society. Primary prevention may include policy changes focused on substantializing mental health resources, reducing stigma placed on mental health, and increasing connections of families and communities (7, 9). The adoption of evidenced-based welfare practices and interventions on a national level is important in addressing adversity in childhood (9). Economic strength may include strengthening financial security and creating family-friendly workplaces for households (9).

Strong communities are necessary in supporting efforts to withstand the negative effects of adversity in childhood. Community involvement and strengthening is vital to its population health. Evidence suggests that juvenile facilities are highly populated with individuals who experienced adversity in their childhood (10). Addressing ACEs would likely benefit the work force and decrease crime and violence of communities. Leaders in medicine, politics, education, business, non-profits, public health, social services, media, and law enforcement should interlink knowledge and skills to form networks to strengthen the health and social system that resists such negative effects (9). Future research and cost analysis on the development and execution of evidence-based interventions that reduce the sources of toxic stress compared to effectiveness of treating costly effects of chronic mental and physical disease resulting from ACEs.

Individuals and families should be well equipped with proper parenting skills to promote adequate social, cognitive, and emotional development in children (4). Health promotion interventions that incorporate regular supportive relationships, adequate sleep, regular exercise, counseling, mindful practices, and balanced nutrition may mitigate the dysregulation developing systems of children suffering negative effects of adversity (4). Active screening is important in the process of mitigating the long-term effects of ACEs (7, 11). Approximately thirty percent of pediatricians fail to ask about any adverse childhood experiences, and only 42% ask families about parental separation and divorce (12). Provider discomfort is a strong barrier in discussing childhood adversity in adults and children (11). Studies suggest that discussing ACEs is empowering to adults and avoiding them may be harmful health (11). Increasing parental resilience, creating social connections in children, increasing parental knowledge on fostering a child's development, and ensuring concrete support in times of need, and fine tuning child's regulation and expression of emotions may optimize familial and individual protection against childhood adversity (12).

Conclusion

The effects of adverse childhood experiences are widespread. Early negative childhood exposures disrupt the developing bodies and minds of childhood that resulting in impaired physical and mental health of individuals. Government policies, community involvement, and shaping strong individuals and families can be the building blocks in forming resilience against the negative forces of childhood adversity. Coordinated efforts in reducing factors contributing to the negative outcomes of adversity is vital to the physical, mental, emotional, and social health of individuals.

References

[1] Substance Abuse and Mental Health Services Administration, Trauma and Justice Strategic Initiative. SAMHSA's working definition of trauma and guidance for trauma-informed approach. Substance Abuse and Mental Health Services Administration, 2014. URL: https://store.samhsa.gov/shin/content/SMA14-4884/SMA14-4884.pdf.

[2] Center for Substance Abuse Treatment (US). Trauma-informed care in behavioral health services. Substance Abuse and Mental Health Services Administration (US), 2014. URL: https://www.ncbi.nlm.nih.gov/books/NBK207192/.

[3] Felitti VJ, Anda RF, Nordenberg DF, Williamson DF, Spitz AM, Edwards V, et al. Relationship of childhood abuse and household dysfunction to many of the leading causes of death in adults: the Adverse Childhood Experiences Study. Am J Prev Med 1998;14:248-58.

[4] Anda RF, Felitti VJ, Bremner JD, Walker JD, Whitfield C, Perry BD, et al. The enduring effects of abuse and related adverse experiences in childhood. Eur Arch Psychiatry Clin Neurosci 2006;256:174-86.

[5] Shonkoff JP, Garner AS. The lifelong effects of early childhood adversity and toxic stress. Pediatrics 2012;129:e232-46.

[6] Flaherty EG, Thompson R, Dubowitz H, Harvey EM, English DJ, Proctor LJ, et al. Adverse childhood experiences and child health in early adolescence. JAMA Pediatr 2013;167(7):622-9.

[7] Ports KA, Merrick MT, Stone DM, Wilkins, NJ, Reed J, et al. Adverse childhood experiences and suicide risk: toward comprehensive prevention. Am J Prev Med 2017;53:400-3.

[8] Dube SR, Anda RF, Felitti VJ, Chapman DP, Williamson DF, Giles WH. Childhood abuse, household dysfunction, and the risk of attempted suicide throughout the life span. JAMA 2001;286:3089-96.

[9] Fortson, BL. Preventing child abuse and neglect: A technical package for policy, norm, and programmatic activities. Centers for Disease Control. URL: https://www.cdc.gov/violenceprevention/pdf/can-prevention-technical-package.pdf.

[10] Duke NN, Pettingell SL, McMorris BJ, Borowsky IW. Adolescent violence perpetration: associations with multiple types of adverse childhood experiences. Pediatrics 2010;125:e778-86.

[11] Bethell CD, Hudziak A, Gombojav N, Powers K. Methods to assess adverse childhood experiences of children and families. Acad Pediatr 2017;17:S51-S69.

[12] Flaherty EG, Stirling J. The pediatrician's role in child maltreatment prevention. Pediatrics 2010;126:833-41.

In: Building Youth for the Future
ISBN: 978-1-53613-768-2
Editors: H. A Omar and J. Merrick

Chapter 13

EATING DISORDERS IN ADOLESCENCE

Mandakini Sadhir*, MD
Division of Adolescent Medicine, Department of Pediatrics,
University of Kentucky, Lexington, Kentucky, US

ABSTRACT

Eating disorder is one of the common chronic conditions in adolescence associated with medical and psychological complications. Suicide is the second most common cause of death in adolescents with eating disorder. Treatment involves a multidisciplinary team approach that includes medical provider, nutritionist, and mental health professional. Family support and their involvement plays a very important role in overall management of eating disorders. The chapter describes different types of eating disorder, signs and symptoms, associated complications and treatment.

* Correspondence: Mandakini Sadhir, MD, Division of Adolescent Medicine, Department of Pediatrics, University of Kentucky, Lexington, KY 40536-0284, United States.
Email: m.sadhir@uky.edu.

Introduction

Growing obesity prevalence has resulted in greater emphasis on healthy eating (1). Further, there is societal and cultural pressure to be thin and online exposure to social media and networking websites that depict photos of emaciated fashion models, celebrities. Some websites provide tips and techniques for maintaining dangerously thin physiques and promote unhealthy eating behaviors in lieu of healthy dieting (2). Thus, it is not uncommon for adolescents to have body image concerns and problematic eating behaviors. According to youth risk behavior surveillance conducted in United States, 18.7% high school females and 7.4% males reported not eating for >24 hours to lose weight or to keep from gaining weight; 6.6% females and 3.4% males took diet pills, powders or liquids and 6.6% females and 2.2% males took laxatives or vomited to lose weight or keep from gaining weight (3).

Table 1. Type of eating disorders

Anorexia nervosa **a) Restriction of energy intake** leading to significantly low body weight that is less than normal or expected for children and adolescents in the context of age, sex, development, physical health **b) Intense fear** of gaining weight or becoming fat, or engaging in persistent behavior that interferes with weight gain **c) Disturbance** in the way in which one's body weight or shape is experienced, undue influence of body weight or shape on self-evaluation, or persistent lack of recognition of the seriousness of the current low body weight. **Classification of severity** **Mild:** BMI > 17 kg/m2 **Moderate**: BMI 16-16.99 kg/m2 **Severe:** BMI 15-15.99 kg/m2 **Extreme:** BMI < 15 kg/m2
Bulimia nervosa **a) Recurrent episodes of binge eating characterized by BOTH :-** 1. Eating an amount of food that is definitely larger than what most individuals would eat in discrete period of time under similar circumstances. 2. Sense of lack of control over eating during an episode. **b) Recurrent inappropriate compensatory behavior** in order to prevent weight gain, such as self-induced vomiting; misuse of laxatives, diuretics, or other medications; fasting; or excessive exercise.

c) The binge eating and inappropriate compensatory behaviors both occur, on average, at least once a week for three months. D. Unduly influenced by body shape and weight for self-evaluation E. The disturbance does not occur exclusively during episodes of anorexia nervosa. **Classification of severity** **Mild:** An average of 1-3 episodes **Moderate:** An average of 4-7 episodes **Severe:** An average of 8-13 episodes **Extreme**: An average of 14 or more episodes
Binge eating disorder **A) Recurrent episodes of binge eating characterized by both** 1. Eating an amount of food that is definitely larger than what most people would eat in a discrete period of time under similar circumstances. 2. A sense of lack of control over eating during the episode **B. The binge-eating episodes are associated with three (or more) of the following:** 1. Eating much more rapidly than normal. 2. Eating until feeling uncomfortably full. 3. Eating large amounts of food when not feeling physically hungry. 4. Eating alone because of feeling embarrassed by how much one is eating. 5. Feeling disgusted with oneself, depressed, or very guilty afterward. **C. Marked distress regarding binge eating is present.** **D. The binge eating occurs, on average, at least once a week for 3 months.** **E. The binge eating is not associated with the recurrent use of inappropriate compensatory behavior** **Classification of severity** **Mild:** 1-3 binge-eating episodes per week **Moderate:** 4-7 binge-eating episodes per week **Severe:** 8-13 binge-eating episodes per week **Extreme:** 14 or more binge-eating episodes per week
Other specified eating disorder • Atypical anorexia nervosa (Met all criteria except weight is within or above normal range) • Bulimia nervosa (of low frequency and/or limited duration): • Binge-eating disorder (of low frequency and/or limited duration): • Purging disorder: Recurrent purging behavior in the absence of binge eating. • Night eating syndrome: – Recurrent episodes of night eating such as eating after awakening from sleep or after the evening meal. – There is awareness and recall of the eating. – Causes significant distress and/or impairment in functioning. – Not associated with other eating disorder, medical condition, and medication. – Not related to changes in the individual's sleep-wake cycle or by local social norms.

Source: American Psychiatric Association. *Diagnostic and statistical manual of mental disorders*, 5th ed. Arlington, VA: American Psychiatric Association, 2013.

The etiology of eating disorder is often complex and multifactorial (4, 5). Family history of eating disorder or other mental health condition such has depression, anxiety, substance use disorders puts an adolescent at higher risk of eating disorder (4). In twin studies, higher concordance rate for anorexia was found in monozygotic twins thus suggesting role of genetic factors. Other risk factors include family dynamics, bullying, sexual or physical abuse, low self-esteem and personal history of anxiety, depression (5, 11). Personality traits of perfectionism, rigid thinking style, obsessive compulsive behaviors, and difficulties regulating emotions can often be predisposing factors (4). In addition, adolescents active in track, gymnastics may be at risk because of extra emphasis on lean body. Adolescents with sexual or gender identity concerns may develop body image concerns and eating disorders due to stigma, discrimination, and body image distress (9, 10).

EPIDEMIOLOGY

According to "Diagnostic and statistical manual (DSM V)", there are different types of eating disorders (see Table 1). Historically, anorexia nervosa is more common in adolescent Caucasian females than males with sex ratio 9:1 and lifetime prevalence was <1% (4, 5). Using newer DSM V diagnostic criteria, however, overall prevalence of anorexia nervosa, bulimia nervosa and binge eating disorder seem to have increased (6-8). Based on systemic review, lifetime prevalence of anorexia nervosa in females ranged from 1.7% to 3.6% with point prevalence of 0.67% to 1.2% (6). Lifetime prevalence of anorexia in males was 0.1%. Bulimia nervosa is found to be common in females with prevalence rate of 0.6%. Binge eating disorder was, however, seen in both males and females with point prevalence of 3.6% in males and females combined (6). Lifetime prevalence rates for other specified feeding and eating disorders ranged from 0.3% in males to 0.6% in females(6). There has been increase in incidence of eating disorder in males and ethnic minorities (8). In a national representative sample, ethnic differences were noted. Anorexia nervosa was common in Non- Hispanic white, bulimia nervosa common in Hispanic and binge eating disorder was more common among ethnic minorities (8). Socio-economic status including parental education, household income, and parental/surrogate marital status was not associated with eating disorder in the study (8). Lesbian and bisexual females as well as gay males are found to have higher prevalence of binging and purging than heterosexual adolescents (9).

SIGNS AND SYMPTOMS

Adolescents with eating disorders may present with variety of behavioral as well as physical symptoms (4, 5). Eating behaviors may include eating smaller portions, refusing to eat meals or wanting to eat alone (11, 12). Food rituals like cutting food into small pieces, chewing each bite an unusually large number of times or eating very slowly can be present (12). Adolescents may want to consume only "safe" or "healthy" food; have new practice with food or fad diets that may include cutting out entire food groups such as no sugar, no carbs, no dairy, become vegetarian or vegan or drink excessive amount of water (11, 12). They may develop interest in cooking shows, collect recipes and engage in cooking elaborate meals for others but refusing to eat meals themselves. Adolescents who engage in binge eating/purging may hide foods, and eat in secret, may use excessive amounts of mouthwash, mints and gum (12). They may engage in excessive exercise regimen and may often continue with their exercise even during sickness (12). As a result of their eating behaviors, adolescent may have changes in weight, stomach issues such as vomiting, diarrhea, period irregularities (often missing periods) (13). Dizziness, lightheadedness, fainting spells and feeling cold all the time are common. Adolescent with purging behaviors may have cuts or calluses across the top of finger joints (Russell's sign) and may have eroded tooth enamel (4, 5, 13). Poor nutrition further results in loss of hair, thin body hair (lanugo), problems with circulation, cool extremities, and slow heart rate (13). Teens become more withdrawn, socially isolated and develop sleep problems

(13). Teens with coexisting anxiety or depression may have suicidal ideation and self- harming behaviors (20, 21).

MEDICAL AND PSYCHOLOGICAL COMPLICATIONS

Anorexia nervosa is the most common and fatal psychiatric Disorder with mortality rate of 1.8% (2-20%) in adolescents which is 6 times higher than normal in adults (5). Majority of deaths result from medical complication of starvation and suicide is second most common cause (11, 12). Cardiovascular complications are associated with high mortality due to sudden death caused by prolonged QTc. Bradycardia is common in anorexia (13, 14). Other arrhythmias include first degree heart block, ectopic atrial foci, and premature ventricular complexes (13, 14). Chronic starvation results in heart changes that may include decrease in left ventricular mass, increase in peripheral vascular resistance, decreased cardiac output. Mitral valve prolapse may also occur (14). Poor nutrition can also lead to cognitive deficits, seizures, myopathy, peripheral neuropathy and grey matter deficits in brain in specific areas including limbic system as well as deficits in serotoninergic and dopaminergic system (15). Anemia particularly normocytic, normochromic is common (16).

Macrocytic/Microcytic anemia, however, may warrant further investigation (16). Mild decrease in white blood cell count is common and it usually resolves with nutrition. Decrease in platelet count, although, less common can be seen and lead to bleeding problems such as easy bruising, gum bleeding, petechiae (16). Gastrointestinal complications include fatty liver from acute weight loss and re-feeding (13). Elevated liver enzymes and high cholesterol may be present. Delayed gastric emptying and decreased intestinal motility often cause bloating and constipation and is common in anorexia (13). Superior Mesenteric Artery Syndrome may develop due to loss of retroperitoneal fat and mimic intestinal obstruction (4, 13, 20). Laxative abuse for weight loss can lead to rectal prolapse and electrolyte abnormalities. Frequent vomiting can cause inflammation and tears of esophagus (13, 20).

Children and adolescents with eating disorders may develop endocrine abnormalities abnormal thyroid function, abnormal adrenal function, low levels of sex steroids, and problems with growth (17, 18). Pre-pubertal children may have pubertal delay and growth retardation (17). Adolescent female may have loss of periods due to weight loss and poor nutrition. Prolonged cessation of menstrual periods can affect bone mineral density leading to osteopenia and osteoporosis with increased risk of stress fractures. Low bone mineral density and risk of fracture may persist in adulthood even after recovery (17, 18).

Mental health comorbidities are common in adolescents with eating disorders and may be present before the onset, co-exist or occur during recovery (19, 20). Common mental health conditions are depression, anxiety, obsessive-compulsive disorder, posttraumatic stress disorder, personality disorders, substance abuse disorders, and self-injurious behaviors (19, 20). In anorexia, the lifetime prevalence of depression and anxiety disorders is 50%-68% and 30%-65% respectively (18, 19). Mood disorders, substance use disorders and personality disorders are common in bulimia nervosa. Suicidal ideation and self-harm behaviors are common (20). Self –harm behaviors typically represent emotion regulation strategy and serves the function of replacing unwanted emotions such as numbness, dissociation or stop unpleasant emotions, avoid an unwanted situation or ask for help. Adolescents who engage in self-injurious behaviors present with more severe eating disorder, depression and anxiety symptoms, perfectionism and less motivation to change (21).

MANAGEMENT OF EATING DISORDERS

Treatment of eating disorders involves multidisciplinary approach with involvement of medical providers, dietician and mental health professionals and intervention often includes medical, psychological and pharmacological (22). Collaboration and support of family is important.

The main goals of treatment include medical stabilization with weight restoration and recovery from medical complications with therapy to eliminate eating behaviors (20, 22). Adolescents are treated based on the severity of disorder and includes inpatient, outpatient, partial or residential treatment (22). Upon presentation, it is important to obtain a detailed history and perform thorough examination. Baseline labs including complete hemogram, electrolytes, hepatic function panel, lipid profile, thyroid studies, electrocardiogram (EKG) should be obtained to screen for complications (22). Inpatient treatment is necessary if medical complications are present or there is suicidal risk (see Table 2). During inpatient hospitalization, adolescents are monitored closely for electrolyte abnormalities and refeeding syndrome (22, 23). Structured meals with supervision are provided and sometimes nasogastric feeding may be necessary if there is refusal to eat or to provide higher calorie for weight restoration (24).

Adolescents who are medically stable but have poor to fair motivation and are preoccupied with constant daily thoughts benefit from residential treatment where there is constant supervision with meals, receive intensive counseling to address eating behaviors (22). Partial hospitalization is a full day outpatient program for adolescents who need some structure to gain weight through daily nutritional and psychological counseling (22, 23). Once adolescents are more stable, it is important that they continue to follow up with their medical, mental health provider and nutritionist on regular and frequent basis (23). Adolescents with eating disorders often have chronic relapsing and remitting disease and may need different levels of care depending on their severity (22, 23).

A family based therapy called Maudsley method is an evidence-based treatment for adolescent anorexia nervosa as well bulimia nervosa (25, 26). The goal of family based therapy is to involve parents or caregivers in overall management of eating disorder. Family based therapy has three phases. In the first phase which is the weight restoration phase, focus is on addressing physical complications and parents assist adolescents in feeding and restoring weight. In the second phase, parents encourage their child to take more control over eating and focus on attaining stable physical health.

Once adolescent establishes healthy identity and ability to maintain weight, parents support increased personal autonomy (25, 26). Other forms psychotherapy such as cognitive behavioral therapy, interpersonal or dialectical therapy may also be utilized in the treatment of eating disorders (22, 23).

Medications have limited role in treatment of eating disorders. A national eating disorder collaborative study found that most teens with anorexia had significant anxiety and depression and were often prescribed medications (27). There was, however, no significant difference in weight restoration as compared to those without medications (27). Selective serotonin reuptake inhibitors (SSRI) are commonly used for associated anxiety and depression (28). Atypical antipsychotics particularly olanzapine has shown to be beneficial for weight gain and improve behavioral symptoms (28). In bulimia and binge eating disorder, medications are useful and can help with improvement of behaviors.

Table 2. Criteria for inpatient hospitalization

1. Severe malnutrition (weight 75% average body weight for age, sex, and height) 2. Dehydration 3. Electrolyte disturbances (hypokalemia, hyponatremia, hypophosphatemia) 4. Cardiac dysrhythmia 5. Physiological instability Severe bradycardia (heart rate 50 beats/minute daytime; <45 beats/minute at night) – Hypotension (80/50 mm Hg) – Hypothermia (body temperature 96° F) – Orthostatic changes in pulse (20 beats per minute) or blood pressure (10 mm Hg) 6. Arrested growth and development	7. Failure of outpatient treatment 8. Acute food refusal 9. Uncontrollable binging and purging 10. Acute medical complications of malnutrition (e.g., syncope, seizures, cardiac failure, pancreatitis, etc.) 11. Acute psychiatric emergencies (e.g., suicidal ideation, acute psychosis) 12. Comorbid diagnosis that interferes with the treatment of the eating disorder (e.g., severe depression, obsessive compulsive disorder, severe family dysfunction)

Source-Position Paper of the Society for Adolescent Health and Medicine: medical management of restrictive eating disorders in adolescents and young adults. *J Adolesc Health* 2015;56(1):121-5.

Recently, lisdexam-fetamine was FDA approved for treatment of binge eating disorderin adults. It is reported to be generally well tolerated and effective (28). But currently research is needed in adolescents regarding its effectiveness in treatment of binge eating disorder. Prolonged absence of period leads to one of most serious complications of low mineral density which can affect bone heath as adults (17). Resumption of menses occurs after weight gain through nutritional intervention that leads to some improvement in bone mineral density. Oral estrogen and progestin supplementation currently has no role in period regulation unless needed for contraception (22, 23, 27). Role of transdermal estrogen is currently being explored (23, 27).

Overall prognosis of eating disorder depends on age of onset, duration of illness, weight at initial presentation and coexisting mental health conditions. Shorter duration of illness before intake and higher percent of mean body weight at initial presentation predicted improved weight outcomes at 1 year for adolescents diagnosed with anorexia (29). Coexisting conditions such as obsessive compulsive disorder, bingeing/purging behaviors and chronicity of disease are unfavorable prognostic factors (30).

Conclusion

Body image concerns and problematic eating behaviors may develop during adolescence. It is thus important to recognize symptoms and seek early intervention for better outcomes. Nutritional rehabilitation and behavioral intervention is the mainstay of treatment. Family support and collaboration is crucial in the management of eating disorder.

References

[1] Golden NH, Schneider M, Wood C. Preventing obesity and eating disorders in adolescents, Pediatrics 2016;138(3). Doi:10.1542/peds.2016-1649.

[2] Oksanen A, Garcia D, Räsänen P. Proanorexia communities on social media. Pediatrics 2016;137(1). Doi: 10.1542/peds.2015-3372.
[3] Kann L, Kinchen S, Shanklin S, Flint KH, Kawkins J, Harris WA, et al. Youth risk behavior surveillance: United States, 2013. MMWR Suppl 2014;63(4):1-168.
[4] Goldstein MA, Dechant EJ, Beresin EV. Eating disorders. Pediatr Rev 2011;32(12):508-21.
[5] Rome E. Eating disorder in children and adolescents. Curr Probl Pediatr Adolesc Health Care 2012;42(2):28-44.
[6] Lindvall Dahlgren C, Wisting L. Feeding and eating disorders in the DSM-5 era: A systematic review of prevalence rates in non-clinical male and female samples. J Eat Disord 2017;28(5):56.
[7] Smink FR, Van Hoeken D, Oldehinkel AJ, Hoek HW. Prevalence and severity of DSM-5 eating disorders in a community cohort of adolescents. Int J Eat Disord 2014;47(6):610-9.
[8] Swanson SA, Crow SJ, Le Grange D, Swendsen J, Merikangas KR. Prevalence and correlates of eating disorders in adolescents. Results from the national comorbidity survey replication adolescent supplement. Arch Gen Psychiatry 2011;68(7):714-23.
[9] Sadhir M, Stockburger S, Omar H. Sexual minority (LGBTQ) youth and role of health care provider. Dyna Hum Health 2016;3:1.
[10] Connolly MD, Zervos MJ, Barone CJ. The mental health of transgender youth: Advances in understanding. J Adolesc Health 2016;59(5):489-95.
[11] Rome ES, Strandjord SE. Eating disorders. Pediatr Rev 2016;37(8):323-36.
[12] National Eating Disorders Association. Emotional and behavioral signs of an eating disorder, NEDA toolkit for parents. URL: https://www.nationaleatingdisorders.org/sites/default/files/Toolkits/parenttoolkit/index.html.
[13] Rosen DS, Identification and management of eating disorders in children and adolescents, Pediatrics 2010;126(6):1240-53.
[14] Casiero D, Frishman WH. Cardiovascular complications of eating disorders. Cardiol Rev 2006;14(5):227-31.
[15] Phillipou A, Rossell SL, Castle DJ. The neurobiology of anorexia nervosa: A systematic review. Aust NZ J Psychiatry 2014;48(2):128-52.
[16] Cleary BS, Gaudiani JL, Mehler PS. Interpreting the complete blood count in anorexia nervosa. Eat Disord 2010;18(2):132-9.
[17] Jayasinghe Y, Grover SR, Zacharin M. Current concepts in bone and reproductive health in adolescents with anorexia nervosa. BJOG 2008;115(3):304-15.
[18] Warren MP. Endocrine manifestations of eating disorders. J Clin Endocrinol Metab 2011;96(2):333-43.
[19] Golden NH, Attia E. Psychopharmacology of eating disorders in children and adolescents. Pediatr Clin North Am 2011;58(1):121–38.
[20] Campbell K, Peebles R. Eating disorders in children and adolescents: state of the art review. Pediatrics 2014;134(3):582-92.

[21] Varela-Besteiro O, Serrano-Troncoso E, Rodríguez-Vicente V, Curet-Santisteban M, Conangla-Rosello G, Cecilia-Costa R, et al. Suicidal ideation and self-injurious behavior in adolescents with eating disorders. Actas Esp Psiquiatr 2017;45(4): 157-66.

[22] Golden NH, Katzman DK, Sawyer SM, Ornstein RM, Rome ES, Garber AK, et al. Position Paper of the Society for Adolescent Health and Medicine: Medical management of restrictive eating disorders in adolescents and young adults. J Adolesc Health 2015;56(1):121-5.

[23] Golden NH, Katzman DK, Sawyer SM, Ornstein RM, Rome ES, Garber AK, et al. Update on the medical management of eating disorders in adolescents. J Adolesc Health 2015;56(4):370-5.

[24] Robb AS, Silber TJ, Orrell-Valente JK, Valadez-Meltzer A, Ellis N, Dadson MJ, et al. Supplemental nocturnal nasogastric re-feeding for better short-term outcome in hospitalized adolescent girls with anorexia nervosa. Am J Psychiatry 2002;159(8):1347-53.

[25] Jewell T, Blessitt E, Stewart C, Simic M, Eisler I. Family therapy for child and adolescent eating disorders: A critical review. Fam Process 2016; 55(3):577-94.

[26] Forsberg S, Lock J, Family-based treatment of child and adolescent eating disorders. Child Adolesc Psychiatr Clin North Am 2015;24(3):617-29.

[27] Monge MC, Forman SF, McKenzie NM, Rosen DS, Mammel KA, Callahan ST, et al. Use of psychopharmacologic medications in adolescents with restrictive eating disorders: Analysis of data from the National Eating Disorder Quality Improvement Collaborative. J Adolesc Health 2015;57(1):66-72.

[28] Davis H, Attia E, Pharmacotherapy of eating disorders. Curr Opin Psychiatry 2017;30(6):452-7.

[29] Forman SF, Grodin LF, Graham DA. An eleven site national quality improvement evaluation of adolescent medicine-based eating disorder programs: predictors of weight outcomes at one year and risk adjustment analyses. J Adolesc Health 2011;49(6):594-600.

[30] Steinhausen HC. Outcome of eating disorders. Child Adolesc Psychiatr Clin North Am 2009;18(1):225-4

In: Building Youth for the Future ISBN: 978-1-53613-768-2
Editors: H. A Omar and J. Merrick

Chapter 14

How to Survive and Thrive: Parenting Children and Adolescents with Mental Health Problems

Stephanie Stockburger*[*], *MD and Alissa Briggs, PhD
Division of Adolescent Medicine, Department of Pediatrics,
University of Kentucky, Lexington, Kentucky, US

Abstract

Parents and guardians of children and adolescents with mental health problems often find themselves navigating challenges in the social, academic, medical, and financial aspects of life. Mental health diagnoses in children and adolescents are relatively common, yet access to quality treatment is rare. Parents and guardians commonly need support as they navigate the journey of parenting a child or adolescent with a mental health diagnosis.

[*] Correspondence: Stephanie Stockburger, MD, Assistant Professor of Pediatrics, Department of Pediatrics, Division of Adolescent Medicine, 740 S Limestone, Lexington, KY 40536-0284, United States. Email: Sjstoc2@uky.edu.

Introduction

Mental health diagnoses in children and adolescents are relatively common. It is also relatively rare that children and adolescents receive appropriate intervention services when symptoms first begin. The prevalence of mental health problems in children is 1 in 5 (1). Within the previous year, 13% of children ages 8-15 had a diagnosable mental illness (1). Yet, it takes 10 years on average before a child or adolescent receives appropriate intervention services after the first onset of symptoms (1). Among the most common mental illness diagnoses are attention deficit hyperactivity disorder (ADHD), anxiety, depression, and behavior disorders.

Parenting a child or adolescent with a mental health problem can be a challenge, to say the least. Problems that parents or guardians may encounter include lack of support in the school system, difficulty finding a health provider to manage medications, difficulty finding a therapist, and a general lack of social and emotional support. In addition, the stress associated with parenting a child with a mental illness can contribute to a parent's own mental illness (2). Below is a discussion of some simple things that parents can do that will help them and their child/adolescent move from surviving to thriving.

Mental Health

Parenting children and adolescents with mental health problems is not something that is extensively discussed in the literature. Thus, parents and guardians of children and adolescents with mental health problems may feel alone and lack support. However, as mentioned in the introduction, they are far from alone. Twenty percent of children will have a serious mental illness (1).

The signs of mental health problems may vary. Common signs include changes in sleeping patterns, changes in eating patterns, irritability, decreased interest in doing things that were previously enjoyed, decreased school performance, school refusal, somatic complaints such as headaches or stomachaches, and neglect of personal appearance or hygiene. Children or adolescents may also voice statements indicating that others around them would be "better off if they weren't there" or engage in self-harm behaviors. It is very important for parents and guardians to take these signs seriously and not brush them off as "attention seeking behaviors." Often, these statements or engaging in self-harm behaviors are cries for help and warrant further assessment by a medical or mental health professional.

When a child or adolescent has been diagnosed with a mental health problem, it is normal for parents and guardians to experience a host of worries and concerns. Guardians may worry about stigma for their child and their family. Medical concerns are common. There are often concerns regarding risks of medication, side effects of medication, running out of medication, and long-term dependency on medication. They may have difficulty finding medical and mental health providers to help manage their child or adolescent's condition. It may also be difficult to find a medical primary care provider who is comfortable caring for their child. Social concerns commonly include worries about meltdowns in public, fear of child protective service referrals, lack of respite care, more than one child with a mental health problem in the family, and a parent or guardian who has also been diagnosed with a mental health problem. Financial concerns may include insurance not covering medication and limited finances. Families caring for a child or adolescent with a mental health problem may experience both objective and subjective burdens. Objective burdens include financial costs, transportation, and housing logistic negotiations in managing child. Subjective burdens may include psychological pain, embarrassment, and mental anguish.

Regardless of the concerns present, there is definitely a need from the guardians and entire family to have ongoing support from a medical provider to assist with problem solving, efficacy, and possible side effects of medication (3). Fortunately, many pediatric practices are moving towards a patient centered medical home (PCMH) model, which enables the medical provider to work as an advocate for the parent and child/adolescent and link them to necessary supports and services (4). In addition to the need for medical care for their child, social support for the parents and guardians is also extremely important. Parents and guardians, and family members may feel alone and isolated after a child is diagnosed or exhibiting symptoms consistent with a mental health problem.

An important initial step after a mental health diagnosis is made in a child or adolescent is to learn all about the diagnosis. In other words, to be armed with information. This is important for a number of reasons. A major reason is that there will be a better understanding of what the child or adolescent is going through. Also, a parent or guardian will be better equipped to advocate for their child. A multitude of professional organizations and mental health organizations have reliable information that is readily accessible on the internet. At the local level, support groups may be available both for the child or adolescent and the guardians. Support groups can be a great way to continue to learn about the mental health diagnosis, available local resources, and also for receiving emotional support.

SCHOOL

Another important step is to reach out to the school. School counselors and school psychologists have training in providing mental health services in schools. There may be resources within the school that parents can access for free, such as individual and group counseling. Many schools are implementing Multi-tiered Systems of Supports, (MTSS), and thus may have systems in place to support students who are struggling with social, emotional, and behavioral functioning in the school environment. In addition, the child or adolescent may be eligible for accommodations and modifications under Section 504 of the Rehabilitation Act of 1973 so that symptoms of their mental illness, such as impaired concentration, do not interfere with their progress. However, symptoms of a mental illness may interfere with academic progress, even given accommodations and modifications, and thus the child or adolescent may be eligible for specialized instruction (special education) under the Individuals with Disabilities Education and Improvement Act (IDEIA) of 2004. If a parent thinks that their child may be eligible for supports or services through a 504 plan or special education, they should communicate their concerns in a letter to the child/adolescent's counselor and/or administrator and request a meeting to discuss evaluation for eligibility for these supports and/or services.

Home

At home, parenting the child or adolescent with a mental health diagnosis may present some challenges. However, many strategies for parenting are similar to managing children and adolescents without a mental health diagnosis. Overall, being attentive and fully present can help strengthen relationships and avert problems. Paying attention to any changes in the child or adolescent's eating, sleeping, interests, or behavior may be an early clue to initiate a conversation about how the child or adolescent is faring. Maintaining a "respectful curiosity" about what is going on in their life can be helpful for staying tuned in to what is going on with them. Keeping open communication: "I am here for you when you are ready" can be a helpful phrase for the child or teen who isn't interested in communicating in the current moment. Noticing strengths in the child or adolescent and building on them and developing them can help build confidence and also avert more negative behaviors.

Monitoring social media use as well as limiting screen time is recommended. Parents and guardians can be a role model for screen time use by turning screens off and having intentional family time. The American Academy of Pediatrics (AAP) recommends that for children ages 2-5 years, screen use should be limited to 1 hour per day of high-quality programs. Parents should co-view media with children to help them understand what they are seeing and apply it to the world around them (5). For children ages 6 years and older, the AAP recommends placing consistent limits on the time spent using media, the types of media, and to make sure media does not take the place of adequate sleep, physical activity and other behaviors essential to health. Another recommendation is to designate media-free times together such as dinner or driving as well as media-free locations at home such as bedrooms (5). Additionally, recent literature suggests that depression rates may be higher in those who engage in visiting a high number of social media sites per week (6).

A major factor in one's ability to control behaviors and regulate mood is sleep. Parents or guardians can be role models also for good sleep habits. Recommendations include setting regular bedtimes and wake-up times and turning off all screens 1-2 hours prior to bedtime. It is not recommended to have electronic devices including televisions, video games, computers, and cell phones in the bedroom. Parents may want to regularly collect cell phones at a set time in the evening to help the child or adolescent establish and maintain good sleep habits.

As all parents and guardians are aware, their number one parenting job is to keep their child safe – no matter how old he or she is. The American Academy of Pediatrics recommends that if there are guns in the household that they be kept separately from the ammunition, both locked up so they are not able to be accessed by the child or adolescent (7). It is also recommended that all medications (even over the counter medications) be kept in a lock box. This is to prevent both children and adolescents from accessing them, whether intentionally or unintentionally. Although over the counter medications may be perceived as safe since they are readily available, they are often far from being safe. Many medications are toxic or deadly if taken by children or misused by adolescents (8).

Communication with the child or adolescent is extremely important. It is important to actively listen to what they are saying. This is more than just simply hearing them. Giving the child or adolescent full attention by stopping what you are doing, and looking them is a physical cue that you are listening. Listening fully without interrupting (which can be challenging sometimes!) is key. Your own thoughts may come into your head but let them go and continue listening to the child or adolescent. In this way, you are showing respect to them as well as modeling a respectful conversation. When they are finished speaking, showing you're interested by nodding or making a comment such as "I see" or "that sounds tricky" helps them know that you are listening (9).

Picking your battles can be another important strategy for keeping as much peace as possible at home. Conflict can be about small things and may not really be worth arguing about. For example, your teen may want to dye their hair blue. There are different ways to look at this. You may ask yourself, does this affect their safety? If the item at hand is not safety-related, consider making it a reward for (attainable) positive behavior (10). Remember that while adolescents may look and act like an adult at times, their brains are still developing. Children tend to think very concretely. Adolescents may have periods of concrete thinking as well and may have difficulty associating certain actions with consequences. Adolescents may have trouble seeing the "big picture" and often think that "bad things happen to other people." Being flexible about little issues may help your child listen and accept guidance when it comes to bigger issues that may affect their safety.

Also, when tempers are getting heated, it can be helpful to take a step away from each other. Dealing with conflict is much easier when you and/or your child are not feeling upset or angry (10). Some call this a "take 5" or "take 10" break to take five or ten minutes in separate rooms in order to calm down before dealing further with the issue at hand. Remember, as the parent or guardian, it is your job to role model staying cool and collected during heated times, not join in the child or teen's chaos. When you are unable to do this, it may be helpful to come back later to the child or adolescent and say something like "I was really angry, I'm sorry I yelled at you. A better thing for me to do would have been to take a break and then come back and talk about it calmly with you."

There are times when children or adolescents with a mental health diagnosis (or without a mental health diagnosis) may have escalating behavior which is concerning for becoming violent. When this occurs, it is important to send a clear message that this behavior is not okay. A parent or guardian can let them know that they are willing to talk to the child or adolescent and work things out together when they have calmed down. A clear message should be conveyed that there will be consequences for the behavior. The parent or guardian can check their own behavior and make sure it is respectful and that they are managing their emotions and modeling self-control. If a situation is escalating out of control, it is a good idea to get help (10). There may be times when taking the child or adolescent to the Emergency Department or calling local law enforcement may be necessary for the safety of themselves or others. Talking with other caregivers to make sure everyone is on the same page about limit setting and handling negative behaviors can help minimize conflict. This shows a "united front" and helps the caregivers show a stronger position and often keeps negotiation simpler (10).

Discipline and setting limits are important whether a child or teen has a mental health diagnosis or not. Limits and boundaries can help teens learn independence, take responsibility for his or her behavior and its outcomes, and solve problems (11). It can help to involve the teen when working out limits and rules as they will be more likely to stick to rules they contributed to. Being clear about the limits and consequences helps the child or teen stick to them. Also, be willing to discuss and adjust rules as the adolescent shows increasing responsibility (11).

There is a flip side of limit-setting and discipline which is strengthening relationships. Without this important piece, limit-setting and discipline methods are often not successful. Showing interest in the child or teen, being there when they need you, being in the moment, and being available when your child needs support are integral to a strong relationship with them. Also, listening without judging or correcting strengthens relationships. Get to know your child or adolescent and truly value them for who they are. Time spent listening to and valuing children and adolescents is never wasted.

CONCLUSION

In conclusion, mental health diagnosis in children and adolescents are relatively common. Parenting children with or without a mental health diagnosis can be a challenge! Parents and guardians of children and adolescents with a mental health diagnosis often need increased support for medical and mental health needs. It is important to listen to these caregivers, appreciate the efforts they are putting forth to parent, and support them whether we are a community member, school professional, or health care professional.

References

[1] National Alliance on Mental Illness. Mental health by the numbers [Internet]. Arlington, VA: National Alliance on Mental Illness, 2018. URL: https://www.nami.org/learn-more/mental-health-by-the-numbers.

[2] National Alliance on Mental Illness. Learning to help your child and your family. Arlington, VA: National Alliance on Mental Illness, 2018. URL: https://www.nami.org/Find-Support/Family-Members-and-Caregivers/Learning-to-Help-Your-Child-and-Your-Family.

[3] Faulkner M. How to support parents of children and adolescents with mental health issues [Internet]. Rockville, MD: Indian Health Service: the federal health program for American Indians and Alaska natives, 2015. URL: https://www.ihs.gov/telebehavioral/includes/themes/newihstheme/display_objects/documents/slides/nationalchildandadolescent/spring2015/supportingparents0215.pdf.

[4] AAP Agenda for children: Medical home. American Academy of Pediatrics, 2018. URL: https://www.aap.org/en-us/about-the-aap/aap-facts/AAP-Agenda-for-Children-Strategic-Plan/pages/AAP-Agenda-for-Children-Strategic-Plan-Medical-Home.aspx.

[5] American Academy of Pediatrics. American Academy of Pediatrics announces new recommendations for children's media use [Internet]. Illinois: American Academy of Pediatrics, 2016. URL: https://www.aap.org/en-us/about-the-aap/aap-press-room/pages/american-academy-of-pediatrics-announces-new-recommendations-for-childrens-media-use.aspx.

[6] Lin LY, Sidani JE, Shensa A, Radovic A, Miller E, Colditz JB. Association between social media use and depression among US young adults. Depress Anxiety 2016;33(4):323-31.

[7] American Academy of Pediatrics. How pediatricians can advocate for children's safety in their communities [Internet]. American Academy of Pediatrics, 2018. URL: https://www.aap.org/en-us/advocacy-and-policy/Pages/How-Pediatricians-Can-Advocate-for-Childrens-Safety-in-Their-Communities.aspx.

[8] Dawson KL. Over-the-counter medication abuse [Internet]. Lexington, KY: University of Kentucky Health Care CE Central, 2017. URL: http://www.cecentral.com/activity/ 12921.

[9] Raising Children Network. Active listening: A skill to promote communication with your child [Internet]. Australia: Raising Children Network, 2015. URL: http:// raisingchildren.net.au/articles/active_listening_teenagers.html/context/1096.

[10] Raising Children Network. Conflict management with teenagers [Internet]. Australia: Raising Children Network, 2017. URL: http://raisingchildren.net.au/articles/ conflict_management_teenagers.html/context/1096.

[11] Raising Children Network. Discipline strategies for teenagers [Internet]. Australia: Raising Children Network, 2017. URL: http://raisingchildren.net.au/articles/ discipline_teenagers.html/context/1123.

In: Building Youth for the Future ISBN: 978-1-53613-768-2
Editors: H. A Omar and J. Merrick

Chapter 15

SLEEP: A TALK FOR EVERY VISIT

Shawn Sorrell*, MD
Division of Adolescent Medicine and Young Parent programs,
J422 Kentucky Clinic, Department of Pediatrics,
Kentucky Children's Hospital,
University of Kentucky College of Medicine,
Lexington, Kentucky, US

ABSTRACT

The importance of sleep is a conversation for every visit to the pediatrician. Adolescents are getting less quantity and quality of sleep than in previous decades. School start times and chronic media use play a significant role in the sleep patterns of adolescents. Poor quality and quantity of sleep can affect all aspects of a child and adolescent. The impact has been seen on overall physical health including obesity and eating patterns. There is also a relationship between mental health and risk taking behaviors and sleep. This chapter hopes to better illustrate the importance of sleep in the life of an adolescent.

* Correspondence: Shawn Sorrell, MD, Adolescent Medicine, University of Kentucky College of Medicine, 740 S Limestone, Lexington, KY 40536, United States.
Email: shawnjsmith@uky.edu.

INTRODUCTION

Sleep is an imperative part of any pediatrician's discussion if he or she is evaluating growth and development in a child or adolescent. It is important to understand what is considered normal for sleep in different ages. It is also very helpful to understand sleep physiology.

There are two different types of sleep, REM (rapid eye movement) and Non-REM sleep. During sleep there are four cycles and the person will go through all four stages in each cycle of sleep. The first stage (Non REM stage 1) can last between 1 and 10 minutes. It consists of very light sleep and one can return to being fully awake if this stage is interrupted. The body's muscles are not inhibited. The eyelids may open slightly and breathing slows while the heartrate is regular. During this stage hypnic jerks may be experienced.

The second stage (Non REM stage 2) is a much deeper sleep than stage 1 and usually is approximately 20 minutes. The heart rate continues to slow. There are characteristics specific for this stage that can be identified on the EEG. There are sleep spindles and K Complexes. The sleep spindles are rapid wax and wane of the EEG waves in 1-2 seconds. The K complexes are large wax and wane of the waves. There are also specific physiologic changes. There is a decrease in body temperature. This is often referred to the preparative stage for deep sleep. It becomes more difficult to wake a person. These first two stages are often referred as light sleep. Most of our sleep is spent in stage 2.

The third stage (Non REM stage 3) starts 30-45 minutes after falling asleep. The brainwaves on an EEG (electroencephalogram) become slower and larger. A person can usually sleep through most noises and movements without any reaction. Often this is the stage that when a person is awakened there is a brief time of disorientation. There are high amplitude waves on the EEG during this stage that is referred to as delta waves. This stage is also referred as the slow-wave sleep.

The fourth stage of sleep is the final stage and known as Rapid Eye Movement (REM). This stage lasts approximately 10 minutes and usually occurs after someone has been asleep for 90 minutes. As the name indicates, the eyes move in all directions and rapidly during this stage. The brain is highly activated during this time and this is reflected on the EEG. The EEG during REM is very similar to the EEG during wakefulness. Dreams usually occur during this stage. Enuresis and sleepwalking also can occur during this stage. There are specific physiological changes including an increase in the heart rate, an increase in respiration rate (1).

SLEEP ARCHITECTURE AND BEHAVIORS

Sleep architecture and behaviors change dramatically from birth through adolescence and understanding these differences allow for improved diagnosing of sleep disturbances and better communication when discussing sleep patterns with patients and families.

From birth through three months of age the average sleep duration is 16-20 hours. Most infants will sleep 1-4 hours at a time and then this is followed by 1-2 hour awake periods. The amount of daytime sleep usually corresponds to the amount of nighttime sleep. There are some exceptions such as birth trauma can be associated with sleep disruption. Infants that are breast fed may have shorter sleep periods (2).

From the ages of three months to 12 months there are s significant differences. At four months there is usually a total of 14-15 hours of sleep. At six months of age there are a total of 13 -14 hours of sleep. This amount of sleep is obtained usually through 11 hours of sleep at night and napping three hours during the day; however, this is usually divided into two hours. From the age of 9-12 months infants will nap 2-4 hours a day. Self-soothing skills begin to develop starting at three months (2).

Sleep continues to decline as the child grows. Toddlers (ages 1-3) will sleep 12-14 hours total and usually nap just once during the day. Nighttime fears often develop during this age. Transitional objects and bedtime routines are important to help lay the foundation for healthy sleep. There is often significant bedtime resistance and limit setting is important for parents and caregivers. Preschool children (ages 3-6 years) will sleep 11-12 hours and napping often declines by the age of five years. Napping patterns may be influenced by parental routines and school practices. Sleep problems including sleepwalking and sleep terrors often occur during this time. This is the age in which obstructive sleep apnea may be present.

During middle childhood and early adolescence (ages 6-12 years) children should be getting an average of 10 hours of sleep. Daytime routines and activities may play a larger role in a child's life and affect duration of sleep. There may be low levels of daytime sleepiness. There is an increased discrepancy between the amount of sleep a child gets during school nights and non-school nights. School and behavior issues may be related to sleep problems including inadequate sleep (2).

There are also significant differences in brain waves from early infancy through puberty. Infants spend 50% of sleep in the REM stage or eight hours of an infant's 24 hour period is spent in REM. Time spent in REM stabilizes at age 10 years and then begins to decline at age 80 years. By age 70 years only 45 minutes of total sleep is spent in REM stage (4).

ADOLESCENT SLEEP

Adolescent sleep is considerably different than early to middle childhood. Teen's onset of sleep is later. Puberty plays a significant role in sleep physiology. With the onset of pubertal development there is a delay of circadian rhythm regulation. At the onset of secondary sexual characteristics there is a peak of delayed circadian rhythm. This correlation has been studied across cultures and mammalian species (4).

SLEEP QUALITY

The discussion of the importance of quality and quantity of sleep has greatly increased over the last several years. Hundreds of books have been published that discuss the effects of sleep restriction and disordered sleep. Only within the last two decades has this discussion led to an increase in research in adolescence and the importance of sleep. The effects of poor sleep are detrimental not only on cognition and behavioral health but also physical affects.

Disordered sleep greatly affects cognition and school performance. This correlation is important to discuss during clinical visits with parents and patients. Often patients will feel that he or she must sacrifice sleep in order to complete academic assignments. It is important to describe the detrimental effects of sleep restriction during this conversation. A meta-analysis was published that studied the correlation between a spectrum of breathing abnormalities (snoring, obstructive sleep apnea, upper airway resistance syndrome) that decrease quality and duration of sleep (5). The impact these abnormalities had on sleep were correlated with negative effects on intelligence (standardized testing), memory, executive function, attention and hyperactivity (5).

Obesity is an extremely common morbidity that results in ongoing conversations between the pediatrician and the patient and family. The prevalence of obesity among children and adolescents has widely increased worldwide and it is now one of the most common chronic disorders of all ages. It is imperative when discussing this morbidity to include the discussion of sleep quality and duration. There is a correlation between increased weight gain among adolescents and decreased sleep. An association between body mass index (BMI kg/m^2) and sleep duration found with each additional hour of sleep a teen obtained a correlation with a decrease in BMI (5). This relationship between obesity and sleep is not completely understood; however, there is research that shows that sleep loss is a risk factor for insulin resistance (6).

Indeed, poor sleep can affect overall physical health. In the past few years research has shown that there is a correlation between increased high risk behaviors among adolescents and decreased sleep. The Center for Disease Control reported that four risky behaviors in teenagers including texting while driving, driving and riding in a car after drinking and not using seatbelts were all significantly more common if the teen were to have seven hours or less or sleep (7).

Another study (8) found that there was a decrease in quality of life of adolescents with decreased duration of sleep. Quality of life was defined with characteristics pertaining to sedentary or active lifestyle, eating behavior, physical activity, ability to join in activities and overall feeling sad or worried. Over 3,000 students were followed and there was a direct correlation between what the researchers defined as improved quality of life and increased duration of sleep (8).

Furthermore, research has shown there is also a correlation between depression, suicidality and self-reports of going to bed one hour later than average. The study defined the average sleep duration in adolescents was seven hours and 53 minutes. In this study, parents and students were interviewed on sleep habits. There was also a relationship between parents' low expectation for a specific bedtime and symptoms of depression (9).

The effects on decreased sleep undoubtedly have significant morbidity in the lives of teenagers. How do we begin to change these patterns and discuss with families and teens the importance of developing a healthy sleep pattern? In 1939, Nathanial Kleitman (1895-199), the "father of modern sleep research" was a professor at the University of Chicago and instrumental in early studies of sleep. He coined the term "sleep hygiene" that is commonly used today. Sleep hygiene refers to the behavioral techniques used for the treatment of insomnia. Kleitman also used the early EEG to determine the REM of sleep (10).

THE NEED FOR SLEEP

Adolescents require 9-11 hours of sleep. Most adolescents receive 7-7½ hours of sleep and thus over time develop a "sleep debt" (2, 3). Due to the known circadian rhythm delay in adolescents, many schools have adopted later start dates. The sleep debt that occurs often results in adolescents having a much different weekend sleep pattern than during the week. Although increased sleep on the weekends does allow for teens to decrease their sleep debt, it causes a disruption in sleep routine that can have a negative impact.

There are some basic principles of sleep hygiene for adolescents that should be discussed during every well child check or annual visit as well as during acute visits when applicable. They should wake up and go to bed at about the same time every night. To reinforce this development of a pattern the difference should not be more than an hour between school and non-school nights. Also, by developing this pattern through the week, it can avoid the needed "catch up" on the weekends which, as mentioned previously, can be detrimental when trying to establish a routine. Try to avoid taking naps as these will also cause disruption in the routine which can in turn delay onset of sleep at bedtime. It is always important to incorporate physical activity in the day. Exercise can help with improving sleep onset and duration. Sunlight plays an important role with circadian rhythm and daily exposure is recommended.

It is recommended to use the bed only for sleeping. Often teens will use the bed for doing homework or watching TV, listening to music, etc. It is recommended to start a routine an hour before going to bed. It is recommended to engage in relaxing activities to improve the onset of sleep such as taking a warm shower, listening to relaxing music, or reading. Avoid engaging in activities that involve screens (phones, pads, TV, computers). It is important to avoid eating or drinking late at night especially products that contain caffeine. Of course, abstinence from alcohol and tobacco is recommended for all teens. If an adolescent engages in these behaviors, participating in the prior to bedtime can have a significant disruption on sleep. Caffeine increases neurotransmitters dopamine, serotonin and acetylcholine. It is recommended to abstain from caffeine two hours before expected onset of sleep.

RECOMMENDATIONS

The best recommendation for improving sleep patterns is to develop healthy sleep hygiene and a routine. There are pharmacologic agents used for improving sleep onset and duration. Despite this, the American Academy of Pediatrics published a consensus statement to address pharmacologic treatment of insomnia in children and adolescents. The basis is that there is not enough research to fully understand the long term consequences and it is not recommended to pharmaceuticals for sleep (11). Despite this recommendation there is wide prevalence of the use of melatonin to aid in sleep disturbances. Melatonin is a naturally synthesized hormone made by the pituitary gland and regulated by the hypothalamus. Short term studies show it to be helpful for use in sleep onset (used for a short duration). There are no long term studies and the recommended dose varies: children have been recommended to use between 2.5 mg and 3 mg and adolescents have been recommended to use between 3 mg and 10 mg (11).

CONCLUSION

In summary, poor sleep has been shown to have dramatic effects on many aspects of the adolescent. There is considerable research that shows the deleterious effects sleep restriction has on not only on behavioral health, physical health but possibly even more considering risk taking behaviors. As we continue to learn more how we can improve sleep, it is important to have this discussion frequently with parents, caregivers and patients.

REFERENCES

[1] Colton HR, Altevogt BM, eds. Sleep disorders and sleep deprivation. An unmet public health problem. Washington, DC: National Academic Press, 2006.

[2] Owens JA. Sleep disorders. In: Behrman R, Kliegman R, Jenson H, eds. Textbook of pediatrics. Philadelphia, PA: Saunders, 2004:75-9.

[3] Jenco M. Recommended amount of sleep for pediatric populations. AAP News: American Academy of Sleep Medicine, June 2016.

[4] Hagenauer MH, Perryman JI, Lee TM, Carskadon MA. Adolescent changes in the homeostatic and circadian regulation of sleep. Dev Neurosci 2009;31(4):276-84.

[5] Galland B, Spruyt K, Dawes P, McDowall PS, Elder D, Schaughency E. Sleep disordered breathing and academic performance: A meta analysis. Pediatrics 2015;136(4):e934-46.

[6] Spiegel K, Knutson K, Leproult R, Tasali E, Van Cauter E. Sleep loss: A novel risk factor for insulin resistance and type 2 diabetes. J App Physiology 2005;99(5): 2008-19.

[7] CDC: Lack of sleep associated with risky behaviors. AAP News 2016 Apr 08. URL: http://www.aappublications.org/news/2016/04/08/TeenSleep040816

[8] Chen G, Ratcliffe J, Olds T, Magarey A, Jones M, Leslie E. BMI, health behaviors and quality of life in children and adolescents: A school based study. Pediatrics 2014;133(4):e868-74.

[9] Gangwisch JE, Babiss LA, Malaspina D, Turner JB, Zammit GK, Posner K. Earlier parental set bedtimes as a protective factor against depression and suicidal ideation. Sleep 2010;33(1):97-106.

[10] Wikipedia. Nathaniel Kleitman. URL: https://en.wikipedia.org/wiki/NathanielKleit man.

[11] Mindell J, Emslie G, Blumer J, Genel M, Glaze D, Ivanenko A, et al. Pharmacologic management of insomnia in children and adolescents: Consensus statement. Pediatrics 2006;117(6):e1223-32.

SECTION THREE: SCHOOLS

In: Building Youth for the Future
Editors: H. A Omar and J. Merrick
ISBN: 978-1-53613-768-2

Chapter 16

PREVENTING SUICIDE: WHAT CAN SCHOOLS DO?

Alissa Briggs**, PhD
Division of Adolescent Medicine, UK Healthcare,
Department of Pediatrics, KY Clinic, Lexington,
Kentucky, US

ABSTRACT

It is a school's responsibility to engage in suicide prevention given that suicide is the second leading cause of death for 10-24 year-olds (1) and school is where they spend most of their day. Suicide prevention will be most effective when implemented within the public health model in schools (2-5), or what literature within education refers to as Multi-Tiered Systems of Support (MTSS). In addition, schools should be prepared to implement postintervention, which involves promoting healing and preventing further trauma and suicide after a suicide. This chapter will discuss implementing suicide prevention within MTSS and postintervention in schools.

---

* Correspondence: Alissa Briggs, PhD, Assistant professor, Division of Adolescent Medicine, UK Healthcare, Department of Pediatrics, KY Clinic, Lexington, KY 40536-0284, United States. Email: alissa.briggs@uky.edu.

INTRODUCTION

Suicide is the second leading cause of death for 10-24 year-olds (1), making it a significant public health concern for this age group (6). According to the 2015 national school-based Youth Risk Behavior Survey (YBRS) conducted by the Centers for Disease Control (CDC), 17.7% of high school students indicated they had seriously considered suicide, 14.6% of high school students indicated they made a plan about how they would attempt suicide, 8.6% of students indicated they had attempted suicide, and 2.8% of students indicated they had made a suicide attempt that required medical attention within the past year (7). Thus, in a high school with 1,000 students, it is possible that within one year around 30 students will make a suicide attempt that requires medical attention. Moreover, a survey of members of the National Association of School Psychologists (NASP) in 2008 found that a third of school psychologists reported that a student in their school died by suicide (8).

These data call schools to action to prevent suicide and suicidal behavior (i.e., ideation and attempts). Schools are a natural location for suicide prevention given that they are accessible to all and where the majority of youth spend the majority of their time. In addition, schools are implicitly contracted to protect the safety of their students (9). In accordance with best practice, prevention in schools should be approached through the public health model (2-5), which distinguishes between primary (tier one), secondary (tier two), and tertiary (tier 3) prevention (10, 11). Literature within education often refers to the public health model as Multi-tiered Systems of Support (MTSS), because implementation of the public health model requires coordination amongst school stakeholders to identify needs of varying intensity, develop interventions to meet those needs, and implement interventions at multiple tiers. At tier one, all students would receive an intervention designed to prevent suicide. At tier two, students who are at higher risk for suicide would receive more intensive interventions. Tier three, students at the greatest risk for suicide would receive individualized interventions. Research-based prevention and intervention strategies are used at each tier and systems of data collection and analysis are employed to determine needs (4). Tiers are overlapping, and thus students at tier three still receive interventions at tier one and can also receive interventions at tier two.

There are many resources on suicide prevention in schools. The purpose of this chapter is to highlight these resources, direct readers to them for more in-depth information, and outline school-based suicide prevention at each tier. While the hope is to prevent suicide, the unfortunate truth is that sometimes, despite best efforts, they occur. Thus, a comprehensive approach should also include postintervention, which will also be discussed.

SUPPORTS FOR PREVENTION WITHIN MTSS

Schools are often bombarded with different initiatives (12). Asking a school to implement MTSS to prevent suicide could be overwhelming (13). In order to support implementation, suicide prevention efforts should be integrated into existing initiatives and should flow from collaboration and teaming (9). A team of key players should get together, review existing systems and initiatives that can support suicide prevention, identify gaps, and develop a plan for implementation. The "Preventing suicide: A toolkit for high schools" (9), available for free online by the Substance Abuse and Mental Health Services Administration (SAMHSA) at http://store.samhsa.gov/product/Preventing-Suicide-A-Toolkit-for-High-Schools/SMA12-4669, provides detailed guidance for these steps.

The team of key players should, at a minimum, include someone from the school with mental health expertise and a school administrator. The team may also include various representatives of school stakeholders, such as teachers, parents, community members, students, and support staff. All stakeholders should have a voice and cultural groups should be represented so that prevention and intervention efforts respect the diversity of the school (9, 14). Different groups may have very different beliefs regarding mental health and suicide. The team may wish to work closely with a school crisis team or suicide prevention activities may be assigned to the school crisis team (9). In fact, it may be best to use or adapt an existing team rather than stretching resources to create another team. Once the team is assembled, they should identify their responsibilities and the responsibilities of school staff members in planning and implementing suicide prevention (9).

In order to keep from stretching resources thin and thus threatening implementation, the team charged with suicide prevention activities should review existing resources and initiatives that can support suicide prevention at each tier. The "Preventing suicide" toolkit (9), provides suggestions for how to proceed with this step and links to further resources and tools. Activities in place to promote a positive school climate, prevent bullying and violence, prevent substance abuse, and enhance school engagement fall under the umbrella of suicide prevention because they address risk factors and promote protective factors (9). These can be organized under MTSS to address suicide prevention and the team charged with suicide prevention can support or collaborate in their implementation.

Once existing resources are identified, it will be easier for the team to identify gaps and priorities and then develop a plan for the implementation of suicide prevention within a MTSS. However, before the team moves on to developing the plan, policies to which the school must conform should be reviewed (9). The "Preventing suicide" toolkit (9), provides guidance for identifying such policies. When identifying gaps, if the team finds that the school does not have a protocol for responding to students at risk of suicide, one must be developed before anything else. The school must be prepared to respond because, based on the YBRS, it is likely that around 150 students in a high school of 1,000 students have been at risk of suicide at some point in time over the course of the school year (7). In the toolkit you will also find guidance for developing a protocol to respond to students at risk of suicide (9).

In identifying specific suicide prevention programs to implement, the team should review evidence-based programs on the National Registry of Evidence-Based Programs and Practices (NREPP, see http://www.nrepp.samhsa.gov/) or the Best Practices Registry (BPR, see http://www.sprc.org/bpr) (9). The team should also keep in mind that research on such programs is relatively new and that there is disagreement on their efficacy. A team member versed in reading primary literature on interventions, such as the school psychologist, should critically review the research in addition to identifying programs on the registries. For example, the "Signs of suicide" (SOS) program is on the registries and widely marketed, yet there is debate regarding the strength of the evidence base for its effectiveness in preventing suicide. A review of the program concluded that there is no evidence that its implementation prevents suicide (15).

PRIMARY PREVENTION

Prevention at tier one targets all students and can involve everyone on the school community, but at a minimum involves all students. Typically, direct approaches to prevention at this level include education regarding statistics, risk factors, and warning signs (2). Education also aims to dispel myths and teach how to respond to someone who may be suicidal (2). Indirect approaches to prevention at this level include efforts to reduce risk factors and promote protective factors. Unfortunately, there are few evidence-based prevention programs that can be implemented at this tier. The "Signs of suicide" (SOS) and "Good behavior game" have been found to reduce suicide attempts (16), but a critical review of SOS debates its effectiveness (15). Other programs have not been found to impact suicidal behavior directly, but support protective factors (16). Katz et al. (16) provide a detailed review of primary prevention programs.

Secondary Prevention

Prevention at tier two targets students who are at higher risk for suicidal behavior than the general population of students, but who are not at immediate risk of suicide. The population of students at this tier can include students with depression, anxiety, a substance abuse disorder, or other mental health problem (2). Students at this tier may also include Hispanic females (7), Native American males, students who demonstrate risk for dropping out of high school or being expelled (2, 8), runaway or homeless youth (8), students who identify as lesbian, gay, bisexual, and/or transgender (LGBT), students who are victims of bullying, and students who have experienced trauma (3). A social justice lens highlights that many groups of students at increased risk for suicide are students who experience oppression and victimization. Thus, in layering secondary prevention on primary prevention, primary prevention efforts should aim to reduce the impact of “isms,” like racism, sexism, ableism, and heterosexism on students’ lives within the school environment.

Screening measures may need to be identified or developed in order to identify populations at increased risk. Once students are identified, the team should review existing data to determine the best course of action for each student. It may even be prudent for a team member to meet with students individually to further assess their needs, as students who appear to be at higher risk for suicidal behavior may actually be at greater risk than screening measures indicated or may already be receiving support in the community.

The specific prevention efforts at this tier depend upon the population of students targeted, but will typically be delivered to selected groups. Thus, there may be multiple prevention efforts at tier two given that students may be at risk of suicide for varied reasons. Just like at tier one, prevention efforts should include evidence-based interventions (e.g., cognitive behavioral therapy or a social-emotional curriculum). They could be delivered through group or individual counseling by a school or community based mental health professional.

Tertiary prevention

Prevention at tier three targets students who have engaged in suicidal behavior (e.g., expressed desire to end their life, made a previous attempt). The focus at tier three is to resolve any immediate crisis and address risk for future suicidal behavior (2). Because of the intensity of need at this level, prevention efforts are delivered to individual students and include conducting thorough risk assessments, working with families to link students with the appropriate level of care, and delivering evidence-based mental health interventions. If the appropriate level of care is hospitalization, or if a student was hospitalized for any psychiatric disorder, there should be a plan in place for the student when they return to school in order to support the student in reentering the school environment and from relapsing into suicidal behavior (17). Indeed, an individual is at the greatest risk for suicide in the week after a psychiatric hospitalization for suicidal behavior (18).

From a social justice perspective, this has the potential to be a disempowering process for the student, as their level of risk likely necessitates a break of confidentiality to a caretaker and perhaps a loss of freedom due to hospitalization. Efforts should be made to respect and empower the student throughout the process by clearly explaining the limits of confidentiality, giving him or her the choice to be a part of the conversation in which the caretaker is informed, helping him or her develop a clear picture of what to expect next, and involving him or her in planning supports for his or her return to school. For example, prior to informing a caretaker, rehearse what will be said with the student. Be prepared to explain various treatment scenarios and answer student questions about them. Have a document describing various supports and accommodations upon a student's return to school that a student can review and select.

POSTINTERVENTION

Hopefully prevention at all three tiers is effective in preventing suicide, but they occur despite our best efforts to prevent them. In order to help school community members cope effectively and prevent a suicide contagion in which at risk students are triggered to commit suicide, protocols must be in place for responding to a suicide (i.e., postintervention) (3). Like prevention efforts, postintervention encapsulates all three tiers as it seeks to support the school community and prevent contagion (tier 1), provide mental health interventions for groups at increased risk or who were close to the person who committed suicide (tier 2), and identify and respond to individuals who are having particular difficulty coping or who are at high risk (tier 3). The American Foundation for Suicide Prevention and the Suicide Prevention Resource Center published a toolkit called "After a suicide: A toolkit for schools," which provides detailed guidance and resources for a school team to follow in implementing postintervention (19), and can be found here http://www.sprc.org/sites/sprc.org/files/library/AfteraSuicideToolkitforSchools.pdf.

CONCLUSION

Utilizing MTSS of support to prevent suicide has the potential to have a significant impact suicidal behavior. The Miami-Dade County Public Schools serves as a model for implementing suicide prevention in alignment with MTSS and demonstrates that doing so can relate to significant reductions in suicides (from 5.5 per 100,000 to 1.4 per 100,000) and suicide attempts (from 45.5 per 100,000 to 9 per 100,000) over an eighteen year period (17). However, implementing MTSS is complex process and takes more time and resources than simply implementing a packaged prevention program, which may be only one piece of the puzzle. Thus, schools must accept that while implementing suicide prevention within this model takes time and effective teaming, doing so is the socially just thing to do because all students have access schools and many, especially marginalized populations, struggle with suicidal behavior.

In order to make the investment in the process more palatable, schools should identify priorities for implementation rather than becoming overwhelmed with the whole system at once. While MTSS is organized around numbered tiers, this does not mean that tier one should be implemented first when implementing suicide prevention in schools (5). In fact, gathering a team and developing or reviewing and revising protocols for addressing a student at risk of suicide and responding to a student suicide are critical, as the school must be prepared to respond effectively should a crisis arise (9). Moreover, screening should not take place until a school is ready to effectively respond to a student in crisis (9). Once the school is ready to respond to a crisis, then the school can consider implementing prevention efforts to the school population in general at tier one or specific groups of students at higher risk at tier two. "Preventing suicide" (9) and "After a suicide" (19) provide resources, tools, templates, and detailed guidance to school teams and should be referenced throughout the process.

REFERENCES

[1] Sullivan EM, Annest JL, Simon TR, Luo F, Dahlberg LL, Centers for Disease C, et al. Suicide trends among persons aged 10-24 years--United States, 1994-2012. MMWR 2015;64(8):201-5.

[2] Miller DN, Eckert TL, Mazza JJ. Suicide prevention programs in the schools: A review and public health perspective. Sch Psychol Rev 2009;38(2):168-88.

[3] Lieberman R, Poland S, Korfield C. Best practices in suicide prevention and intervention. In: Harrison PL, Thomas A, eds. Best practices in school psychology: Systems-level services. Bethesda, MD: National Association of School Psychologists, 2014:273-88.

[4] Ysseldyke J, Burns M, Dawson P, Kelly B, Morrison D, Ortiz S, et al. School psychology: A blueprint for training and practice III. Bethesda, MD: National Association of School Psychologists, 2006.

[5] Desrochers JF, Houck GM. Depression: A quiet crisis. Principal Leadership 2013;4:12-6.

[6] Crepeau-Hobson F. An exploratory study of suicide risk assessment practices in the school setting. Psychol Sch 2013;50(8):810-22.

[7] CDC. Youth risk behavior surveillance: United States, 2015. MMWR 2016;65(6): 1-180.

[8] Berman AL. School-based suicide prevention: Research advances and practice implications. Sch Psychol Rev 2009;38(2):233-8.

[9] Administration SAaMHS. Preventing suicide: A toolkit for high schools. Rockville, MD: Center for Mental Health Services, Substance Abuse and Mental Health Services Administration, 2012.

[10] Sugai G. Promoting behavioral competence in schools: A commentary on exemplary practices. Psychol Sch 2007;44(1):113-8.

[11] Walker HM, Horner RH, Sugai G, Bullis M, Sprague JR, Bricker D, et al. Integrated approaches to preventing antisocial behavior patterns among school-age children and youth. J Emot Behav Disord 1996;4(4):194-209.

[12] Sarason S. Revisiting "the culture of the school and the problem of change." New York: Teachers College Press, 1996.

[13] Senge P. The fifth discipline: The art and practice of the learning organization. New York: Doubleday; 1990.

[14] North CE. More than words? Delving into the substantive meaning(s) of "social justice" in education. Rev Educ Res 2006;76(4):507-35.

[15] Wei Y, Kutcher S, LeBlanc JC. Hot idea or hot air: A systematic review of evidence for two widely marketed youth Suicide prevention programs and recommendations for implementation. J Can Acad Child Adolesc Psychiatry 2015;21(1):5-16.

[16] Katz C, Bolton SL, Katz LY, Isaak C, Tilston-Jones T, Sareen J, et al. A systematic review of school-based suicide prevention programs. Depress Anxiety 2013;30(10):1030-45.

[17] Zenere FJ. The sustained reduction of youth suicidal behavior in an urban, multicultural school district. Sch Psychol Rev 2009;38(2):189-99.

[18] Qin P, Nordentoft M. Suicide risk in relation to psychiatric hospitalization: Evidence based on longitudinal registers. Arch Gen Psychiatry 2005;62(4):427-32.

[19] Center AFfSPaSPR. After a suicide: A toolkit for schools. Newton, MA: Education Development Center, 2011.

In: Building Youth for the Future ISBN: 978-1-53613-768-2
Editors: H. A Omar and J. Merrick

Chapter 17

SCHOOL HEALTH PROGRAMS AS A MEANS OF SUICIDE PREVENTION

Eva Stone**, MSN, APRN
Jefferson County Public Schools, Director Health Services,
Louisville, Kentucky, US

ABSTRACT

Suicide is an ongoing problem in American adolescents. According to 2015 Youth Risk Behavior Survey (YRBS) data, 1 in 7 high school students in Kentucky has seriously considered suicide in the past twelve months and 1 in 5 middle school students reported they had seriously considered killing themselves in their lifetime. While there are some requirements for education regarding suicide prevention among middle and high school staff and students, there is no consistent school-based intervention which has significantly decreased suicide rates in the United States. In addition there is no requirement in Kentucky for nurses or other health staff to be present in schools. Poor school attendance can be indicative of psychopathology. A consistent process of screening children for at-risk behaviors and connecting them with appropriate referrals and treatment can lead to improved outcomes for middle and high school students in Kentucky.

* Correspondence: Eva Caseman Stone, MSN, APRN, Jefferson County Public Schools 4309 Bishop Lane, Louisville KY, 40218, United States. Email: eva.stone@jefferson.kyschools.us.

Introduction

Education is one of the strongest predictors of long term health. Successful education can increase longevity, prevent sickness, decrease risk-taking behaviors and reduce health disparities (1-3) Chronic absenteeism, defined as missing ten percent or more of school, can be predictive of school failure and dropout (4) and a possible indicator of mental health concerns (2). In the earliest years students who miss ten percent or more of school are less likely to read at the expected level by the end of third grade and more likely to be retained (4). Chronically absent high school students are less likely to enroll and stay in college after graduating (4). Although many factors impact school attendance, research shows the presence of school nurses performing targeted activities can help decrease absenteeism. In 2016-2017 over 17,000 children (grades K -12) in Jefferson County missed 10% or more of school. (5) thus increasing their risk for school failure or dropout, potential risk for mental illness (2) and likelihood of poor health.

An important solution to absenteeism is the presence of school nurses. Studies by Jacobson et al. (6), Rodriguez et al. (7), Telljohann et al. (8) and Telljohann et al. (9) showed improved school attendance when a nurse was present throughout the school day and Allen, Pennington and Delaney (10) and Wyman (11) showed that fewer students were dismissed from school when nurses were present. Case management, asthma programs and family support are all interventions that decrease the amount of school missed (12-15). Case management and family support are interventions that can lead to increased identification of mental illness and/or suicidal ideations.

Prevention and Intervention

In Kentucky, school health services must be provided by a physician, advanced practice registered nurse, registered nurse or licensed practical nurse, a non-licensed health technician that has the health services identified as part of his/her job or a school employee who is delegated responsibility for health services (16).There is no requirement for health licensed health care providers to be present throughout the school day, or requirement for screening of adolescents for suicide risk.

School nurses can be key identifiers of mental illness, risk taking behaviors or suicidal thoughts. Somatic complaints in teenagers often translate to underlying depression or anxiety. Interaction with registered nurses in schools can lead to the development of relationships for vulnerable children.

The Perkins Adolescent Risk Screen (PARS) is a 16 item assessment for risk and protective factors in children which has been validated as an instrument to assess these elements (17). The PARS is conducted in a 1:1 interview between an adolescent and adult which takes 7-10 minutes to complete. Registered nurses can easily conduct these screenings during interactions with students or through a scheduled program to screen children who are exhibiting high incidence of absenteeism from school.

An increased focus on school absenteeism secondary to the "Every Student Succeeds Act" (ESSA) (18) in the United States will enhance emphasis on student attendance. This is an opportunity for schools to acknowledge the need for additional health personnel in schools and measures to intervene when students have a high incidence of absence from school. Screening can help identify risk-taking behaviors in children as well as suicidal thoughts or ideations and decrease the consideration or completion of suicide in adolescents.

CONCLUSION

In conclusion, schools are an ideal place to provide health services for children. The presence of registered nurses who can screen at-risk children for risk and protective behaviors can help identify those students in need of referral for additional care. Community partnerships with local providers and health care systems are essential to meet the needs of the whole child. Poor school attendance is a risk factor for mental health concerns including anxiety and depression which place children at increased risk for suicide.

Targeting those children with screening programs can decrease the incidence of youth suicide, suicidal thoughts and improve overall school performance.

REFERENCES

[1] Youth Risk behavior survey. YRBSS results, 2015. URL: https://www.cdc.gov/healthyyouth/data/yrbs/results.htm.

[2] Wood JJ, Lynne-Landsman SD, Langer DA, Wood PA, Clark SL, Eddy JM, et al. School attendance problems and youth psychopathology: structural cross-lagged regression models in three longitudinal data sets. Child Dev 2012;83(1):351-65.

[3] Freudenburg N, Ruglis J. Reframing school dropout as a public health issue. Preventing chronic disease. Public Health Res Pract Policy 2007;4(4):1-11.

[4] Attendance works. Chronic absence: Our top pick for the ESSA school quality or student success indicator, a policy brief, 2016. URL: http://www.attendanceworks.org/wordpress/wp-content/uploads/2016/08/ESSA-Brief_083016-1.pdf.

[5] Jefferson County Public Schools. Data books, 2016-2017. Chronic absenteeism. URL: https://www.jefferson.kyschools.us/departments/data-management-research/data-books.

[6] Jacobsen K, Meeder L, Voskuil VR. Chronic student absenteeism. NASN Sch Nurs 2016;31(3):178-85.

[7] Rodriguez E, Rivera D, Periroth D, Becker E, Wang N. School nurse's role in asthma management, school absenteeism, and cost-savings. A demonstration project. J Sch Health 2013;(83)12:842-50.

[8] Telljohann SK, Dake JA, Price JH. Effect of full-time versus part-time school nurses on attendance of elementary students with asthma. J Sch Nurs 2004;20(6):331-4.

[9] Telljohann SK, Price JH, Dake JA, Durgin J. Access to school health services: Differences between full-time and part-time school nurses. J Sch Nurs 2004;20(3);176-81.

[10] Allen G. The impact of elementary school nurses on student attendance. J Sch Nurs 2003;19(4);225-31.

[11] Wyman LL. Comparing the number of ill or injured students who are released early from school by school nursing and nonnursing personnel. J Sch Nurs 2005;21(6), 350-355.

[12] Bonaiuto MM. School nurse case management: achieving health and educational outcomes. J Sch Nurs 2007;23(4):202-9.

[13] Cicutto L, To T, Murphy S. A randomized controlled trial of a public health nurse-delivered asthma program to elementary schools. J Sch Health 2013;83(12):876-84.

[14] Kerr J, Price M, Kotch J, Willis S, Fisher M, Silva S. Does contact by a family nurse practitioner decrease early school absence? J Sch Nurs 2012;28(1):38-46.
[15] Long G, Whitman C, Johansson M, Williams C, Tuthill R. Evaluation of a school health program directed to children with high history of absence. Am J Public Health 1975;65(4):388-93.
[16] Health services in school setting-designated provider-liability protection, 2014. URL: http://www.lrc.ky.gov/Statutes/statute.aspx?id=42933.
[17] Adams CD, Perkins KC, Lumley V, Hughes C, Burns JJ, Omar HA. Validation of the Perkins Adolescent Risk Screen (PARS). J Adolesc Health 2003;33(6):462-70.
[18] US Department of Education. Every student succeeds act. URL: https://www.ed.gov/esea.

In: Building Youth for the Future ISBN: 978-1-53613-768-2
Editors: H. A Omar and J. Merrick

Chapter 18

WELCOMING AND SAFE SCHOOLS/ COMMUNITIES FOR LGBTQ YOUTH

Nicole A Begg*[*], PhD, NCSP
Division of Adolescent Medicine, Department of Pediatrics,
University of Kentucky, Lexington, Kentucky, US

ABSTRACT

Many adolescents encounter obstacles on their path to adulthood that may include family problems, school stress, peer pressure, and poor self-esteem. For LGBTQ youth, these challenges are often intensified due to harassment, discrimination, and bullying. It has been established that LGBTQ youth are at significant risk relative to non-LGBTQ peers for poor educational outcomes, homelessness, adverse health outcomes, and experiences with violence. Though they represent a smaller percentage of the school population, they are at greater risk for victimization, mental health problems, and suicide highlighting the need for safe schools and communities for LGBTQ youth. This chapter describes the prevalence of risk and poor outcomes for LGBTQ youth and the institutional barriers

[*] Correspondence: Assistant professor Nicole A Begg, PhD, Division of Adolescent Medicine, Department of Pediatrics, University of Kentucky, Lexington, KY 40536-0284, United States. Email: Nicole.Begg@uky.edu.

they face but also provides strategies for safeguarding youth including universal and targeted supports to ensure that they are protected and affirmed in their schools and communities.

INTRODUCTION

Multiple challenges confront today's youth that may include family problems, school stress, peer pressure, and poor self- esteem. For lesbian, gay, bisexual, transgender, and queer (LGBTQ) youth, prejudice, stigma, and discrimination potentially magnify and exacerbate these psychosocial stressors. LGBTQ youth experience threats to safety and face rejection by others that can disrupt developmental tasks that mark adolescence. Adjusting to puberty, moving toward independence, developing deeper peer relationships, understanding and expressing complex emotions, establishing aspects of identity, and acquiring personal values and beliefs are not simple tasks. Navigating this journey is particularly arduous for LGBTQ youth who are vulnerable to discrimination and violence. Basic human needs for safety, security, and belongingness underscore the importance of welcoming and safe schools/communities for LGBTQ youth.

EXPERIENCES OF LGBTQ YOUTH

All individuals require safety to survive and acceptance to thrive. However, LGBTQ youth often encounter physical assault, verbal harassment, and biased language that can negatively affect their physical and mental health and adversely influence their educational outcomes and overall well-being. The 2015 National School Climate Survey investigated the experiences of 10,528 students in grades 6 through 12 from schools across the US Distressing numbers of LGBTQ students perceived their school climate as hostile due to a number of factors (1). Concerns about feeling unsafe at school were reported by more than 57.6% due to sexual orientation; and 43.3% due to gender expression. Nearly 60% reported being sexually harassed at school while 13% reported being physically assaulted. More than 48% indicated that they were cyberbullied. It is markedly concerning that over 63% who reported these incidents at school said no action was taken in response to their report. Further, nearly 58% who were harassed or assaulted chose not to report due to fear that the situation would worsen or distrust that the school would intervene effectively. According to results, high numbers of anti-LGBT remarks were heard at school and included remarks from school staff. LGBTQ students also reported discriminatory school policies and practices pertaining to disciplinary procedures, dress code, participation in extra-curricular activities, and school functions.

It is no surprise that a hostile environment at school is associated with poor educational outcomes and social-emotional problems for LGBTQ youth, according to the 2015 National School Climate Survey (1). LGBTQ students who experienced discrimination based on sexual orientation or gender identity were at least three times more likely to have been absent from school in the past month relative to those who did not experience discrimination. Further, they also had lower grade point averages, were less likely to report plans to pursue higher education, incurred a greater number of disciplinary actions, had lower self-esteem, lower school belonging, and higher levels of depression. School policies and practices that contribute to hostile school climate were reported as a significant factor in 32% of LGBTQ student's consideration or plans of dropping out.

According to the Centers for Disease Control and Prevention, the second leading cause of death of young persons aged 10-24 is suicide (2). Relative to non-LGB youth, LGB youth are three times more likely to seriously contemplate suicide and five times more likely to have attempted suicide (3). Further, research has shown that LGB youth suicidality is associated with family acceptance or rejection of their sexual orientation. LGB youth whose families are highly rejecting were at 8.4 times greater risk of suicidality than LGB whose families were more accepting (4). With respect to victimization, each occurrence of physical or verbal harassment increases the risk by 2.5 times on average that LGBT youth will engage in self-harm (5).

Safeguards for LGBTQ youth: Knowledge and awareness

The onus is on everyone, families, peers, educators, medical providers, mental health professionals, law enforcement, government officials, and communities to support and protect LGBTQ youth. Increased knowledge and awareness is the foundation for creating safe schools and communities for LGBTQ youth. Familiarity with sexual identity and gender identity development, LGBTQ language and terminology, multicultural competence, and overcoming personal bias are the building blocks that foster acceptance and appreciation of sexual and gender diversity.

Sexual and gender identity

Assumptions and misunderstandings persist regarding sex, sexual orientation, gender identity, and gender expression. The American Psychological Association has defined these terms based on developing conceptual understandings of sexual orientation and gender diversity. Sex is typically categorized as male, female, or intersex and refers to biological status indicated by sex chromosomes, gonads, internal reproductive organs, and external genitalia (6). Biological sex assigned at birth is not always male or female but may also be categorized as intersex. Some infants are born with characteristics of both male and female biological and anatomical traits. Intersex refers to being born with variations in male and female biological markers. Sexual orientation is defined as sexual and romantic attraction, which may include attraction to members of the other sex, members of one's own sex, members of both sexes, or members outside of the gender binary of "male" and "female" (6). Gender identity is defined as an individual's internal sense of self as male, female, or something else (6). Gender identity and sex do not always align with one another. For individuals whose sex assigned at birth and gender identity do not align, they may identify as transgender or along the transgender spectrum (6, 7). Gender expression refers to how an individual chooses to present aspects of gender identity or role that may include physical appearance, clothing and accessories, and behaviors (6). Gender expression and gender identity may not necessarily be congruent with one another.

Language and terminology

The foundation of understanding and connection with others begins with communication. Sharing a common language conveys respect and affirmation, whereas an unwillingness to do so communicates disdain or rejection. Words have the power to bring people together or create division and cause pain. Therefore, ensuring that schools and communities are safe and welcoming requires use of language that affirms LGBTQ youth. The National LGBT Health Education Center, a program of the Fenway Institute, Glossary of LGBT Terms for Health Care Teams provides a relevant list of terminology (8). However, it is important to be aware that language evolves and terms/definitions do change. LGBT glossaries are also available through Amnesty International (9) and the Human Rights Campaign (10). GLAAD, an advocacy organization whose mission is cultural change to promote acceptance through entertainment, news, and digital media, published an online media reference guide that includes a glossary of lesbian, gay, bisexual, and queer terms but also specifies terms to avoid and defamatory language (11).

LGBTQ youth deserve the dignity and respect to be called by their preferred name and preferred pronouns. When making introductions, consider stating your preferred pronouns along with your name to communicate acceptance. For example, "My name is Nicole. My preferred pronouns are she, her, hers. What do you like to be called?" Some individuals may be uncertain of how to ask the question but doing so conveys genuine interest and sensitivity to others' needs and is likely to be well received by LGBTQ youth.

Avoid gendered terms and use gender-neutral language to communicate acceptance and inclusivity. Instead of "mother" or "father," use "parent" to recognize that adolescents' families are diverse and they may have same-sex parents. Use of the terms "boyfriend" or "girlfriend" makes assumptions about sexual preference. Consider asking open-ended questions such as, "Are you in a relationship? Do you like boys, girls, or both?" Taking the time to choose words carefully reduces the chances of alienating LGBTQ youth during verbal exchanges.

Multicultural competence

Understanding the myriad ways that multiple minority identities intersect and complicate sexual identity and gender identity is important in establishing safe, welcoming schools/communities for LGBTQ youth. Intersectionality refers to the merging of multiple identities for members of historically oppressed groups that may include race/ethnicity, limited English proficiency, refugee/immigration status, religious affiliation, disability, socioeconomic status, and sexual orientation/gender identity (12). It has been well established that membership in any one of these marginalized groups is associated with inequity but the intersection of multiple identities significantly increases the likelihood of discrimination and oppression. For example, Rosario et al. 2004 found that fewer Black and Latino LGB youth disclosed their sexual identity than did White youths (13). LGBTQ racial minority youth report having to choose either their sexual or ethnic identity and fewer are involved in LGB social activities when compared to white youth who are LGBTQ (13,14). According to Wade et al. (15), LGBTQ youth of Asian American and Pacific Islander descent feel that they have shamed their families if they do not marry and have children in accordance with cultural expectations (15). In schools, specifically, Black students are disproportionately suspended relative to White students (16), LGBTQI2-S youth are overrepresented in the criminal justice system, particularly racial minority youth and females (17). Racial minority and religious minority students are more likely to experience bias and harassment in schools and immigrant or refugee students are at higher risk for bullying because many are members of racial/religious minority groups (18).

Addressing a single aspect of marginalization without considering the cumulative effects of intersecting identities is insufficient. Rather, schools and communities must view LGBTQ students through a broader lens to acknowledge differences and address complex needs. For any person, sexual identity and gender identity are just two of many aspects that make each one unique.

Overcoming personal bias – self-reflection

If we are to work to ensure that schools and communities are safe and affirming for LGBTQ youth, we must explore and acknowledge our own personal biases. There are a number of policies, practice parameters, position statements, and professional ethics principles that reference the importance of addressing implicit biases through self-examination, training, and/or consultation. (19-23). There are many questions that one might consider to assess personal attitudes that affect our perceptions, interactions, and behaviors. What overt and covert messages about sexual orientation and gender identity did I receive growing up? What factors influenced these messages? What stereotypes do I hold about LGBTQ people? How do these stereotypes shape my interactions? Upon initial meeting, do I assume that a person is cisgender or heterosexual? Have I ever had to worry about negative consequences because of someone discovering my sexual orientation or gender identity? What steps have I taken to educate myself about LGBTQ students and their experiences at school and in my community? Do I believe that LGBTQ youth have the right to be out and open at school and in their community? Through careful introspection, we can increase our awareness of attitudes and stereotypes we hold and be intentional about reducing opportunities for biases to operate or compensate for biases.

Implicit biases are subconscious, involuntary, and inaccessible through introspection. Project Implicit is a non-profit organization and international collaboration between researchers who are interested in implicit social cognition – thoughts and feelings outside of conscious awareness and control (24). The mission of the organization is to educate the public about hidden biases and to provide a "virtual laboratory" for collecting data on the Internet. The Implicit Association Test (IAT) is a well-validated measure that is designed to assess the strengths of associations between concepts (e.g., black people, gay people) and evaluations (good, bad) or stereotypes (athletic, clumsy) (25). Many different IAT tests are available for individuals to learn more about their covert biases, including tests that measure social attitudes toward or beliefs about sexual orientation and gender. Individuals who take the IAT are encouraged to attempt to compensate or use strategies to reduce the chances that implicit biases influence decisions.

In summary, families, peers, educators, medical providers, mental health professionals, law enforcement, government officials, and community members have the power and the responsibility to protect and support LGBTQ youth. Understanding that sexual and gender diversity exist on a spectrum and using gender-neutral, inclusive language and preferred names and pronouns conveys to LGBTQ youth that they are understood, respected, and valued. Developing multicultural competence with attention to intersecting identities and attending to personal bias with self-reflection combats pervasive negative attitudes and threats to the safety of LGBTQ youth.

BREAKING DOWN INSTITUTIONAL BARRIERS

No child should face unfair treatment yet LGBTQ youth experience restricted access to freedoms and are singled out based on their sexual and gender diversity. In 2016, the Human Rights Watch interviewed over 500 students, teachers, administrators, parents, service providers, and advocates in Alabama, Pennsylvania, South Dakota, Texas, and Utah and documented problems LGBT youth experience in US schools (26). They found that LGBTQ youth are unable to access information about LGBT topics at school whether by talking to school staff or searching for materials in the school library or school-based information technology. School staff are reluctant to engage students in classroom discussion about LGBT topics and, when they do, they tread carefully due to fear of backlash or lack of education. When discussion and debate is initiated, LGBTQ youth may be silenced, redirected, or disciplined. Furthermore, they report being put in unfair positions that they must defend or open themselves up to scrutiny. One might expect that these limitations relate to health/sex education; however, this extends to LGBT themes in English, history, civics, and psychology. Findings indicated that state law expressly prohibits discussion of LGBT topics at school in eight US states including Alabama, Texas, and Utah. Further, the Human Rights Watch found that gay/straight alliances are subject to more requirements and restrictions as compared to non-LGBTQ peers. Further, LGBTQ encounter more obstacles from school administration to form and operate a gay/straight alliance. Overall, these institutional barriers single out LGBTQ youth from their non-LGBTQ peers and communicate the negative message that they are not okay as they are.

Legal protections

Laws and policies that prohibit discrimination based on sexual orientation and gender identity/expression exist at the federal, state, and local levels. Advocates for LGBTQ youth need to be familiar with these protections as well as school district policies in order to be a strong voice in ensuring safe and welcoming schools/communities.

At the broadest level, the Fourteenth Amendment of the US Constitution includes the Equal Protection Clause (§ 1983), which guarantees equal protection for all people (27). Therefore, LGBTQ youth are entitled to the same protections and treatment afforded to their non-LGBTQ peers. As such, it holds that schools cannot single out LGBTQ students when it comes to discipline, participation in school activities, or protections from discrimination or harassment. State constitutions hold similar protections for all. LGBT students surveyed reported incurring disciplinary infractions for public displays of affection; and reported unfair discipline based solely on being LGBT (1). Federal level protections include Title IX of the Educational Amendments of 1972 (20 U.S.C. §1681), which expressly addresses sexual harassment of students. Further, constitutional protections of the first amendment guarantee LGBTQ students' basic liberties including freedom of speech, assembly, and petition. Non-LGBTQ individuals have the right to voice support for LGBTQ youth in schools and communities. LGBTQ youth have the right to express their gender identity, to write about LGBTQ issues in the student newspaper, to have access to educational materials related to LGBTQ issues, and to advertise and convene LGBTQ groups in the same manner as other student clubs. Further, if a school receives federal funding, under the Equal Access Act (US § 4071), LGBTQ groups or clubs must be permitted to meet on school property if the school allows any other extracurricular group or club to meet on school property. Despite explicit protections, LGBT students surveyed indicated that they were not permitted to focus on LGBT topics in assignments or in extracurricular activities, they were not allowed to bring a date of the same gender to a school dance, they were prohibited from wearing clothes supporting LGBT issues, and they were discouraged from participating in school sports (1).

Though state laws vary, state constitutions contain equal protections similar to the US Constitution. There has been a shift to protect LGBTQ youth from discrimination and harassment in schools by explicitly addressing sexual orientation and gender identity/expression in the state laws. While some states require school boards to enact specific policies to protect LGBTQ youth, other states have not expressly mentioned sexual orientation or gender identity/expression but have antibullying laws. Therefore, based on equal protections, LGBTQ and non-LGBTQ youth must be equally protected. However, eight in ten LGBTQ students surveyed reported that their school's policies or practices were discriminatory based on sexual identity or gender identity/expression; whereas two-thirds reported that they had experienced discriminatory policies personally (1). Research has shown that lesbian and gay youth living in communities with fewer antibullying policies specific to sexual orientation and gender identity are two times more likely to report suicide attempts in the past year than youth who live in communities with targeted policies (27). The ever-changing landscape of state law requires that advocates for LGBTQ youth keep current with local legislation. Lambda Legal (https://www.lambdalegal.org) and the Human Rights Campaign (www.hrc.org) are two resources committed to civil rights that maintain up to date information on state laws as well as specific antidiscrimination and antibullying policies at the local and district level.

At the local level, advocates for safe and welcoming schools/ communities can get involved by attending school board meetings or being active in city or municipal government. Other useful strategies might include consulting with school officials and becoming familiar with legal resources in the community.

Need for safe spaces

According to Merriam Webster, a safe space is a place intended to be free of bias, conflict, criticism, or potentially threatening actions, ideas, or conversations. While laws and protections for LGBTQ youth afford safety and equal protections and access, they do not guarantee safe spaces. At least two-thirds to one-half of LGBTQ students surveyed in the US heard homophobic, derogatory remarks such as "gay," "fag," or "dyke" (1). More than half of those surveyed heard homophobic remarks from school staff. Nearly two-thirds of students surveyed reported that they frequently heard disapproving remarks about gender expression such as not behaving in a manner that is "masculine enough" or "feminine enough." (1). Further, students surveyed reported minimal intervention by school staff when overhearing homophobic or derogatory remarks about gender expression

(1). Significant numbers of students surveyed also reported commonly hearing sexist or racist remarks at school (1).

PROMOTE SOCIAL CHANGE

Family members, peers, educators, medical providers, mental health professionals, law enforcement, government officials, and community advocates all have a responsibility to take an active role to ensure the safety and well-being of LGBTQ youth. There are countless ways that key allies of LGBTQ youth can make positive and lasting change in schools and communities. Efforts focused on celebrating diversity, inclusion, and affirmation are universally beneficial and foster a positive climate in schools and communities. Minority stress theory (28, 29) posits that poor mental health outcomes for LGBTQ youth are related to the additive effects of prejudice, discrimination, and victimization in addition to universal stressors. Therefore, school-wide and community-wide efforts to reduce or eliminate stigma associated with prejudice, discrimination, and victimization can positively influence overall climate as well as moderate harmful stressors that are associated with poor mental health.

Universal supports

Core programs and strategies that benefit all students, regardless of sexual or gender identity/expression, are universal supports. The goal of universal supports is to promote student success and prevent negative outcomes. School-wide policies that protect LGBTQ youth and improve school climate include staff training in diversity/inclusion, positive behavior intervention supports that address bullying, and incorporating topics of diversity/inclusion into the curriculum.

Fisher and Kennedy (30) and Kosciw et al. (1) found that implementation of inclusive school policies that outline specific protections for LGBTQ students is the most important step that a school can take to affirm and protect LGBTQ students. A comprehensive policy that explicitly safeguards students based on actual or perceived sexual orientation and gender identity/expression should outline unacceptable behaviors, consequences for violation of the policy, standardized protocols for handling violations, and disciplinary actions. All school staff, students, and parents need to be aware of the policy and it must be consistently enforced (30, 31).

In a study that surveyed teachers, administrators, and school counselors about their attitudes and knowledge about LGBTQ students, respondents reported limited awareness of LGBTQ student issues, policies, and identities (32). Whitman (33) reported a lack of training across educational disciplines in LGBTQ issues in preparation programs and, thus, the need for professional development. Trainings should focus on knowledge of LGBTQ language and terminology, of sexual development and gender identity development, and the school experiences and outcomes for LGBTQ youth (33). Awareness of personal biases and attitudes about LGBTQ students should be explored by staff to determine how their assumptions may influence their beliefs and to encourage openness and questioning (33). Finally, training should address several skills including how to increase visibility as a support, how to respond to harassment and bullying, how to incorporate LGBTQ topics in classroom activities and curricula, and how schools can provide supportive, affirmative counseling to LGBTQ students.

Efforts devoted to bullying prevention and intervention initiatives have yielded modest results (34). However, the role of bystanders is an area of increased interest in the research (35). Although this research has not focused specifically on LGBTQ students, elements are consistent with positive behavior intervention supports (PBIS). PBIS is a framework for school wide discipline with an emphasis on defining, explicitly teaching, and rewarding appropriate behavior to create a positive school culture (36). Teaching prosocial behaviors and on practicing how to intervene appropriately when witnessing bullying are social-emotional skills that should be embedded in the PBIS framework.

In recent years, there has been increasing attention devoted to appreciating and celebrating diversity. Efforts to be more inclusive and address diversity in educational curricula have generally focused on race, ethnicity, culture, or language (30). LGBTQ students can feel invisible unless schools are intentional about integrating LGBTQ topics into the curriculum. Educators have endless ideas and creativity when it comes to designing curriculum, though they may be limited by having to follow specific guidelines. Educators might consider using language that is reflective of LGBTQ terminology on written materials for class, studying historical events/civil rights movement through the LGBTQ lens, exploring the LGBTQ voice in history, art, literature, media, music, etc. Using inclusive and gender-neutral language in the classroom communicates inclusivity and expands acceptance beyond the heteronormative perspective.

Targeted supports

For students that are unsuccessful with universal supports, targeted supports are indicated. Targeted supports are secondary strategies aimed at providing a more intensive focus and may be individualized to meet a student's specific needs. Secondary supports might include Gay-Straight Alliances, community agencies, and counseling.

Gay-Straight Alliances are student-led groups at school that support LGBTQ students and all students (37). According to the GLSEN 2015 National School Survey, LGBTQ students who had a GSA at their school reported that they were less likely to hear derogatory or homophobic remarks, were more likely to report that school staff intervened when hearing homophobic remarks, experienced lower levels of victimization related to LGBTQ status, felt safer, reported greater numbers of supportive staff and accepting peers, and felt more connected to their school than students who did not have a GSA at their school (1). Gay Straight Alliances provide LGBTQ students with social support from peers where they can learn how to celebrate individuality, to handle challenges, to explore their identity, and to access LGBTQ information. Student members of Gay-Straight Alliances often get involved in community activism or participate in important events or celebrations such as Pride.

Access to community resources can serve as a protective factor for LGBTQ youth. Helping youth connect with agencies, national or local organizations, or advocacy groups provides them with an array of services that schools may not be able to offer. LGBTQ youth who are not out to many others often feel isolated and achieve a sense of belonging when they are able to connect with others who are accepting and affirming. The Gay Lesbian Straight Education Network (GLSEN) is an organization whose mission is to create safe and affirming schools for all, regardless of sexual orientation, gender identity, or gender expression (www.glsen.org). GLSEN offers resources for students and for educators and provides information about policy and research related to LGBTQ issues. The Trevor Project provides crisis intervention and suicide prevention for LGBTQ youth and offers a variety of supports including crisis intervention via phone, chat, or text and a social networking site (http://www.thetrevor project.org). The Trevor Project website has a support center with access to frequently asked questions and resources related to sexual orientation and gender identity. LGBTQ youth may also need access to community homeless shelters or healthcare providers so it is important to be familiar with local resources in the community.

Intensive supports may be indicated for LGBTQ youth who are struggling with significant psychosocial stressors or mental health issues. Youth who are referred for counseling often seek help for issues related to exploring their sexual orientation or gender identity, coping with family stressors, handling peer difficulties, and treatment of mood disturbance or anxiety that may or may not be related to their LGBTQ status. Counseling may provide a supportive environment where LGBTQ youth can explore their identity at their own pace and process their thoughts and feelings. Common issues that arise might include shifting identities, exploring positive or negative internalized messages about LGBTQ people, coping with stigma, prejudice, harassment, or bullying, building self-esteem, and making connections with LGBTQ community.

For LGBTQ youth who exhibit warning signs for suicidality, immediate intervention is critical. Suicide warning signs might include talking about or threatening to hurt or kill oneself, looking for ways to kill oneself by seeking access to firearms, pills, or other means, talking or writing about death, dying or suicide, feeling hopeless, feeling rage or uncontrolled anger or seeking revenge, acting reckless or engaging in risky activities, feeling trapped, increasing alcohol or drug use, withdrawing from friends, family, and society, feeling anxious, agitated, or unable to sleep, or sleeping all the time, experiencing dramatic mood changes, and/or seeing no reason for living or having no sense of purpose in life (38). Crisis intervention for LGBTQ youth at high risk necessitates a risk assessment by a trained mental health or medical professional who can make a determination about the youth's safety and immediate medical and mental health needs. There are many actions that family members, peers, educators, law enforcement, government officials, and community advocates can take to prevent suicide. Talking about suicide, providing support, directing LGBTQ youth to help (crisis hotline, crisis center, counseling resources), reducing access to means of self-harm, following up with loved ones, and providing support services can prevent suicides and save lives (39).

CONCLUSION

LGBTQ youth have the right to feel safe and welcome in their schools and communities where they are free from discrimination, harassment, and victimization. All youth are entitled to a free and appropriate education and the pursuit of life, liberty, and happiness. Many of the poor outcomes experienced by LGBTQ youth are not related to perceptions of their own sexual or gender identity but the experience of stigma, prejudice, and discrimination that they experience based on their sexual orientation or gender identity/expression. Though LGBTQ youth represent a relatively small percentage of the school/community population, they are at greater risk for victimization, mental health problems, and suicide. Thus, it is critical that families, peers, educators, mental health/medical professionals, law enforcement, and communities to advocate for these vulnerable youth and celebrate diversity and inclusivity. By doing our part to ensure that schools and communities are welcoming and safe, we can make a positive difference in the lives of LGBTQ youth.

REFERENCES

[1] Kosciw JG, Greytak EA, Giga NM, Villenas C, Danischewski DJ. The experiences of lesbian, gay, bisexual, transgender, and queer youth in our nation's schools. The 2015 National School Climate Survey, 2016. URL: https://www.glsen.org.

[2] CDC. Web-based injury statistics query and reporting system (WISQARS). Available at http://www.cdc.gov/injury/wisquars/index.html.

[3] James SE, Herman JL, Rankin S, Keisling M, Mottet L, Anafi M. (2016). The report of the 2015 U.S. transgender survey. Washington, DC: National Center for Transgender Equality.

[4] Family Acceptance Project. Family rejection as a predictor of negative health outcomes in white and Latino lesbian, gay, and bisexual young adults. Pediatrics. 2009:123(1):346-52.

[5] IMPACT. Mental health disorders, psychological distress, and suicidality in a diverse sample of lesbian, gay, bisexual, and transgender youths. Am J Public Health. 2010:100(12):2426-32.

[6] American Psychological Association. Definitions related to sexual orientation and gender diversity in APA Documents. American Psychological Association. URL: https://www.apa.org/pi/lgbt/resources/sexuality-definitions.pdf.

[7] Gainor KA. Including transgender issues in lesbian, gay, and bisexual psychology: Implications for clinical practice and training. In: Greene B, Croom GL, eds. Psychological perspectives on lesbian and gay issues: Vol 5: Education, research, and practice in lesbian, gay, bisexual, and transgendered psychology: A resource manual. Thousand Oaks, CA: Sage, 2000:131-60.

[8] National LGBT Health Education Center. Glossary of LGBT terms for health care teams, 2016. URL: https://www.lgbthealtheducation.org/wp-content/uploads/LGBT-Glossary_March2016.pdf.

[9] Amnesty International USA. LGBT Glossary. URL: LGBT Glossary - Amnesty International USA.

[10] Human Rights Campaign. Glossary of terms. URL: https://www.hrc.org/resources/glossary-of-terms.

[11] GLAAD. GLAAD Media Reference Guide: Lesbian/Gay/Bisexual Glossary of Terms. URL: GLAAD Media Reference Guide - Lesbian / Gay / Bisexual Glossary.

[12] National Association of School Psychologists. Understanding intersectionality. [handout]. Bethesda, MD: NASP, 2017.

[13] Rosario M, Schrimshaw EW, Hunter J. Ethnic/racial differences in the coming out process of lesbian, gay, and bisexual youths: a comparison of sexual identity development over time. Cultural Diversity Ethnic Minority Psychol 2004;10(3): 215-28.

[14] Dube E, Savin-Williams RC. Sexual identity development among sexual minority male youths. Dev Psychol 1999;35(6):1389-98.

[15] Wade S, Watt SE, Mo B. Cultural expectations and experiences: three views. Open Hands 1991;6(3):8-9.

[16] African American Policy Forum. Black girls matter: Pushed out, over policed and under protected, 2014. URL: https://static1.squarespace.com/static/53f20d90e4b0b80451158d8c/t/54dcc1ece4b001c03e323448/1423753708557/AAPF_BlackGirlsMatterReport.pdf.

[17] Center for American Progress, Movement Advancement Project and Youth First. Unjust: LGBTQ youth incarcerated in the juvenile justice system, 2017. URL: http://lgbtmap.org/file/lgbtq-incarcerated-youth.pdf.

[18] Bridging Refugee Youth and Children's Services. (n.d.). Refugee children in U.S. schools: A toolkit for teachers and school personnel. Retrieved from http://www.brycs.org/documents/upload/bullying.pdf.

[19] Adelson SL, ed. Practice parameter on gay, lesbian, or bisexual sexual orientation, gender nonconformity, and gender discordance in children and adolescents. J Am Acad Child Adolesc Psychiatry 2012;51(9):957-74.

[20] Association of Lesbian, Gay, Bisexual, and Transgender Issues in Counseling. Competencies for counseling with transgender clients. Alexandria, VA: Author, 2009.

[21] Haldeman D. Guidelines for psychological practice with lesbian, gay, and bisexual clients. Am Psychologist 2012;67(1):10-42.

[22] Anonymous. National Association of School Psychologists Principles for Professional Ethics. Sch Psychol Rev 2010;39(2):302-19.

[23] Estrada R, Marksamer J. The legal rights of LGBT youth in state custody: What child welfare and juvenile justice professionals need to know. Child Welfare 2006;85(2):171-94.

[24] Project Implicit. URL: https://implicit.harvard.edu/implicit/.

[25] Greenwald AG, McGhee DE, Schwartz JLK. Measuring individual differences in implicit cognition: The Implicit Association Test. J Pers Soc Psychol 1998;74(6):1464–80.

[26] Human Rights Watch. Like walking through a hailstorm: Discrimination against LGBT youth in US Schools, 2016. URL: https://www.hrw.org/report/2016/12/07/walking-through-hailstorm/discrimination-against-lgbt-youth-us-schools.

[27] Hatzenbuehler ML, Keyes KM. Inclusive anti-bullying policies and reduced risk of suicide attempts in lesbian and gay youth. J Adolesc Health 2013;53:S21–6.

[28] Meyer IH. Minority stress and mental health in gay men. J Health Soc Behav 1995;36:38–56.

[29] Meyer IH. Prejudice, social stress, and mental health in lesbian, gay, and bisexual populations: conceptual issues and research evidence. Psychol Bull 2003;129:674–97.

[30] Fisher E, Kennedy K. Responsive school practices to support lesbian, gay, bisexual, transgender, and questioning students and families. New York: Routledge, 2012.

[31] Fisher E. Best practices in supporting students who are lesbian, gay, bisexual, transgender, and questioning. In: Thomas A, Grimes J, eds. Best practices in school psychology. Bethesda, MD: National Association of School Psychologists, 2008.

[32] Mollura J. School personnel attitudes and knowledge towards LGBTQ students, 2017. URL: https://digitalcommons.brockport.edu/edc_capstone/49.

[33] Whitman JS. Training school professionals to work with lesbian, gay, bisexual, transgender, and questioning students and parents. In: Fisher ES, Komosa-Hawkins K, eds. Creating safe and supportive learning environments: A guide for working with lesbian, gay, bisexual, and questioning youth and families. New York: Routledge, 2013:123-39.

[34] Merrell KW, Gueldner BA, Ross SW, Isava DM. How effective are school bullying intervention programs: A meta-analysis of intervention research. Sch Psychol Quart 2008;23:26-42. doi:10.1037/1045-3830.23.1.26.

[35] Espalage DL, Rao MA. Safe schools: Prevention and intervention for bullying and harassment. In: Fisher ES, Komosa-Hawkins K, eds. Creating safe and supportive learning environments: A guide for working with lesbian, gay, bisexual, and questioning youth and families. New York: Routledge, 2013:140-55.

[36] OSEP Technical Assistance Center on Positive Behavioral Interventions and Supports (2017). Positive Behavioral Interventions & Supports [Website]. Retrieved from www.pbis.org.

[37] Kennedy, KS. Accessing community resources: Providing support for all. In: Fisher ES, Komosa-Hawkins K, eds. Creating safe and supportive learning environments: A guide for working with lesbian, gay, bisexual, and questioning youth and families. New York: Routledge, 2013:243-55.

[38] Substance Abuse and Mental Health Services Administration. Suicide prevention [Website]. Retrieved from https://www.samhsa.gov/suicide-prevention.

[39] The National Suicide Prevention Lifeline. We can all prevent suicide. [Website]. Retrieved from https://suicidepreventionlifeline.org/how-we-can-all-prevent-suicide/

In: Building Youth for the Future ISBN: 978-1-53613-768-2
Editors: H. A Omar and J. Merrick

Chapter 19

TRAUMA SENSITIVE SCHOOLS: A SAFE HOME FOR ALL STUDENTS

Alissa Briggs**, *PhD
Division of Adolescent Medicine, UK Healthcare, Department of Pediatrics, KY Clinic, Lexington, Kentucky, US

ABSTRACT

Estimates of the percentage of the population who have experienced a traumatic childhood experience varies. What is clear is that a large percentage of the population have experienced at least one adverse event during childhood. Given that stress can interfere with a child or adolescent's development in multiple domains, it is the responsibility of the school to create a trauma-sensitive environment and implement trauma-informed care.

---

* Correspondence: Alissa Briggs, PhD, Assistant professor, Division of Adolescent Medicine, UK Healthcare, Department of Pediatrics, KY Clinic, Lexington, KY 40536-0284, United States. Email: alissa.briggs@uky.edu.

INTRODUCTION

In the literature on trauma-informed schools, Adverse Childhood Experiences (ACEs) are commonly referenced. An ACE is a stressful or traumatic event that occurs during childhood (first 18 years of life) (1). They include abuse, neglect, and household changes. The Centers for Disease Control and Prevention (CDC) regularly assesses the number of ACEs in the general population. Their most recent ACEs survey data suggest that 26% of the population have experienced an ACE, and about 12.5% of the population have experienced four or more (1).

There are more opporutnities for traumatic and stressful events than what are assessed by an ACEs questionnaire, because trauama can result from any actual or perceived harm to one's well-being (2). Trauma requires the occurrence of a stressful event, plus the inability to cope, and impairment in daily functioning (2). This may explain why estimates of adverse experiences during childhood are even higher in other studies. Eric Rossen and Katherine Cowan cite studies with prevalence estimates near 70% (3).

However, we need to give children and adolescents credit. They can be incredibly resilient the face of adverse experiences. Few develop post-traumatic stress disorder (3). That being said, adversity can affect their academic, social, emotional, and behavioral well-being (3). If adversity is driving academic failure and acting out behaviors, increasing instruction and discipline will not work (4). A continuum of supports for students who have experienced adverse events is necessary in order to minimize the impact of trauma and teach children and adolescents skills that will help them manage life's stressors as they age.

In education, a continuum of supports for children and adolescents who have experienced adverse events can fall under Multi-tiered Systems of Supports (MTSS) (5). Throughout this continuum exists an underlying *philosophy*. At each tier in the continuum there are *systems* that support evidence-based *practices* whose efficacy is evaluated through *data* on a variety of *outcomes* (5). The literature generally addresses three tiers within MTSS. Tier 1 generally includes low intensity preventative interventions for all. Tier 2 generally consists of moderate intensity interventions for some. Tier 3 generally consists of high intensity interventions for a few.

The underlying approach and philosophy and examples of practices at each tier will be discussed. Examples of systems and resources for implementing these systems are provided. However, it is up to each individual school to research different approaches, determine outcomes they would like to address, identify data sources they can monitor, and create teaming structures and systems to support identified practices that they would like to implement. There is no one, clear prescribed path to this work (6). However, there are guiding questions, a recommended philosophy, and evidence-based practices.

APPROACH AND PHILOSOPHY

The Substance Abuse and Mental Health Services Administration (SAMHSA) outlined a recommended approach for implementing trauma-informed practices in any organization, called the four "R's" (7). The four "R's" serves as a common language for trauma-informed service-delivery so that schools and other organizations have a guide to follow throughout this complex systems change process (5). The four "R's" dictate that those within the school system *realize* the impact of trauma and understand potential avenues for recovery, *recognize* the signs and symptoms of trauma in others, *responds* by integrating knowledge of trauma into policies, procedures, and practices, and *resists* re-traumatization (7). The response to trauma in schools can take place at each tier (5). All individuals involved in the school system should receive education such that they understand the impact of trauma and potential for recovery and can identify signs and symptoms of trauma. All school policies should be reviewed to ensure that they do not unwittingly re-traumatize students. Discpline practices, such as corporeal punishment and suspension, are a common source of retraumatization.

The four "R's" support a necessary philosophical shift. A philosophical shift that must occur is a change in mentality from "what is wrong with you?" to "what happened to you?" (8). When the question is "what happened to you?", the blame for the maladaptive behavior is taken away from the child or adolescent and the adults who care for them at school and at home are more compassionate and open to finding ways to support them.

PRIMARY PREVENTION

Primary prevention, or tier one, includes practices that support all students and staff (5, 8). Systems at this level include those that support positive behavior supports (system for teaching and acknowledging expected behavior), restorative justice, and instruction in appropriate social behavior and emotion regulation (social-emotional learning curricula) (5, 8). Overall, it is critical that these systems and the practices they support create a welcome, supportive community where students feel connected to others in order to ameliorate the sense of disconnection many children who have experienced trauma feel (6). Simple things that a school can do to create the sense of a welcome, supportive community are to have school personnel greet students warmly as they arrive and school and to have every teacher greet students at the door before class. Schools can also create tip-lines and counseling drop-in times so that students can communicate concerns and reach out for support. Moreover, at this tier, teachers and other school professionals need to be prepared to administer psychological first aid (5). Anyone at any time can experience a stressful event and need brief support. Websites with information regarding these systems mentioned in this paragraph are listed in the appendix.

Regular professional development is also a necessary component of tier one, and should include training in trauma-sensitive practices as well as strategies for staff and caregivers to address their own stress (8). Working in a school where the majority of children have experienced adverse events and are depicting behavioral symptoms of trauma can be draining and lead to burn-out. Raising a child with signs and symptoms of trauma is also stressful. Teachers, other school professionals, and caregivers need to learn how working with trauma-impacted children and adolescents affects their own well-being and identify and implement self-care strategies so that they can be mentally and emotionally present for the children and adolescents who need their support (8).

SECONDARY PREVENTION

Secondary prevention, or tier two, includes practices that support students at-risk of developing a trauma and stressor related disorder or students who may be having difficulty emotionally, behaviorally, or socially but whose needs could be met through group intervention (5,8). A group intervention could include a supportive adult in the school working with a group of students to set and monitor goals (behavioral and academic) and progress (e.g., Check and Connect and Check-in/Check-out) and cognitive behavioral therapy delivered in a group therapy setting (e.g., Cognitive Behavioral Intervention for Trauma in Schools [CBITS], Support for Students Exposed to Trauma (SSET), and Multimodal Trauma Treatment [MMT]). Again, teachers, school staff, and caregivers are included in secondary prevention (8). Supports for them may include wellness groups, support groups, and even group exercise and/or yoga classes after school. Links for more information on recommended group interventions for students at this tier are included in the appendix.

TERTIARY PREVENTION

Tertiary prevention, or tier three, includes practices that support students who are experiencing signs and symptoms consistent with a trauma and stressor related disorder and require individualized support (5, 8). The gold standard at this tier is cognitive behavioral therapy (5). Cognitive behavioral therapy delivered in groups (tier two) or individually (tier three) is evidence-based and time-limited, and thus ideal for school-based delivery (5). The cognitive behavioral therapy interventions mentioned above under secondary prevention can be delivered individually. In addition, trauma-focused cognitive behavioral therapy (tf-CBT) is an intervention with a strong evidence base (5). A link to a web-based course in tf-CBT is provided in the appendix. The cost of the course is minimal ($35) compared to the number of resources and continuing education credits (11) provided.

Adults may also depict signs and symptoms of secondary trauma that require individual support. Adults can experience symptoms of a trauma and stressor related disorder due to exposure to traumatic material they may encounter when working with children and adolescents who have experienced traumatic events (9). They may wish to engage in cognitive behavioral therapy with their own individual therapist. Mindfulness Based Stress Reduction (MBSR) can also be a great way for adults experiencing signs and symptoms of secondary trauma to reduce stress at their own pace and in line with their own busy schedules. A free eight week mindfulness based stress reduction course is available here: https://palousemindfulness.com/.

EXAMPLE

The University of California, San Francisco's Healthy Environments and Response to Trauma in Schools (HEARTS) Program is an excellent example of the creation of trauma-informed schools using MTSS (8). The UCSF HEARTS program collaborates with schools and districts to create trauma-informed schools. In the study referenced above, they collaborated with San Francisco Unified School District. Of note is that before their work with schools could begin, principals had to buy-in (e.g., "…believe that social emotional skills and wellness is crucial to academic achievement, and that addressing trauma would help promote school success" (7).) and there needed to be a coordinated care team that included key school stakeholders who met regularly (8). Leadership and an existing method of working with those who represent the school are critical to beginning systems change. When implementing trauma-informed care within MTSS, which included supports for adults and children, Dorado et al. (8) found that school personnel's knowledge about trauma and trauma sensitive practices and indicators of student engagement increased. They found that behavioral incidents involving physical aggression decreased by 32% after one year and 86% after five years (8). Out of school suspensions decreased by 95% (8). And, importantly, students with trauma symptoms experienced a reduction in their symptoms (8).

CONCLUSION

Creating a trauma-sensitive school environment within MTSS can support the well-being of children and foster resilience in the face of traumatic stress. However, doing so requires systems change – a complex and challenging endeavor that takes time (6). In order for such an endeavor to move forward, there must be: a) consensus on the part of the school administration and faculty that implementing trauma-informed service delivery is necessary, b) professionals within the school or who can work closely with the school with expertise in trauma, and c) professional development for all faculty and staff. In order to determine if a school is ready to begin the important journeying of implementing trauma-informed practices, and to assess progress along the way, the Attitudes Related to Trauma-Informed Care (ARTIC) scale can be used (see http://traumaticstressinstitute.org/artic-scale/).

Other resources include *Helping Traumatized Children Learn* (see https://traumasensitiveschools.org/). In volume two of *Helping Traumatized Children Learn*, there are four guiding questions that can be used when creating a trauma-sensitive school (6). These are:

1) Why do we feel an urgency to become a trauma-sensitive school?
2) How do we know we are ready to create a trauma sensitive school?

3) What actions will address staff priorities and help us become a trauma sensitive school?
4) How do we know we are becoming a trauma sensitive school?

In fact, both volumes of *Healing Traumatized Children Learn* (6, 10) are free and a necessary read before beginning the process of creating a trauma-sensitive school. They recognize and address the challenge of changing a school culture and the time it takes to do so. Changing the school culture is necessary if a school is going to become a trauma-sensitive learning community (6).

While it is clear that this journey is a challenging process that takes time, doing so will foster academic, social, emotional, and behavioral growth and prevent the behavioral incidents that add stress to a teacher's and administrator's work day. There is no doubt that there are students in each school who have experienced adverse events and who are having difficulty regulating their emotions and behaviors so that they can learn, and thus it is the responsibility of the school to create an environment that can promote resilience so that children and adolescents can enter adulthood with the skills they need.

REFERENCES

[1] Centers for Disesase Control and Prevention, Kaiser Permanente. The ACE studey survey data [unpublished data]. US Department of Health and Human Services, Centers for Disease Control 2016. URL: https://www.cdc.gov/violenceprevention/acestudy/about.html.

[2] Blaustein M. Childhood trauma and a framework for intervention. In: Rossen E, Hull R, eds. Supporting and educationing traumatized students: A guide for school-based professionals. New York: Oxford University Press, 2013:3-21.

[3] Rossen E, Cowan K. The role of schools in supporting traumatized students. Principal's Res Rev 2013;8(6):1-8.

[4] Porche MV, Constello DM, Rosen-Reynoso M. Adverse family experiences, child mental health, and educational outcomes for a national sample of students. Sch Ment Health 2016;8:44-60.

[5] Chafouleas SM, Johnson AH, Overstreet S, Santos NM. Toward a blueprint for trauma-informed service delivery. Sch Ment Health 2016;8:144-62.
[6] Cole SF, Eisner A, Gregory M, Ristuccia J. Helping traumatized children learn: Creating and adovcating for trauma-sensitive schools. Boston, MA: Massachusetts Advocates for Children, 2013.
[7] Substance Abuse and Mental Health Services Administration. SAMHSA's concept of trauma and guidance for a trauma-informed approach. Rockville, MD: Substance Abuse and Mental Health Services Administration, 2014.
[8] Dorado JS, Martinez M, McArthur LE, Leibovitz T. Healthy environments and response to trauma in schools (HEARTS): a whole-school, multi-level, prevention and intervention program for creating trauma-informed, safe and supportive schools. Sch Ment Health 2016;8:163-76.
[9] National Child Traumatic Stress Network. Secondary traumatic stress. URL: http://www.nctsn.org/resources/topics/secondary-traumatic-stress.
[10] Cole SF, O'Brien JG, Gadd MG, Ristuccia J, Wallace DL, Gregory M. Helping traumatized children learn: A report and policy agenda. Boston, MA: Massachusetts Advocates for Children, 2005.

APPENDIX

Primary Prevention

- Positive Behavior Interventions and Supports: http://www.pbis.org/
- Restorative Justice: https://www.edutopia.org/blog/restorative-justice-resources-matt-davis
- Social-Emotional Learning: https://casel.org/

Secondary Prevention

- Check and Connect: http://checkandconnect.umn.edu/
- Check-in/Check-out: https://www.interventioncentral.org/behavior_management_check_in_check_out

- Cognitive Behavioral Intervention for Trauma in Schools (CBITS): https://cbitsprogram.org/
- Support for Students Exposed to Trauma (SSET): http://sset program.org/
- Multimodal Trauma Treatment (MMT): http://www.nctsnet.org/ nctsn_assets/pdfs/promising_practices/MMTT_General.pdf

Tertiary Prevention

- Trauma-Focused Cognitive Behavioral Therapy (tf-CBT): https:// tfcbt2.musc.edu/
- Secondary Traumatic Stress: http://www.nctsn.org/resources/ topics/secondary-traumatic-stress.

SECTION FOUR: ACKNOWLEDGMENTS

In: Building Youth for the Future ISBN: 978-1-53613-768-2
Editors: H. A Omar and J. Merrick

Chapter 20

ABOUT THE EDITORS

Hatim A Omar, MD, FAAP, Professor of Pediatrics and Obstetrics and Gynecology; Professor of Family Studies; and Chief of the Division of Adolescent Medicine, Department of Pediatrics, University of Kentucky, Lexington. He is the holder of the Children's Miracle Network Endowed Chair in Pediatrics. Dr. Omar has completed residency training in obstetrics and gynecology as well as pediatrics. He has also completed fellowships in vascular physiology and adolescent medicine. Dr. Omar is the founder and chairman of the Stop Youth Suicide Campaign. He is the recipient of the Commonwealth of Kentucky Governor's Award for community service and volunteerism in 2000, Kentucky Teen Pregnancy Coalition Award for outstanding service 2002, Awards for suicide prevention from the Ohio Valley Society for Adolescent Medicine and Kentucky Pediatric Society in 2005 and 2007, Sexual Abuse Awareness Month Award for his work with sexual abuse victims from the Kentucky Association of Sexual Assault Professionals in 2007, Special Achievement Award from the American Academy of Pediatrics 2007 and the Founders of Adolescent Medicine Award from the AAP in 2007. He is well known internationally with numerous publications in child health, public health, pediatrics, adolescent medicine, pediatric and adolescent gynecology. Email: haomar2@uky.edu

Joav Merrick, MD, MMedSci, DMSc, born and educated in Denmark is professor of pediatrics, Division of Pediatrics, Hadassah Hebrew University Medical Center, Mt Scopus Campus, Jerusalem, Israel and Kentucky Children's Hospital, University of Kentucky, Lexington, Kentucky United States and professor of public health at the Center for Healthy Development, School of Public Health, Georgia State University, Atlanta, United States, the former medical director of the Health Services, Division for Intellectual and Developmental Disabilities, Ministry of Social Affairs and Social Services, Jerusalem, the founder and director of the National Institute of Child Health and Human Development in Israel. Numerous publications in the field of pediatrics, child health and human development, rehabilitation, intellectual disability, disability, health, welfare, abuse, advocacy, quality of life and prevention. Received the Peter Sabroe Child Award for outstanding work on behalf of Danish Children in 1985 and the International LEGO-Prize ("The Children's Nobel Prize") for an extraordinary contribution towards improvement in child welfare and well-being in 1987. In 2017 appointed a Kentucky Colonel by the Commonwealth of Kentucky, the highest honor the governor can bestow to a person. Email: jmerrick@zahav.net.il

In: Building Youth for the Future
Editors: H. A Omar and J. Merrick
ISBN: 978-1-53613-768-2

Chapter 21

About the Division of Adolescent Medicine, Kentucky Children's Hospital at the University of Kentucky, Lexington, Kentucky, United States

The Kentucky Children's Hospital is the only facility in central and eastern Kentucky dedicated to the expert medical and surgical care of infants, children and adolescents. The University of Kentucky (UK) has a proud and distinguished history of providing comprehensive programs and innovative care to the children of the region. Although patients are referred from every county of the Commonwealth of Kentucky and from every adjacent state, the majority of patients are from the Bluegrass region around Lexington and from Appalachian counties in the eastern part of Kentucky. The Department of Pediatrics has provided service and education from the opening of UK College of Medicine in 1961.

The passion for teaching is palpable at the Kentucky Children's Hospital. Most years about 15% of our graduates or more choose to train in pediatrics. The University of Kentucky had one of the earliest combined Internal Medicine-Pediatrics residency program with "med-peds" graduates very well represented throughout the faculty. This, in addition to a strong adolescent medicine program, is among factors which have led to a focus upon adolescent and adult graduates of pediatric care from Kentucky Children's Hospital.

The approach at the Kentucky Children's Hospital (KCH) is focused on family-centered care. Full-time child life coverage, facilities for families to stay with children overnight, age-appropriate playrooms, children's library facilities, in-hospital school services, a dedicated television channel, a computer laboratory and many other features provide the special environment to provide the best of care for children. The Kentucky Children's Hospital includes a 12-bed Pediatric Intensive Care Unit, a 66 bed Level 3 Neonatal Intensive Care Unit, 44 acute care pediatric beds, a 26 bed normal newborn nursery, and an 8 bed short stay admissions/observation unit. KCH has grown from about 3,750 discharges per year in 2004 to about 5,400 in 2009.

Pediatric medical and surgical outpatient facilities are primarily located in the Kentucky Clinic, which is attached to the hospital. Each year, the pediatric clinic has over 46,000 patient visits. Of these, over 15,300 patient visits are in the general pediatric and continuity clinics, over 17,400 occur in the various subspecialty clinics. Kentucky Children's Twilight Clinic is open all but two days of the year in addition to the state-of –the-art pediatric emergency center.

Specialty care includes medical and surgical cardiac care, endocrinology, pediatric kidney disease, developmental pediatrics, pediatric allergy and immunology, solid organ transplantation, behavioral pediatrics, pediatric emergency medicine, intensive care pediatrics, neonatology, gastroenterology and hepatology, dysmorphology, biochemical genetics, pediatric rheumatology, oncology, hematology, infectious diseases, hospitalist care, adolescent medicine, adolescent gynecology, child neurology, pediatric surgery, pediatric orthopedics, pediatric imaging, child psychiatry, pediatric anesthesiology, pediatric otorhinolaryngology, speech disorders, pediatric pathology, pediatric physical medicine, pediatric neurosurgery and many other fields. The Young Parents Program is an innovative service of the Adolescent

Medicine Division, which has been very successful. Many of these specialties cover outreach clinics throughout underserved Appalachian counties of Kentucky as well as in Lexington. New facilities are in preparation, because of the remarkable growth in clinical programs for children.

The growth of clinical programs and service capability has been matched by considerable growth in pediatric research at UK. Substantial programs in vascular biology and diabetes, pediatric inflammatory biology, molecular pediatrics, developmental biology, pediatric health policy research, epidemiology, prevention, cancer research and pediatric pharmacology are growing rapidly. The Kentucky Children's Hospital is located on the UK campus. Access to faculty in the other colleges including social sciences and humanities enhances the Kentucky Children's Hospital scholarly environment and provides unique opportunities for collaborative work.

As we approach our 50th year anniversary, we remain committed to improving the lives and health of young people of the Commonwealth and improving the future for their families.

DIVISION OF ADOLESCENT MEDICINE

The Division of Adolescent Medicine was founded in 1998 to provide state of the art care for adolescent patients from all areas of the commonwealth of Kentucky, to serve as a state wide resource for education and training for local providers on adolescent issues, to study specific factors on the local level affecting youth in the state, to help teach medical students and residents and to provide community service to help improve teen future in the commonwealth.

The division provides comprehensive, holistic team approach to adolescents, where teens receive all aspects of care from mental health to routine care from a team of professionals including physicians, mental health providers, social workers, psychologists, nutritionists and nursing staff. One unique program within the division is the Young Parent

Program, where pregnant teens are cared for throughout pregnancy then they and their babies are cared for together in the program.

The division is active in research with many peer reviewed articles published each year as well as several books and special journal editions.

In the community, the program has founded several grass route programs to help prevent youth suicide, teen pregnancy, accidental death and substance abuse among adolescents in Kentucky.

The division has provided more than 300 lectures, workshops, media events and teaching for community providers, parents, teachers and school counselors. It also provides advocacy work on behalf of teens with active work at the state legislative and executive government as well as local governments to help improve the lives of teens.

COLLABORATIONS

The Division of Adolescent Medicine collaborates locally with school boards, youth service centers, state and local governments, other universities and child advocacy centers as well as with regional adolescent medicine programs.

Internationally with the Institute for Child Health and Human Development in Israel, the Division of Adolescent Medicine at Santa Casa University, Brazil, Quality of Life Research Center and Nordic School of Holistic Health, Copenhagen, Denmark, Department of Applied Social Sciences, The Hong Kong Polytechnic University, Hong Kong.

THE VISION

The vision of the Division of Adolescent Medicine is to improve the health and long term wellbeing of Kentucky Youth to grow into productive adults. We also envision global work to help positive youth development world wide.

TARGET AREAS OF INTERESTS

The interest areas of the division are all aspects of youth development and adolescent health with focus on prevention and community involvement in collaboration on the local, national and global level with programs having the same goal.

CONTACT

Hatim Omar, MD, FAAP
Professor of Pediatrics and Obstetrics/Gynecology
Director of Adolescent Medicine & Young Parent programs
J422, Kentucky Clinic
Department of Pediatrics, Kentucky Children's Hospital
University of Kentucky College of Medicine
Lexington, KY 40536
Email: haomar2@uky.edu
Website: http://www.mc.uky.edu/

In: Building Youth for the Future ISBN: 978-1-53613-768-2
Editors: H. A Omar and J. Merrick

Chapter 22

The Annual "Stop Youth Suicide" Conference, Lexington, Kentucky, United States

In October 2000, the Stop Youth Suicide Campaign was launched (see stopyouthuicide.com) with the following goals in mind:

- Increase awareness about youth suicide in the community, schools and homes
- Advocacy to create state wide suicide prevention
- Develop a grassroots program to actually reduce teen suicide completions and attempts

As part of the effort, a state conference was held in February 2001. Although we never had actual funding, we still wanted parents, teens and school personnel to be able to attend at little or no cost. I recruited caring experts from around the world to help by being speakers with no financial compensation. The initial conference was a great success, which led me to organize another one in November 2001 and to make it an annual event since.

The conference is held in the month of November each year in Lexington, Kentucky, generally the 1st week unless there is a conflict with other events in the city.

A total of 18 conferences have been held since then and every topic related to teen health is usually addressed. We want to educate people about teen development, and the factors leading to risky behavior including suicide. Throughout the years, we have always been filled to capacity and the evaluations are always very positive.

Moving forward, we will continue to update participants on the newest knowledge about teens and engage the community as a whole in overall prevention of risk behavior.

CONTACT

Hatim Omar, MD, FAAP
Professor of Pediatrics and Obstetrics/Gynecology
Director of Adolescent Medicine & Young Parent programs
J422, Kentucky Clinic
Department of Pediatrics, Kentucky Children's Hospital
University of Kentucky College of Medicine
Lexington, KY 40536
Email: haomar2@uky.edu
Website://www.mc.uky.edu/

In: Building Youth for the Future ISBN: 978-1-53613-768-2
Editors: H. A Omar and J. Merrick

Chapter 23

About the National Institute of Child Health and Human Development in Israel

The National Institute of Child Health and Human Development (NICHD) in Israel was established in 1998 as a virtual institute under the auspices of the Medical Director, Ministry of Social Affairs and Social Services in order to function as the research arm for the Office of the Medical Director. In 1998 the National Council for Child Health and Pediatrics, Ministry of Health and in 1999 the Director General and Deputy Director General of the Ministry of Health endorsed the establishment of the NICHD.

Mission

The mission of a National Institute for Child Health and Human Development in Israel is to provide an academic focal point for the scholarly interdisciplinary study of child life, health, public health, welfare, disability, rehabilitation, intellectual disability and related aspects of human development. This mission includes research, teaching, clinical work, information and public service activities in the field of child health and human development.

SERVICE AND ACADEMIC ACTIVITIES

Over the years many activities became focused in the south of Israel due to collaboration with various professionals at the Faculty of Health Sciences (FOHS) at the Ben Gurion University of the Negev (BGU). Since 2000 an affiliation with the Zusman Child Development Center at the Pediatric Division of Soroka University Medical Center has resulted in collaboration around the establishment of the Down Syndrome Clinic at that center. In 2002 a full course on "Disability" was established at the Recanati School for Allied Professions in the Community, FOHS, BGU and in 2005 collaboration was started with the Primary Care Unit of the faculty and disability became part of the master of public health course on "Children and society". In the academic year 2005-2006 a one semester course on "Aging with disability" was started as part of the master of science program in gerontology in our collaboration with the Center for Multidisciplinary Research in Aging. In 2010 collaborations with the Division of Pediatrics, Hadassah Hebrew University Medical Center, Jerusalem, Israel around the National Down Syndrome Center and teaching students and residents about intellectual and developmental disabilities as part of their training at this campus.

RESEARCH ACTIVITIES

The affiliated staff have over the years published work from projects and research activities in this national and international collaboration. In the year 2000 the International Journal of Adolescent Medicine and Health and in 2005 the International Journal on Disability and Human Development of De Gruyter Publishing House (Berlin and New York) were affiliated with the National Institute of Child Health and Human Development. From 2008 also the International Journal of Child Health and Human Development (Nova Science, New York), the International Journal of Child and Adolescent Health (Nova Science) and the Journal of Pain Management (Nova Science) affiliated and from 2009 the International Public Health Journal (Nova Science) and Journal of Alternative Medicine Research (Nova Science). All peer-reviewed international journals.

NATIONAL COLLABORATIONS

Nationally the NICHD works in collaboration with the Faculty of Health Sciences, Ben Gurion University of the Negev; Department of Physical Therapy, Sackler School of Medicine, Tel Aviv University; Autism Center, Assaf HaRofeh Medical Center; National Rett and PKU Centers at Chaim Sheba Medical Center, Tel HaShomer; Department of Physiotherapy, Haifa University; Department of Education, Bar Ilan University, Ramat Gan, Faculty of Social Sciences and Health Sciences; College of Judea and Samaria in Ariel and in 2011 affiliation with Center for Pediatric Chronic Diseases and National Center for Down Syndrome, Department of Pediatrics, Hadassah Hebrew University Medical Center, Mount Scopus Campus, Jerusalem.

INTERNATIONAL COLLABORATIONS

Internationally with the Department of Disability and Human Development, College of Applied Health Sciences, University of Illinois at Chicago; Strong Center for Developmental Disabilities, Golisano Children's Hospital at Strong, University of Rochester School of Medicine and Dentistry, New York; Centre on Intellectual Disabilities, University of Albany, New York; Centre for Chronic Disease Prevention and Control, Health Canada, Ottawa; Chandler Medical Center and Children's Hospital, Kentucky Children's Hospital, Section of Adolescent Medicine, University of Kentucky, Lexington; Chronic Disease Prevention and Control Research Center, Baylor College of Medicine, Houston, Texas; Division of Neuroscience, Department of Psychiatry, Columbia University, New York; Institute for the Study of Disadvantage and Disability, Atlanta; Center for Autism and Related Disorders, Department Psychiatry, Children's Hospital Boston, Boston; Department of Pediatric and Adolescent Medicine, Western Michigan University Homer Stryker MD School of Medicine, Kalamazoo, Michigan, United States; Department of Paediatrics, Child Health and Adolescent Medicine, Children's Hospital at Westmead, Westmead, Australia; International Centre for the Study of Occupational and Mental Health, Düsseldorf, Germany; Centre for Advanced Studies in Nursing, Department of General Practice and Primary Care, University of Aberdeen, Aberdeen, United Kingdom; Quality of Life Research Center, Copenhagen, Denmark; Nordic School of Public Health, Gottenburg, Sweden, Scandinavian Institute of Quality of Working Life, Oslo, Norway; The Department of Applied Social Sciences (APSS) of The Hong Kong Polytechnic University Hong Kong.

TARGETS

Our focus is on research, international collaborations, clinical work, teaching and policy in health, disability and human development and to establish the NICHD as a permanent institute in Israel in order to conduct model research and provide policy aspects in the field of interest.

CONTACT

Professor Joav Merrick, MD, MMedSci, DMSc
Former Medical Director, Health Services, Division for Intellectual and Developmental Disabilities, Ministry of Social Affairs and Social Services, POB 1260, IL-91012 Jerusalem, Israel. Email: jmerrick@zahav.net.il

In: Building Youth for the Future ISBN: 978-1-53613-768-2
Editors: H. A Omar and J. Merrick

Chapter 24

ABOUT THE BOOK SERIES "PEDIATRICS, CHILD AND ADOLESCENT HEALTH"

Pediatrics, child and adolescent health is a book series with publications from a multidisciplinary group of researchers, practitioners and clinicians for an international professional forum interested in the broad spectrum of pediatric medicine, child health, adolescent health and human development.

- Merrick J, ed. *Child and adolescent health yearbook 2011*. New York: Nova Science, 2012.
- Merrick J, ed. *Child and adolescent health yearbook 2012*. New York: Nova Science, 2012.
- Roach RR, Greydanus DE, Patel DR, Homnick DN, Merrick J, eds. *Tropical pediatrics: A public health concern of international proportions*. New York: Nova Science, 2012.
- Merrick J, ed. *Child health and human development yearbook 2011*. New York: Nova Science, 2012.
- Merrick J, ed. *Child health and human development yearbook 2012*. New York: Nova Science, 2012.
- Shek DTL, Sun RCF, Merrick J, eds. *Developmental issues in Chinese adolescents*. New York: Nova Science, 2012.

- Shek DTL, Sun RCF, Merrick J, eds. *Positive youth development: Theory, research and application.* New York: Nova Science, 2012.
- Zachor DA, Merrick J, eds. *Understanding autism spectrum disorder: Current research aspects.* New York: Nova Science, 2012.
- Ma HK, Shek DTL, Merrick J, eds. *Positive youth development: A new school curriculum to tackle adolescent developmental issues.* New York: Nova Science, 2012.
- Wood D, Reiss JG, Ferris ME, Edwards LR, Merrick J, eds. *Transition from pediatric to adult medical care.* New York: Nova Science, 2012.
- Isenberg Y. *Guidelines for the healthy integration of the ill child in the educational system: Experience from Israel.* New York: Nova Science, 2013.
- Shek DTL, Sun RCF, Merrick J, eds. *Chinese adolescent development: Economic disadvantages, parents and intrapersonal development.* New York: Nova Science, 2013.
- Shek DTL, Sun RCF, Merrick J, eds. *University and college students: Health and development issues for the leaders of tomorrow.* New York: Nova Science, 2013.
- Shek DTL, Sun RCF, Merrick J, eds. *Adolescence and behavior issues in a Chinese context.* New York: Nova Science, 2013.
- Sun J, Buys N, Merrick J. *Advances in preterm infant research.* New York: Nova Science, 2013.
- Tsitsika A, Janikian M, Greydanus DE, Omar HA, Merrick J, eds. *Internet addiction: A public health concern in adolescence.* New York: Nova Science, 2013.
- Shek, DTL, Lee TY, Merrick J, eds. *Promotion of holistic development of young people in Hong Kong.* New York: Nova Science, 2013.
- Shek DTL, Ma C, Lu Y, Merrick J, eds. *Human developmental research: Experience from research in Hong Kong.* New York: Nova Science, 2013.
- Rubin IL, Merrick J, eds. *Child health and human development: Social, economic and environmental factors.* New York: Nova Science, 2013.
- Merrick J, ed. *Chronic disease and disability in childhood.* New York: Nova Science, 2013.

- Rubin IL, Merrick J, eds. *Break the cycle of environmental health disparities: Maternal and child health aspects.* New York: Nova Science, 2013.
- Rubin IL, Merrick J, eds. *Environmental health disparities in children: Asthma, obesity and food.* New York: Nova Science, 2013.
- Rubin IL, Merrick J, eds. *Environmental health: Home, school and community.* New York: Nova Science, 2013.
- Merrick J, Kandel I, Omar HA, eds. *Children, violence and bullying: International perspectives.* New York: Nova Science, 2013.
- Omar HA, Bowling CH, Merrick J, eds. *Playing with fire: Children, adolescents and firesetting.* New York: Nova Science, 2013.
- Merrick J, Tenenbaum A, Omar HA, eds. *School, adolescence and health issues.* New York: Nova Science, 2014.
- Merrick J, Tenenbaum A, Omar HA, eds. *Adolescence and sexuality: International perspectives.* New York: Nova Science, 2014.
- Diamond G, Arbel E. *Adoption: The search for a new parenthood adoption*. New York: Nova Science, 2014.
- Taylor MF, Pooley JA, Merrick J, eds. *Adolescence: Places and spaces.* New York: Nova Science, 2014.
- Greydanus DE, Feinberg AN, Merrick J, eds. *Born into this world: Health issues*. New York: Nova Science, 2014.
- Greydanus DE, Feinberg AN, Merrick J, eds. *Caring for the newborn: A comprehensive guide for the clinician*. New York: Nova Science, 2014.
- Rubin IL, Merrick J, eds. *Environment and hope: Improving health, reducing AIDS and promoting food security in the world.* New York: Nova Science, 2014.
- Greydanus DE, Feinberg AN, Merrick J, eds. *Pediatric and adolescent dermatology: Some current issues*. New York: Nova Science, 2014.
- Roach RR, Greydanus DE, Patel DR, Merrick J, eds. *Tropical pediatrics: A public health concern of international proportions,* Second edition. New York: Nova Science, 2015.
- Merrick J, ed. *Child and adolescent health issues: A tribute to the pediatrician Donald E Greydanus*. New York: Nova Science, 2015.

- Feinberg AN. *A pediatric resident pocket guide: Making the most of morning reports*. New York: Nova Science, 2015.
- Greydanus DE, Patel DR, Pratt HD, Calles Jr JL, Nazeer A, Merrick J, eds. *Behavioral pediatrics, 4th edition*. New York: Nova Science, 2015.
- Merrick J, ed. *Disability, chronic disease and human development.* New York: Nova Science, 2015.
- Hegamin-Younger C, Merrick J, eds. *Caribbean adolescents: Some public health concerns*. New York: Nova Science, 2015.
- Merrick J, ed. *Adolescence and health: Some international perspectives*. New York: Nova Science, 2015.
- Omar HA. *Youth suicide prevention: Everybody's business*. New York: Nova Science, 2015.
- Greydanus DE, Raj VMS, Merrick J, eds. *Chronic disease and disability: The pediatric kidney.* New York: Nova Science, 2015.
- Merrick J, ed. *Children and childhood: Some international aspects*. New York: Nova Science, 2016.
- Shek DTL, Lee TY, Merrick J, eds. *Children and adolescents: Future challenges.* New York: Nova Science, 2016.
- Shek DTL, Wu FKU, Leung JTY, Merrick J, eds. *Adolescence: Positive youth development programs in Chinese communities.* New York: Nova Science, 2016.
- Merrick J, Greydanus DE, eds. *Sexuality: Some international aspects.* New York: Nova Science, 2016.
- Harel-Fisch Y, Abdeen Z, Navot M. *Growing up in the Middle East: The daily lives and well-being of Israeli and Palestinian youth.* New York: Nova Science, 2016.
- Greydanus DE, Malhotra D, Merrick J, eds. *Chronic disease and disability: The pediatric heart.* New York: Nova Science, 2016.
- Greydanus DE, Kamboj MK, Merrick J, eds. *Chronic disease and disability: The pediatric pancreas*. New York: Nova Science, 2016.
- Kamboj MK, Greydanus DE, Merrick J, eds. *Diabetes mellitus: Childhood and adolescence.* New York: Nova Science, 2016.
- Greydanus DE, Palusci VJ, Merrick J, eds. *Chronic disease and disability: Abuse and neglect in childhood and adolescence*. New York: Nova Science, 2016.
- Greydanus DE, Calles JL Jr, Patel DR, Nazeer A, Merrick J, eds. *Clinical aspects of psychopharmacology in childhood and adolescence*, second ed. New York: Nova Science, 2016.

- Greydanus DE, Apple RW, White K, Merrick J, eds. *Children and youth: Post-traumatic stress disorder and motor vehicle crashes.* New York: Nova Science, 2017.
- Mazaba ML, Siziya S, Merrick J, eds. *Suicide: A global view on suicidal ideation among adolescents.* New York: Nova Science, 2017.
- Chow R, Merrick J, eds. *Adolescence: Bicycle and helmet use of adolescents and young adults.* New York: Nova Science, 2017.
- Chow R, Borean M, Hollenberg D, Viehweger J, Anpalagan T, Rzepka A, Merrick J, eds. *Bicycles: Helmet use and adolescents at independent schools.* New York: Nova Science, 2017.
- Shek DTL, Ma CMS, Leung JTY, Merrick J, eds. *Positive youth development: Long term effects in a Chinese program.* New York: Nova Science, 2017.

CONTACT

Professor Joav Merrick, MD, MMedSci, DMSc
Medical Director, Medical Services
Division for Intellectual and Developmental Disabilities
Ministry of Social Affairs and Social Services
POBox 1260, IL-91012 Jerusalem, Israel
Email: jmerrick@zahav.net.il

SECTION FIVE: INDEX

Index

A

B

C

D

E

F

G

H

I

J

L

M

Q

R

S

T

U

V

W

Y